# Relentless

· 2017 ·

AMBER~
THANKS FOR YOUR SUPPORT. MAY
YOU TO BE RELENTLESS IN THAT
WHICH SPEAKS TO YOUR HEART.

— Kevin Searcy

# Relentless

## A Journey of Forgiveness

## Kellie Springer, RN

Relentless

Published by:
Anam Cara Kellie
P.O. Box 311
Lyndell, PA 19354
www.anamcarakellie.com

Cover image by Getty Images: Tricycle by DNY59/E+/Getty Images
Author Image by: Rebekah Viola Photography

Please visit the author's blog at www.kelliespringer.com

ISBN-13: 9781535291651
ISBN-10: 1535291656
Printed in the United States of America

*"Either I will find a way,*
*Or I will make one."*
–Philip Sydney

# Acknowledgements

First, and always, is my gratitude and love to my three favorite guys–Craig, Nate, and Cole. I've searched the wide world but cannot find the words fitting to express the importance of your unwavering support and encouragement as I embarked on this leg of my life's adventures.

Craig, no one has, or could have, loved me better. Thank you for always holding my hand no matter where we've roamed in this life together. You're still my sunshine.

Nate and Cole, you both fill my days with endless wonder, and it has been through you that my heart has known the purest love. Nothing I have done, or will ever do, can compare to the marvel of being your mom.

Thank you to Angie and Holly, my beacons of sanity and compassion as I made my way back to myself and my truth. There is a special place in my heart reserved for each of you.

Many thanks and much love to Jen McLamb for always being around to read, re-read, listen, suggest, support, and encourage time after time, year after year. You, and your friendship, are priceless.

My appreciation to Cheryl Krass of Alexemi Publishing for listening to my ramblings in this process and for guiding me through the ins and outs of turning a manuscript into a book.

To my editor, Dawn Shuler, I offer my gratitude for seeing the possibilities in my rough manuscript and for providing its finishing touches.

A shout out to Susan Weidener and the members of the Women's Writing Circle. Thanks to all of you for the kindness and encouragement as you listened to my story and my attempts at putting pen to paper.

This page would not be complete without sharing my appreciation to Jody March for her willingness to read the very crude beginnings of the book you now hold in your hands. Thank you for seeing the value in what I've come to share.

*For the children that never made it out
and whose story will never be told.*

## Words for It

I wish I could take language
And fold it like cool, moist rags.
I would lay words on your forehead.
I would wrap words on your wrists.
"There, there" my words would say–
Or something better.
I would ask them to murmur,
"Hush" and "Shh, shh, it's all right."
I would ask them to hold you tight.
I wish I could take language
And daub and soothe and cool
Where fever blisters and burns,
Where fever turns yourself against you.
I wish I could take language
And heal the words that were the wounds
You have no names for.

–Julia Cameron

# Introductions

## We Meet At Last

How do you put over twenty years of purging, insight, and growth into a book? I'm about to find out, and I thank you for joining me.

I'm not a writer, nor do I pretend to be. In fact, while I admire the ability of those who can spin a spectacular tale, I don't aspire to be that. If I bog my mind down with the rules of eloquent writing, I'll lose my truth. And the truth is I've followed no road map to get me here as it's often been my own private excursion, a pioneer of my own landscape. No how-to manual was placed in my hands. There were no classes to take. I just took one step and then another, and so that's how I'll write, clear on my purpose and trusting that the path will be laid before me if I only have the courage to begin. What you now hold in your hands is the contents of the compartments of my life.

I've sought the help and guidance of others when I needed it and fearfully shunned support in other moments. My travels have been solely my own, but will be familiar to many, and shocking to some.

I knew, twenty years before, that we'd be having this conversation, albeit a bit one sided. I also knew the time for our meeting had not yet arrived. I understood and sensed this was a part of my destination all those many years ago. I have no more of a clue now how to proceed than I did then, but I feel driven. I awaited the green light that would signal my soul, always aware of my writing off in the distance of linear time. I wasn't yet prepared to share my secret with you but was indeed in preparation. But the time has come. I've been awakened by the unseen forces of nature like a hibernating bear, and it is now. I feel it most assuredly in the core of my being, as real as my feet planted upon the ground, that we were destined to share this next chapter with one another and confidences must be revealed.

I'm going to tell you the dark, complicated truth of my life both then and now. There's no glamorizing with frilly words or phrases. It's vile and disturbing at times, most times, but this is the woven tapestry of my life that as a whole has become a unique work of art. My words may not flow like smooth rivers, nor will I be quoted in literary circles, but they are wholly my words, profoundly raw. They belong to me and I share them with you.

I don't always recall every detail surrounding what I'm about to share with you, but in this case the devil isn't in the details but had instead taken up residence in my childhood home. At times, as a child, I believed my father was the devil. Truly. You know the classic image of the devil: goatee; slicked-back black hair; and a penetratingly, steely stare. That was my father, except he wasn't red nor did he sport horns. He was the monster of my childhood, and he wasn't make believe. Monsters are real and I called him 'Dad,' his sidekick was 'Mom.'

It's frightening, this telling, but something pulls me forward as if I'm magnetized to the path that is part of my soul's purpose. What is the purpose of the step I'm about to take? I catch glimmers of potential meaning but feel the full impact of this sharing will not be humanly known to me in this life. Nevertheless, there is an unwavering faith that this is part of my master plan, now our master plan.

## To Each His Own

It will soon come as no surprise, but my family doesn't see and remember things from my point of view. As has always been the case, they believe my perspective is a bit skewed. For me, I call their take on things denial. It's one of the strongest coping skills we possess as humans, and it has allowed my family, and countless others, to distance themselves from their actions and the consequences of those behaviors.

So, I've no motivation for proving that my version of events is the right way, and certainly they've no intentions of viewing things from my line of sight. It simply comes down to the truth that they believe what they need to hold as their story. This story… this one is mine. If they wish to tell the world their take on things, well, then they can write a book, too.

Let it be known that I fought valiantly to get them to agree with my version. With the most innocent intentions, I had hoped that if I shared with them my process and newest understandings, waved the banner of truth right in their faces, they would willing trot along beside me.

What I failed to realize was that while I was hell bent on learning, discovering, healing, and growing–all those glorious things–the rest of my family apparently enjoyed where they were hanging out in their world and saw not one reason to change things or learn anew. My unfolding would be a solo act.

And so, if I could no longer live in their world and they had not an inkling of moving out of their familiar stomping grounds, we were at an impasse. I had to let them go, floating on the ethers of denial, as I clawed a bloody trail to new and higher ground. Their place of residence was home to them; for me, hell. I wept as I waved my imaginary good bye to them, never to return to that level of self-deception and unconsciousness.

As I battled to gain my own freedom, I allowed them theirs. If I have the right to cope and deal with our lives together in the fashion that suits me best, then I must afford them the same.

## Vengeance Is Not Mine

This book isn't an act of revenge; it's always been about healing and freeing myself from my past, releasing the vice grip of my parents. I was desperate to no longer carry them and their burdens in every cell of my being, everywhere I traveled. No matter where I turned, it felt as if their actions and misdeeds were some gelatinous parasite that had fused itself to my being.

If I was motivated by revenge, then I would never have sought a way out. I would simply have acted and continued to act from my place of rage, the place that wanted to fight back and hurt in turn. I would not have been the seeker of understanding, processing, and compassion. I would have lashed out again and again, never satisfied with the level of chaos and pain I inflicted, always wanting to make them squirm in agony as they had done to me so many times before.

Let's be realistic: I had fantasies of just that. It would have been so easy to go with what had become the norm, the stormy waters, but easy was never my way. Instead, I learned to surf the emotional rogue wave. I refused to allow it to completely pull me under, drown my spirit, or wreak a lifetime of havoc and emotional torture to anyone that got in my way. I was taught by a master, but remotely I knew that I am not him, nor am I what he taught me.

I caught that wave again and again until it carried me to the mystical land of forgiveness, for myself and them, where I finally released the anchor that bound me to the hope that the past could be rewritten. So far it's taken me more than twenty-five years to unlearn what I was schooled in as a student. For me, this book is about remembering and re-learning who and what is my truth and having the courage to share that with the world, often feeling emotionally stripped and naked. I said he was a master, but what he didn't realize was that I am as well. But unlike him, I chose not to master others, only myself.

What if others judge me? They surely will, at least some, as that seems to be the nature of humanity. We live in a plane where we are taught to assess and evaluate the "good" and the "bad" of both people and situations.

Even worse, what if I believe their judgments?

Such ponderings lead me nowhere fast, which is a long distance from that which I seek. All that I am left to do is share with you my ride, the times I crashed, as well as the glory of my triumphs. Most certainly I have intentions and hopes for this writing, but ultimately you will take out of these words and this encounter what best serves you and as seen through the lens of your own life lived. I pray I serve you well, and the rest is out of my hands.

"We must dare to think 'unthinkable' thoughts. We must learn
to explore all the options and possibilities that confront us
in a complex and rapidly changing world. We must learn to
welcome and not fear the voices of dissent. We must dare to
think about 'unthinkable things' because when things become
unthinkable, thinking stops and action becomes mindless."
—JAMES WILLIAM FULBRIGHT

## The Cast of Characters

The father of my youth stood at least six feet and was not slight in figure. He possessed a strong intelligence, which he readily and often pointed out, yet he had dropped out of school as a teen. He shared that he was never interested in what they taught in school, especially the poetry they made part of his curriculum, but became a learned man from years of reading various sources of information about a wide variety of subjects.

Nature and the outdoors seemed to feed him on some level, the wild being a perfect fit for his untamed persona. Hunting and trapping were mainstream in his life, providing many a creative meal for us; I would not recommend raccoon with sauerkraut. I learned a reverence for our Mother Earth thanks to my father as he was adamant about the need to never litter, many times picking up the trash others had carelessly tossed. Throughout my youth, he became adept at working our large organic garden, tending to his honeybees, and exploring the concepts of solar energy. In some ways, he was ahead of his time.

His woodcarvings shone with his creative and artistic talents, all self-taught. He also learned to refurbish antique furniture and cane chairs, a skill he taught us to help earn household income. He fancied himself a clever cook whenever he stepped into the kitchen, and I would have to agree with his assessment.

While my father never shied away from hard work, keeping a job was a challenge for him for many years. Being told what to do does not come easy to him. When I was a young girl, my mother shared with me that he was always challenging his bosses and the system, and losing his job as a result. Needless to say, money strains became a very realistic issue in our house, and I heard many a fight about my mother's struggles to pay the bills. "I have to rob Peter to pay Paul," she often complained. I, in turn, added money to my list of worries. Because of our low income status, we were participants of the school lunch program. My cheeks flushed with embarrassment every time I hurriedly handed over that turquoise token to pay for my meal, making every effort to not bring attention to myself and avoiding eye contact with others lest they see the disgrace that was me.

Willpower runs through my father like a steel beam. Once he sets his mind to something, there's no wavering in his actions. Smoking was a pleasure for my father ever since he was a teenager, but as the prices of cigarettes continued to build, he declared that he would quit smoking if they reached a dollar a pack. As we well know, they indeed reached that limit, and so my father held true to his word and quit, never to smoke again. He was able to quit people just as readily if he felt slighted in the least. There were no variances of gray in any situation for him, only his way, and that was the only way.

Unlike the other dads, he wore his hair long and refused to shave. I've never seen my father without a beard. As that beard greyed he would sport a Kris Kringle outfit at various Christmas gatherings or for the elderly in a nursing home, showing his softer side and the man I believed he longed to routinely be, if only life hadn't gotten in his way.

2

Shocking people was one of his main sources of entertainment, anything for attention, the more bizarre the better. Dressing like a "mountain man" in our rural town gave him a sense of brotherhood, bonding him to the then popular TV character, Grizzly Adams. Part of his jewelry was a raccoon penis bone necklace that he had created from a raccoon he had trapped. I kid you not. Momentarily fancying raccoon penis bone as his artistic material of choice, he also fashioned a toothpick or two out of them. He even went so far as to encourage a young man that he wasn't too fond of to use the toothpick he had carved, only to take great pleasure in his disgust and humiliation after he told him of its origins.

While working as a TV cable installer, he would enter a residence with the cable wrapped around his head, telling the residents that he was Jesus because he was sporting his own crown of thorns, the image befitting the persecution complex that seemed to be ever present in his mind. I learned of this years later when I met my future husband whose college house my father had installed cable in. Once he set eyes on my father again, he remembered his first encounter with him quite well; he always left a lasting impression.

A smoldering sensuality emanated from my father, especially in his younger years. He was fond of blatantly, and embarrassingly to me, flirting with the opposite sex, no matter the age. There were no boundaries for his sexuality or flirtatious nature; his energy like unseen hands come to accost any female that caught his attention.

His favorite past time was to intimidate others; there need not be a reason and anyone could be victim to his sordid game. Many would cower as he glared at them, lowered his voice a few notches, and puffed out his chest. He relished the discomfort of others, most especially children. Scaring them was *always* his intention. He simply lacked social skills and the ability to even care about it. A deep scowl seemed to be his most natural facial expression, never welcoming to another person, but instead sending a warning signal their way to keep their distance.

As with anyone else on this Earth, he also had moments of tenderness. Music was a release for him and allowed for a more gentle expression of the emotions his words and actions could not convey. The memory that can bring me to tears is that of him singing in the car to the likes of Patsy Cline, Gene Autry, or Eddy Arnold. I can still hear his heart-rendering rendition of "The Prisoner's Song," as he sang of the longing to have angels' wings so that he might fly over the prison walls to die in in the arms of his love. I sensed he was a prisoner of sorts too, longing for wings to set him free. The feelings were palpable as he sang and created an aching in my heart. It thrilled me to sing along, stealing glances at him, as I enthusiastically tried to copy his passion and intensity. In other instances, I simply allowed myself to be swept along in what felt like a deeply personal moment for him. Those were the times I relished just being by his side. It seemed to me he was his truest self when he sang.

His spirit also seemed to soar when he danced, his face beaming with an unbridled joy as the armor temporarily fell away. The truth of the powerful soul that he is saturated the room during those moments, and it was only then that he seemed most comfortable being in this world.

For her part, my mother stood barely over five feet and always seemed somehow lesser than the force that was my father. For many years she dyed her hair a vibrant auburn in order to satisfy my father's preferences, but in time she returned to a run-of-the mill brown that was more her natural color. Moderate weight issues hounded her all of her adult life and were the subject of many contentious talks my parents had over the years, my father longing for the petite teenage girl she had been when they first met. She bounced in and out of Weight Watchers many times over, and each time I had renewed hope that she would overcome this obstacle, but always the weight won the battle.

Many a comment from my father implied his intelligence was superior to hers. I don't know if it's true, but I can tell you I believed it was true as a child, and I judged her harshly for that and her weight struggles, which at the time I understood to simply be a matter of will.

There always seemed to be an impenetrable blanket of bleakness about my mother for a large portion of my early years, sort of like the cloud that follows Pig-Pen around from the *Peanuts* cartoon. She would walk around the house twisting her hair and mumbling to herself, the ringlets left springing off her head where she had been repeatedly twirling the hair about her fingers. I often wondered what she was actually muttering and would sometimes make covert attempts to get physically closer to her so that I might solve the mystery. As kids, we poked fun at her for her crazy behavior. I got a sense that her behavior was a sign of a larger problem, but it was much more comforting to laugh at her then to admit what my worry spoke, that my mother was deeply troubled in some way.

After having me, she decided to quit her secretarial job and open an at home daycare. All of my days were spent with her before I started kindergarten. Her affectionate name for me was Kel Bell, and when she would go to her job on Saturdays at the local meat market, I would long for her return. The roller derby and *WWF* were my sources of distraction until she came home, but given a moment to notice her absence, my stomach would clench and ache. Until she came home, I felt lost, a part of me ripped away.

Birthdays were always special and planned through her concerned efforts, a homemade cake filling our special request. She put thought into what gifts she bought and their presentation was important to her. One of my relatives was notorious for giving us our gift in the plastic Kmart bag she received at the store. This was insulting to my mother. The message I learned? If you're giving a gift, do it like you mean it and you care. Not a bad lesson, thanks to my mother.

My favorite game to play with her happened upon her return from working at the meat market. I would pretend to be asleep on the living room chair when she came home, fighting the smile that threatened to appear on my face. After her failed attempts to wake me, she would then tickle me awake. Immediately, my anxiety would evaporate, and I would feel whole again. This is the only game I can recall playing with my mother, but it is one of the times that I *felt* like the child and she an adult. This was a role reversal for us because many of my moments as her daughter were spent mothering and comforting her after one of my parents' brawls.

Perhaps that's why the game memory holds a special place in my heart; things were as they ought to be in those brief moments. I got to be a kid.

My mother took cake decorating lessons and later sold her cakes to earn some spare change. She sold some adult versions wearing bikinis, while others bore naked breasts and penises. My cakes were rated 'G,' and she made the best deep chocolate icing for my many *Scooby Doo* birthday cakes. Her life, and ours, was also filled with canning, pickling and freezing all the vegetables from our garden. Homemade jellies, fruit leather, and various baked goods were a staple in our house. In my teen years she insisted I do some cooking and baking. I was quite resentful as it felt like one more instance where I was being forced to do something I didn't enjoy or have interest in doing. I would say that that sentiment still rings true, but I am now able to appreciate the fact that because of those times I am capable of making foods that I enjoy, food being a great source of pleasure for me, even if I still don't necessarily fancy the process of making it.

I felt the happiest in my mother's company when I would sit at the kitchen table with her as she worked on the various interests she had over the years, like decorating her cakes or painting my father's carvings. My heart constricted every time my father critiqued her work on his carvings, for what she was able to produce could never compare to his natural abilities. I knew what he said to be true, but internally I rallied for my mother, rooting for the underdog. Going with her to her ceramic class was also considered a special treat, and it was during those times that I was in awe of her and her talents, my father not able to steal the spotlight in this setting.

But there was a darker side to both my parents, one that overshadowed everything, its presence looming in my life and threatening to swallow me whole. They were two walking, breathing vats of shame, and they unleashed that shame upon us in many ways and many times. It was the cumulative effect of their cruelty that made it hard to look at the loving moments with an open heart.

No one is "all good" or "all bad"; we all possess polarities in every aspect, but there's a limit to how far we should allow ourselves to go.

When the innocent in our lives begin to routinely suffer, their very lives in jeopardy, it's time to do a check and take some responsibility for our actions.

Looking back, my father's behaviors were the most consistently and obviously extreme. As a teen, he was arrested for shooting cats out of a car window. As a result, he was given the choice to go to jail or join the Marines. He chose the Marines, where his hatred of authority could have only be fueled all the more. When I was a child, he told me that it was there that he was labeled as having an anti-social personality. He shared this story with laughter and wore the label like a badge of honor. Knowing how he led his life and embraced the label, I would have to guess it may not have been far from the truth. When he was violent or controlling, it wasn't shocking that he behaved that way. For me, there was always trauma surrounding the way he acted, but it was no great surprise that violence was his go-to state of being.

My mother, on the other hand, had more frequent moments of kindness and nurturing. So when she acted malevolent in some way, it was confusing to me as a child, and I felt the fool for falling for her trickery once again. There was an internal conflict because, like any child, I craved love and attention. In those instances when she was loving and warm, I whole heartedly embraced her. During other situations she could be just as sadistic as my father and was even his partner in the abuses. If you did what she wanted, she was saccharin sweet, but cross her and she became coldly vicious. It seemed as long as she wasn't his victim, she was able to look past his behaviors and together they derived some type of sick pleasure in controlling us and watching us writhe.

A classic example of this involved my mother threatening the daycare children that my father would hang those who misbehaved on a hook in the basement. She thought this was funny, and, of course, the children were petrified. She wanted to frighten them into behaving. She helped to feed the image of my father as villainous and indeed, when my father came home from work, she would tell him of all the children's misdeeds that day as he proceeded to glower at them. There were times that he would take the kids into the basement and show them the hook to terrify them further, and even one instance when he in fact did hang one boy on a hook. There Justin hung, helpless, with tears streaming down his face. My heart ached for him as I stood watching, powerless to save him.

My parents, however, would laugh about it all. This was a game to them, and they were, and dare I suggest still are, unaware how this was out and out abuse. If they were bold enough to do this to other people's children, my siblings and I had the proverbial snowball's chance in hell. We were sitting ducks. We didn't have a prayer. However you choose to say it, we were fucked.

To the outside world, my mother was the chubby motherly figure and my father ornery and eccentric. People would wonder how she managed to put up with him. My mother would giggle, glowing with martyrdom, when people talked of her trials in being married to my father. My father, for his part, would become frustrated and claim to her in private that it wasn't all him, that she was just as difficult to deal with in her own right. His perception was accurate; it was just that she played a smarter social game than him.

It's clear to me that something in both my parents' lives helped to support and create this extreme level of shame and acting out. I can't speak of their story, only about the fact that their story inevitably became intertwined with mine, like a poison ivy vine that threatens to squeeze the life out of a sapling. Someone had to put a stop to this wretched tale that was spinning out of control. Over time that someone would be me, but only after the damage had been done.

## Uninvited Guest

And now for me... Let's start at my beginning, shall we? That's what beginnings are for.

My first offense was coming to this plane of existence. I wasn't planned; instead my presence inserted itself into the life of my parents like the eternal uninvited guest. Needy, dependent, challenging, and defiant.

My mother said my father didn't want me. "Why?" I asked.

Her face contorted into a look of disbelief, how could I *not* know? "Well, because he knew he wasn't good..." she began.

"Good with what?" I wondered out loud to her.

"With kids," was her clipped response. Her eyes cast downward, and guilt washed over her face as though she'd revealed some long-ago entrusted personal confession.

So I enraged him from the beginning, not the best entrance to this thing we call life. Who knew a fetus could be so powerful, stripping the power of an adult, and only a cluster of microscopic cells to speak of.

I don't know her motivation for telling me this, but I do know the outcome. I felt as if someone had viciously stomped on my tender heart as a part of me withered from the weight of my deep sadness. Loud and clear the message I heard was, "You weren't wanted." I wasn't a source of delight, but was instead a burden to the very people that created me. I wanted to beg forgiveness, "I'm sorry. I'm sorry I'm here. I'm sorry I bothered you."

Understand this wasn't a thought on my part, but instead it became a truth in my mind, one that I replayed over and over again in my attempts to connect in the world. I could find no value within my being that was worthy of being wanted or loved. I had no frame of reference for being wanted, from my very conception I was swimming in the energies of being less than desirable. I simply didn't know it could be true that I was loveable, instead of barely tolerable.

Later, in my adulthood, I revisited this conversation with my mother. She shared with me that he was indeed resentful and told her, "If you get pregnant again, I'll leave you." As if she got pregnant on her own? This was a shining example of my father's inability to take responsibility for his choices, the building blocks of my very existence. The foundation of my life being formed of quicksand.

It was also an example of the poor parenting choices both my parents made. Advice to other parents: don't tell your children they weren't wanted. It was the modus operandi of my mother. She couldn't see how her actions were hurtful, but only how my father was the villain. She was caught up in how his actions wronged her, instead of how her sharing pained me.

He didn't want me.

I often wonder if on some level he knew, he knew I would become his greatest challenger in this world. The one to say, "No more." The one to shove all his demented beliefs and behaviors right up his ass.

That my father wasn't "good with children" is an understatement if there ever was one, as you're about to see.

# Born to Be Wild

It seemed to me I was born from a place of defiance. Officially, I was to be born towards the end of April. Two weeks past that date I made my entrance in May. No one tells me what to do, not ever. If I listen to you, it's only after careful consideration on my part.

As if conjoined twins, betrayal felt to be defiance's constant companion. Deep within my being, I had a feeling of betrayal at my birth. Of course I didn't have a conscious memory of this event, but residing in my core were feelings of resentment and betrayal as I was torn out of my unconscious mother. Torn. This was to be my first experience with physical assault and the first time my mother failed to protect me. My mother made the choice to be sedated for my birth, a common practice at the time. "I was so miserable and uncomfortable when I was pregnant with you. When I got to the hospital to have you, I told them to knock me out and wake me when it was over," she told me as a child.

I was left with rage. Rage at the first time someone forced their will upon me with no regard for my wellbeing, no regard for my glory or the spectacular process of birth, when the entrance of another spirit into this world is known. My birth and I were an unpleasant, painful event meant to be blocked out and avoided. What a somber and lonely entrance.

In the depths of my being, I sensed my soul trusted, believed in those I'd chosen to be my human caregivers, only to be betrayed and abandoned at the onset. Deep in my bones I felt disrespected and waged a battle against the continuous onslaught of abuse and misuse those who "loved me" barraged me with.

And this was their way. True, they may have never learned anything different, but I make no excuses for their behavior, nor should you. They were entrusted with the nurturing of a beautiful spirit, a fellow human being, and they failed miserably. Perhaps I convey an inflated representation of myself, but I speak of my glory just as I speak of all children being brought to this plane. None is more glorious than another, but all are glorious just the same. To deny the sanctity of creating, birthing, and parenting a dynamic soul was their first step in unconscious parenting.

## Proof of Evidence Lies Within

There were troublesome secrets stowed away inside me, but it wasn't until I became a teenager that I was able to occasionally peek inside those boxes, ever cautious lest their contents spring from the darkness that had imprisoned them for so long. With age, I was finally able to put into words what was before indescribable–I had been sexually abused. I had no date to stamp on my life's timeline, but I felt as though I was about four years old. Like most victims of early childhood abuses, I didn't have a direct link to the entire memory. That is… I couldn't say that the abuse was a clear and distinctly defined event, but was instead a collage of sensations and flashes of images. Thus the term flashback, as the flashes took me back, back to this:

> In my mind's eye, a patch of black pubic hair stares me in the face and my body seems to record what my mind cannot comprehend. The corners of my lips are stretched beyond their limits, feeling as though they are going to split, while 'something' was forced between them that should have had no place in my child-sized mouth. It hurts. I taste the salt from my tears as they trickle into my mouth. I feel a hand wrap behind my head and forcibly move it back and forth. I gag as that 'something' hits the reflex in the back

*of my throat. I feel the bullseye in the back of my throat where a warm, foreign substance squirts explosively into it.*

*Above all else, I am overwhelmingly confused and panicked. I don't know what 'this' is or what is expected of me. I sense he's mad because I don't know what I'm supposed to do, and because I cried. This isn't in my field of comprehension. I have no words for it. I feel violated and scared. I don't like it, whatever it is called.*

*In another flashback I feel wet whiskers scraping the inside of my thighs. It feels soggy and revolting to me. I don't like the mess. My legs kick and scramble in a vain attempt to break free, but my body proves to be weak and powerless against him, and it was in that moment that I began the hate-filled relationship with the flesh that housed me. It had let me down when I needed it most. I feel strong hands grab me by my hips and pull me back, holding me in place. Peering through the bottom of my eyes I see the black hair on the tops of his hands and I feel its coarseness as I push against those hands in another desperately futile measure to make my escape.*

*Lastly, embedded in my memory is the pain on my pubic bone as something rigid moves and presses against it. And always, the panic. Just trying to get away, get away. It feels as though I am fighting for my very life.*

While my brain blocked the image of the perpetrator's face, I knew. I knew who he was. I had the sense that because I was so young he didn't think I would remember, that this was his security. I also believed that because he never actually penetrated me vaginally he convinced himself that he didn't sexually abuse me, a lie he told himself and believes to this day.

## Sleep Tight, Bed Bugs Will Bite

As I grew, so too did my ability to recall in detail other incidents that were to follow, and soon I was all too familiar with the many faces of molestation.

I continued to sleep in a crib well beyond that which is typical for a child, until I was perhaps four or five. I don't know the reasons behind this, but I'd venture to guess it was something my parents considered practical and may have been financially based. One night, while lying in my crib, I was molested.

Charlie was several years older than I, a close teenage family acquaintance. I adored him with the wonder befitting a young child that had built a life-long relationship with another older child. My mother told me that the admiration was mutual. "He thought you were cute and funny," she shared. I no doubt thrived on his attention. Sadly, it was his attention that soon crossed what should have been an impassable boundary.

As I lay ready for sleep, body curled on my right side and back to the wall, I stared at the bunk beds that were across the room from my crib. I watched as Charlie slid under my bed. An internal alarm sounded. I knew this was terribly wrong, and I even had an understanding that he was going to do something to me that was of a sexual nature. My heart beat an increasingly rapid rhythm in my chest, but the rest of my body lay in a frozen panic. I waited, wide eyed and clutching tightly to my stuffed animals.

I listened with a heightened apprehension as his hand rubbed along the wall, trying to awkwardly make his way through the slats of my crib. As his fingers clawed through the bars, he began to pull up my nightgown. Slowly and clumsily, he shifted my underwear and began to fondle me; it was then that I bolted upright. I stood screaming, a death grip on the top crib rail.

My parents rushed into my bedroom. When it was clear what had happened, my parents removed Charlie from my bedroom. I've no idea what was said to him about that night, but I do know different sleeping arrangements ensued. The incident was never discussed again and the relationship Charlie and I once shared was irreparably demolished.

I believe Charlie got in trouble to some degree, more shamed is my guess, and he blamed me for being a tattletale. I imagine he felt betrayed, believing we shared a special bond. He continued to be a part of my life every day, but over the course of years, the distance between us stretched longer and wider, akin to true contempt many times. We argued about almost everything. There seemed to be no common ground. So much so that when we were adults, he made a threat to my physical safety. "Be careful if you're ever alone with me," was his direct threat. I took him at his word, for I knew he had a switch that could cast his heart and his actions into an artic freeze.

I mentioned the conversation to my sister and father, wanting to ensure witnesses "just in case." They too took it seriously, encouraging me to not engage myself in any argument with Charlie, most especially if it was just the two of us. They insisted I walk away, not an easy feat for me.

The impact of sexual abuse and poor sexual boundaries knows no limits; it seems to ooze into every crevice of the lives it touches, an insidious partner to those that perpetrate it. I later learned that children often times mimic the abuses they witness. I suspected that this was true for Charlie and as a result, a deep connection between two innocent children was abruptly severed, never to be the same again. There were times as an adult that I cried because I missed Charlie, or what he had been to me before this incident. My little girl still grieves his loss, one that can never be recovered.

From that night forward, I lined up my stuffed animals along my back as I slept, in order that they might protect me. I did this throughout my entire childhood. My fierce protectors, my stuffed animals. I believed in them the way only a child can, my magical thinking serving me well as it lessened my uneasiness by a small degree each night as I struggled to fall asleep.

One of my most treasured animals was handmade by my mother, a small dog sewn with red ears and a body of red gingham to match. Somehow my mind associated it with my mother being there to comfort me, my imagination taking me to places that reality couldn't. Most often snuggled between me and my little dog was the tiniest bunny, measuring just over four inches and sporting lopsided ears. Its fur, once the palest of baby blues, had turned a dingy gray and was in scattered patches over its body, as though it had mange. The areas that lay exposed due to its missing coat bear the watery marks of stains from the places it had been led. One of its thread-stitched yellow and black eyes was missing several strands. I felt a strong need to protect what I perceived as the most vulnerable in my entourage, squeezing it tightly to me.

Looking at my bunny now, I can see that it conveyed what I had not been able to put into words as a child: That people you love can change you in ways that make you unrecognizable, a sorry expression of your original beauty. That they forever leave their mark on your soul, and when they're through with you, you will never see things the same way ever again. I was the bunny.

As I entered my teens, I faced the reality that my personal army wasn't the indestructible force of protection I once thought them to be, but I was still unable to stop the habit of placing them along me as I felt too exposed and vulnerable with my backside unprotected. Eventually, I said a very painful good bye to my friends and a well-placed blanket became my shield. My stuffed animals brought me comfort and safety in a way no human ever had, and I felt a deep sense of loyalty and unbridled love towards them. Truth be told, I still do today.

## Picture Perfect

Picture day of my kindergarten year proved to be my warped but accurate Kodak moment of everything that had come before. I sat waiting in the cafeteria as the photographer's female assistant gently tended to my hair, pony tails adorned with yellow wool ribbons and perfectly straight bangs thanks to my father's hand, so that I might look my best. I then sat before the photographer as guided, awkward and uncomfortable with the direct attention, and heard the words, "Smile, cutie."

The camera captured the moment well. My understanding of those words at that time, while clearly innocent and typical of something to say to a five year old, were perceived in my young mind as sexual. I sighed inwardly as I thought, "Not him, too." Even getting my picture taken wasn't safe. It felt to me as though he was commenting on my body and its desirability. I believed he wanted me, and thus, that look and feeling was captured in my photograph and for all eternity. At the age of five, I knew my body as an object of desire; this had become a truth in my world, and my body the burden that I believed attracted the attention of grown men. Why would a five year old even have the concept of being sexually desirable? Because someone had taught me that I was, and I've always been a fast learner.

My parents thought the captured expression was funny: my mouth twisted in disgruntlement. It was called my Fuzzhead look; Fuzzhead being my nickname, and that look often conveying my displeasure. But it wasn't cute this time, not to me. I felt disgusting and disgusted.

## Blurred Lines

Throughout my childhood the sexual boundaries in my home were routinely muddied, leaving me to feel soiled each and every time, until inside I, too, felt just as murky.

"I see your heinie, all white and shiny. Don't try to hide it. I'm going to bite it!" my father gleefully spouted. That was the rhyme my father would sing-song before he played his game with me, pulling down my pants and biting my bare bottom when I was a small girl. I could hear my mother chuckling in the kitchen as I giggled in the living room because his beard tickled me as he bit my buttocks, and because I was just so delighted to have a happy daddy. How would Norman Rockwell have painted that scene?

Another conflicting part of me caught my laughter short because I somehow sensed something wasn't okay about our game, despite the playfulness that emanated from him. Guilt that I would enjoy something that was wrong swirled amongst the elation that I felt because my father was paying attention to me.

My father wasn't the only one to dirty the waters, however. We had no air conditioning in our house, and during the hottest months of summer my mother would walk around the house in her underwear and without a bra in order to cope with the heat. As a young girl, I simply didn't want to see this. It unnerved me and left me feeling deep shame because even though I was horrified that her breasts were on full display in the kitchen, I couldn't look away. I shamefully wondered what was wrong with me that I felt this need to stare at my mother's breasts despite my discomfort.

Often times when I was younger, my father would ask my mother to come into the bathroom with him to "wash his back." Wink, wink. I knew and understood what they were doing wasn't about backs and washing. It felt yucky, and I hated the knowing.

During other affectionate moments, my father would sit in a living room chair and my mother would kneel in front of him with a wanton smile. Immediately my mind pictured my mother kneeling before him for oral sex. Where had I gotten this reference? This wasn't something a young child, say at age seven or eight, should know about, but I had experienced it somewhere before. I was mortified and felt like a voyeur in their sex lives.

As my sister's and my body matured, we were often the brunt of teasing from both parents. Many times they would point out the development, or lack of in my case, of our breasts. They would laugh when we would get upset and say, "Stop being so sensitive."

My mother went so far as to make me model a new bra for my father when I was a teen. To say I was humiliated doesn't do it justice. I stood baffled that my own mother would intentionally expose me in this way. I was trapped into a time warp where each second had become an agonizing hour. Every fiber in my being wanted to scream and run from the spot where I stood on display, but I kept it in and held my head down, simply too mortified to make eye contact. As I turned to leave the living room and go hide in my bedroom, I caught a glimpse of my parents, my father smiling broadly and my mother softly chuckling, as if they were sharing a proud parental moment.

Hugging my father when I was a teen was fraught with trepidation as he would often plant a kiss on my neck while we embraced, a kiss that felt as though he had instead taken yet another bite out of me in his efforts to consume me. I didn't believe I could refuse the hug, nor did I want to hurt his feelings or endure more taunting over my discomfort. It seemed easier and quicker to just take it. I would brace myself, cringing internally, as I forced myself to engage in the demented display of affection. Again, there was an internal conflict as part of me knew the interaction was far from acceptable, yet the guilt I felt because I didn't want to hug my father always took me to a place of self-judgment and shame. I hugged him because it was expected, and, just as powerful, because I wanted to prove to myself that I was a loving individual.

We didn't have a shower in my childhood home, so we had to lean over the tub to wash our hair, our bottoms on full display. Often times I would find my father standing at the end of the hall simply watching as I was bent over the tub. It felt lewd and vile. I wanted to jump up and shut the door, but I knew he would only take more jabs at me for being overly sensitive once again. So instead I tried unsuccessfully to convince myself that perhaps I was being too uptight and paranoid, that word "perhaps" a tenuous link to my sanity.

There were several instances when I was a teen that my father would suddenly need to discuss something with me while I sat naked in the bath. My first instinct was to cover up, of course, but he would proceed to tell me I was being silly as he'd seen me naked many times over when I was little, making some reference to changing my diapers. I sat in the tub, in sheer horror and feeling successfully trapped as his prey. I sensed his feelings of power at having made me squirm, triumph glimmering in his eyes, and always that smug grin playing on his lips. From that point forward, I gathered every ounce of courage I had to sit tall and not attempt to cover myself when he came into that bathroom. I utilized the only tool I had at hand, defiance. I would not allow him to win and see me writhe in humiliation and degradation. My insides told a different story, however, as they quivered while I sat being visually raped.

My brother was allowed to hang various calendars of naked women up in the basement. While it might have been developmentally appropriate for him, it wasn't for me who was eight years his junior. I felt uneasy, as if by seeing and enjoying pictures of these nude women, they were somehow taking pleasure in my female body as well. It felt as if I too stood disrobed, as exposed as those women. The message I understood was that women were objects and, therefore, by association, I was too. There was no sense of respect for the beauty of these women's bodies. These weren't glorifying works of art; this was pornography intended for adults, not children. I wanted those pictures put away and innately knew something was perverse about them hanging in our basement for all to see.

I wish I could end my story there, as though that might have been enough for one lifetime, but that was not to be my truth or the limit to their dysfunction.

## Battle Royale

My father, without the slightest degree of exaggeration, was also a raging lunatic. His fury created a wake of lasting traumatic destruction that held us all emotionally bound and hostage.

In our younger years, spanking was my parents' form of discipline for us, and as was typical for the time, they always said, "This hurts me more than it hurts you," before the punishment began. I doubted that very much because my backside and my heart both remained tender each time the ordeal had come to an end.

If I got in trouble during the day while my father was at work, I had to sit on the sofa, for a time that felt no shorter than an eternity, waiting for him to come home and hit me. The entire time I would be tearful, begging my mother to hit me instead. I would awkwardly hiccup for air because I was crying so hard, and she would yell at me to, "Knock it off!" The more I tried to stop, the harder the tears fell, my attempts to breathe coming out in short stutters.

I know this was a source of conflict between my parents, her making me wait for him to come home to dole out my punishment. He would come home unaware of the day's trespasses and not upset with me in the least, yet he would have to deal out the beating for the offense. Quite often he would angrily voice to my mother, "You're making me the bad guy!" Indeed she was by playing the more passive role in the spankings, failing to see how she was just as responsible as he for what happened to me. She allowed it all and had, in fact, orchestrated it.

Before he would spank me, he would make a production out of taking off his black, cracked leather belt and snap it directly in front of me. He smiled as he watched my heightening fear and anticipation, knowing he had succeeded in his goal; apparently scaring me was amusement for him. He would then make me pull down my pants and lean naked over his knee so he could strike me with his belt.

Oftentimes when my father would spank me, I would pee myself, and ultimately all over him. He wasn't pleased about that, so it then became standard operating procedure that I was forced to go to the bathroom before he used his belt on me. I remember one particular time I devised a plan to stay in that bathroom as long as possible, trying to delay the inevitable. I sat in the bathroom petrified, foolishly hoping that out of sight meant out of mind. They quickly caught on to my scheme and called me out into the living room, "Kellie, get out here!" When I hesitantly stepped into the living room, they were shaking their heads side to side, snickering at me and my efforts to avoid the spanking, as if I had done something cute and not desperate. My sadness grew to the size of a mammoth boulder, its weight causing me to implode until I stood in a sinkhole of loneliness. I saw very clearly that my anguish hadn't touched their hearts, only their funny bone. There was nothing left for me to do but assume the position and take my beating.

One particular day the children that my mother watched as part of her daycare stood watch as I was hit, a public flogging of sorts. I felt my face flush with embarrassment and shame, turning the same color as my beaten bottom, as the other kids in the living room stood witness to my exposed naked behind and extreme humiliation.

Sometimes my mother did take part in the discipline, and her tools of the trade for hitting were a marbled, red hairbrush or the orange fly swatter that bore the remnants of its victims' blood and guts. Making me stand in the kitchen corner for extended periods of time and yanking my ear or pulling my hair were also techniques she employed. Another go-to in her arsenal was soap in the mouth–a gritty bar of pink or pale green Lava if it was from the kitchen, or a gold bar of Dial if it came from the bathroom sink. I found the Lava to be more tolerable because it was a naturally drier soap, and so it didn't coat my tongue as readily.

I know there are many of you reading this that can relate to spankings and the soap in the mouth; they're seen as typical childhood punishments. My belief is that these types of punishments belong nowhere in a parents' form of discipline and does nothing but strain the parent-child relationship and shame the child. When these punishments were combined with all the other dynamics and behaviors swirling around my house, I just got more poison for that toxic soup I was being fed. It all became one more thing to suffer in an already intolerable situation.

For the first decade plus of my life, when my parents fought, it became a war to be won at all costs on my father's part. The shouting was the early warning system as it was most often the precursor to the violence. I don't recall what most of my parents' fights were about, and I don't know what specific trigger would send him over the edge, or even if there was one, but once he took that leap, he was maniacal. Regularly strangling my mother with his bare hands was how he chose to express himself and his rage.

The look on his face as he strangled her was, of course, murderous–like hate on steroids. Witnessing her tears and degradation was a pain that cut to my core; each and every time it felt as though he had another set of hands that had ripped into my chest and begun to simultaneously squeeze the life out of my beating heart. To say she looked helpless and pathetic against the ferocious violence that fueled him is my ludicrous attempt at trying to convey the glare of torment in her eyes and the agonizing emotional death she endured, and I witnessed, many times over.

I recall one particular incident when they were fighting that my brother forced my sister and me to stay planted on our moss green-colored couch. I was on the sofa's far right, my brother and I sandwiching my sister between us both. Looking back, I suppose he didn't want us to get hurt too, but at the time I only knew that he was telling me to do something that I wanted no part of. I was incensed at him for his command and furious with my sister as well for so obediently doing as told. I fought the urge to get up from that spot with Herculean willpower. I couldn't fathom how they could just sit there and not at least *try* to help her; I believed we were leaving her abandoned and completely alone. I was overwhelmed with such intense fear for her life and emotion that I had an out-of-body experience.

Without any thought on my part, some level of my consciousness sailed effortlessly to the corner of our living room just above our cabinet TV. From that vantage point I could see the three of us seated on the sofa across the room, a colorful afghan covering the couch and giving the false impression of comfort. It was the shiny faux wood panels behind it that told the true tale of a most unnatural scene. As I hovered close to the ceiling, I could also witness my father strangling my mother while holding her against the side of our refrigerator, which stood just outside their bedroom door. The photo album of my mind still holds the snapshot of her mask of torment—her mouth drawn downward with the weight of defeat as the tears of resignation leaked from her eyes and down her cheeks. It was a pitiful sight. Based on where my physical body was sitting, I wouldn't have been able to see any of this because there was a wall that blocked the view from the couch into the kitchen. Having seen enough, I unconsciously returned to my body that still sat in the same spot and position as I had left it.

Not surprisingly, there were many more violent scenes in the years to come. No longer would I sit idly on the sidelines, but would instead make a mad dash to my mother's side where she was lying on the floor, straddled by my unhinged father. I pleaded with him to stop, sitting beside her on the living room floor as he tried to strangle her into submission. Although I was the youngest in the family, I tried valiantly to stop him, fueled by my desperation to prevent an outcome that for me would have been fatal as well. I was wild-eyed with sheer panic that he would indeed kill her; it seemed a likely outcome, no matter how many times I witnessed the abuse.

I was rewarded for my valor as she soon viewed me as her little hero and fierce protector throughout those violent years. The love that seemed to beam from her eyes and straight into my heart was my sustenance and well worth any price I paid. I took great pride and honor in my role as her personal savior. I felt stronger, bigger, and more powerful than my chronological age. I became quite certain that I possessed the internal strength she was lacking. I was elated to pull her up and out of the hole that had claimed her, as often as was needed. My goal was to rescue her and prove to her that she was not as forsaken as she most certainly felt. My commitment to her was, without question, unwavering–the stone pillar where my only purpose remained docked. I knew full well the agony of standing in the midst of hell all alone, and so I did for her what no one had ever done for me.

Now I know the sad truth of that role, which is that little bit of a girl should never have been in a situation where she was the protector. The roles of parent and child had become horribly reversed, and instead I was put in harm's way by trying to pull my father off my mother.

What stopped him from turning on me in those instances? I'll never know. I don't think he could offer a rational explanation either, then or now. Perhaps it was my sheer audacity to think I could overpower and control him, stop it in its tracks? But my will to save my mother overrode the danger to my very life. I cared more about her than I did myself. She was an inextricable part of what made me whole.

After one particularly intense fight, my mother rushed out of the house, and I followed her. She hopped in the car to drive away, and as she backed up in her state of panic, she slammed into the back of my brother's pickup truck. My stomach sank as I realized the gravity of what she had done. This mistake sent her fear over the edge; she began shaking and crying harder as we stood on the driveway to assess the damage.

My father heard the loud bang. Soon he stood on the front porch and began shrieking at her for her stupidity. He ranted and demanded that we get back inside. It was another out-of-body event for me as I stood briefly behind my own physical form, watching me as I stood gazing up at my maniacal father.

The only word I have to describe my emotion as my mother started making her way back into the house, with me in tow, is terrified, but it was so much more harrowing than that word can depict. There was *no* doubt in my mind he was going to kill us both. I was a dead man walking, certain my death would take place once we shut the front door. Where I found the courage, at the age of about nine, to take those steps back inside I've not a clue. Perhaps it wasn't courage, but instead the emotional super glue that bound me so tightly to my mother; it never even crossed my mind to allow her to re-enter the house by herself.

What happened after we got back inside has escaped my recollection, but to live with the person that could easily be your executioner, and call him "Dad," was an aberration. The two pieces of the mental puzzle did not seem to fit no matter how I turned them and only proved to confuse and petrify me.

My father's rage was our puppet master for a multitude of years. Everything was about trying not to catapult him into some vicious course of anger and brutality. Each time one of us did something that could potentially infuriate him, no matter how minor, my apprehension soared as I waited for the fall out. My stomach would twist upon itself as I cautiously and quietly made my way around our home, lest I be the one to trigger the landmine, eyes ever on my father's facial expressions, words, and body language for a telltale sign of imminent danger.

To a child witnessing violence, it is just as damaging and traumatic as if the abuse happened directly to them. My father was an equal opportunity guy, however, and provided me with many more chances to witness just how far he was willing to go in his efforts to pummel another – and to experience it firsthand.

## Uncharitable

In time, or at least one time that I know of, my mother did reach her limit for my father's abuses. Looking back at the scene, I can't say what world she was living in, only that it was her own.

One afternoon while on summer break from elementary school, I noticed my mother gathering clothes that belonged to my sister and me and putting them into a trash bag. I became quite alarmed when I noticed her pack the latest pair of berry-embellished bell bottoms that had been handed down to me from my sister. I coveted those jeans and was thrilled to know that my sister had outgrown them.

"What are you doing with those clothes?" I asked her.

"Donating them to charity," she mumbled.

"But I want those jeans!" I cried, "I just got them!" She gave no response and continued to stare only at the bag she was stuffing. My personal security system went on high alert because I knew that something was amiss and being kept secret from me.

That afternoon we went grocery shopping at the small store just five minutes from my parents' house. While we stood taking the groceries out of the cart and placing them in the car, my mother appeared quite despondent, as if someone had died. Before finishing our task she posed a question to me and my sister, "I'm leaving your dad. Do you want to come with me or stay with him?" Again, no eye contact.

Suddenly I understood her secrecy and the true intentions behind her collecting our clothes. Naturally, my sister and I were quite upset and became tearful. I certainly didn't feel safe staying alone with him and soon began to fear for the loss of my family as a unit if she walked out the door. I begged her not to leave.

In the end we wiped our tears, went home rather shell-shocked, and she stayed. The matter was never discussed again until I was a teen and she said with an accusatory tone, "I stayed for you kids," as though we were to blame for those years of her suffering.

Her tactic worked; I felt guilty for the misery she endured because of me. *How selfish of me to ask her to remain with him*, I thought.

Now with many years behind me, I understand she gave two young girls a choice that they never could have made. It was quite unfair of her to put us in a position to choose loyalties and make a decision that belonged to an adult. What I find most shocking is that she was willing to leave her children with a man that was extremely abusive; there should never have been a question in her mind as to where we would live. Did she not know charity began at home?

For my part, questions became a mainstay of my life as I tried to understand and sort through their incomprehensible actions year after tragic year.

## Before MADD, there was Madness

There were, of course, many things I couldn't pretend to grasp or forget, like my father stomping on my brother's head.

My teenage brother had come home drunk. Worse, he had been drinking and driving. My parents were on attack as soon as he walked through the kitchen door. He was forced to sit in a kitchen chair that faced the living room. Always in the mix of things, I stood to my brother's right. I may have been about ten at the time.

Both of my parents proceeded to repeatedly yell at him about the danger and stupidity of his actions. I was worried for him because he had clearly done something horribly dangerous. This was before the days of MADD campaigns and drunk driving education.

At some point during the lecture, my brother fell out of the chair and onto the kitchen floor, landing on his left side. I don't recall if my father had hit him, causing him to fall or if he was simply that drunk, but my father's reaction to my brother lying on the floor was to lift his own leg high in the air and stomp on the side of my brother's head. There's a recording in my brain that I cannot erase, one where I can still hear my brother scream out in pain and the sound of him sobbing as my father continued his tirade. My mother stood by my father's side and made no efforts to stop him. The violence was surreal and gruesome to behold, the shock left me frozen in place. All I could manage to do was stare and brace myself to witness my brother's death; I couldn't imagine how he would survive someone crushing his skull.

I desperately wanted to beg for mercy for my brother, but I felt emotionally paralyzed as this was the first time I had witnessed a physical assault by my father against my brother. Attacks on my mother were commonplace, but this was out of my scope of experience. My brother had outgrown spankings and the like many years ago, and so, the days of my brother's physical punishments were not in my memory bank.

Each time my father acted violently, I expected the death of someone in my family. How we survived his intense attacks is a marvel to me, a true miracle of sorts. As strange as it may sound, I always wanted to pose the question to him, "How did you know when to stop? Could you sense that fine line between life and death?" Perhaps I gave him more credit than he deserves; there was no skill involved, only luck.

The other piece that remains etched in my mind about that night is the fleeting awareness of my father's omnipotence. He seemed unstoppable, a battering force of nature. At this point in my brother's life, he was physically comparable to my father. I wondered to myself, *What stopped him from lashing out at my father? What prevented him from fighting back?* Perhaps the alcohol left him incapacitated, but more than anything it felt like it was this unwritten rule that my father was allowed to do and say anything as we remained utterly devoid of power, pounded into surrender. He was our merciless dictator. He made the rules and he was the enforcer. It felt as though he was our personal Goliath and possessed a strength that was far greater than all of us combined.

## Equal Opportunity

Certainly if the humans in our household had not a chance against my father, any animal was an easy mark as well. And so our family beagle, Barney, became one more victim of my father's rampages.

It seemed every time we left the house, Barney would root through the trash, leaving it strewn across the kitchen floor. Those incidents left me with yet another image to add to my photo collage, the pieces of discarded orange peels and coffee grounds lying about the kitchen floor. I can still recall the sweet citrus scent that was overpowered by the rich aroma of brewed coffee grounds, as though the photo was a scratch and sniff. Just in case there was any threat of me forgetting the entire frightful story, Barney's cries continue to loop on playback for my listening pleasure.

Barney didn't know the rules, but he was seen as a flagrant violator, and my father took it all very personally. His remedy to the situation? Pick Barney up by the throat, strangle him as he held him in mid-air and hurl him across the room. A helpless animal became just another victim in my father's path of destruction. There is no word I know that can describe the brutality of that scene. I was desperate to go to Barney, but feared enraging my father all the more, perhaps putting Barney in further danger by bringing attention to him and what would be perceived as the greater offense, my comfort. Instead, Barney suffered alone, and I was left with the heavy burden of shame for abandoning him during his time of dire need.

Trying to prevent this horror show, my sister and I developed a solution. We would try to race into the house after our outings, and before our father got inside, so we could try to clean up any evidence of the trash foraging. I can recall glancing at my father as I hurried past him, what he would have called a "shit-eating grin" planted across his face because he knew our purpose and somehow found that comical. The urgency to get into that house and remove any traces of trash felt as though Barney's life lay in our hands. We were on a rescue mission, truly.

The solution was never a logical one: buy a trashcan and stop putting the trash in a brown paper grocery bag tucked in the corner. No, my parents were determined they were going to "teach this dog a lesson," not find a solution. They seemed to think Barney was challenging their authority because he kept doing it time and again. Lost on them was the fact that he was a dog with food remains readily available to him, that he was simply being a dog. Their twisted logic was, and remains, incomprehensible.

## Without Liberty and Justice for All

What they could not control with physical aggression they attempted to rule with emotional domination. Living with them was a constant exercise in being controlled, day in and day out. There was no middle ground, only their black and white dogma. Negotiations were unheard of, and we were forbidden to voice any disagreement with what they dictated. The only voices allowed were theirs, and only their thoughts mattered. It was infuriating to me, to put it mildly. No one likes to be disregarded, child or not, most especially not by people that seemed to have their own sick interpretation of the world.

When my mother made supper, we were all required to eat whatever she put in front of us. My sister and I spent a noticeable amount of time shuffling the foods we disliked upon our plates, but never were we permitted to pass on what was a displeasure to our palates. The typical rule applied: "Sit and finish what's on your plate." And sit we did.

My father was most fond of fried calves' liver and onions; my sister and I were most definitely not, and my mother happily made this dish to please him. It was one of the few things she could get right without fail. This was where my parents took the dinner rule to a whole new level.

No matter how hard I tried I could not swallow the gray, chalky mush that had become the chewed liver in my mouth. I would sit there and heave, tears filling my eyes, at every attempt to get even the smallest portions down my throat. Eventually particles of liver could be seen floating around my glass of water, like snow in a snow globe, because I kept taking gulp after gulp in an effort to moisten the dry paste in my mouth in hopes that it would soften and flow more easily pass my gag reflex. Well, I can confirm that it did indeed moisten what I had in my mouth because when I did gag once again I was left with a muddy puddle upon my plate, which I then had to scoop up with my spoon so that I might try, try again. It was a foul, degrading, and harsh display of force.

Another shining example of how they controlled us was when we were grounded. My father would ground us for whatever offense was deemed worthy and not give a time frame for the punishment. There was no, "You're grounded for a week." We were simply grounded, and the only way to get ungrounded was to go and ask him permission to be set free. It was all a manipulative mind game, another way for him to feel like he was the almighty in our household. He relished our groveling to him.

I would spend days getting up the courage to talk to him about not being grounded. When I would finally speak to him, my stomach would be queasy, churning with apprehension because, of course, he couldn't make that part easy either. He wouldn't give the respect of any eye contact as I stood internally trembling in front him and asked, "Can I be ungrounded?"

The only response this self-appointed god would bestow upon me would be to deeply growl a hesitant, "Yeah," just to make sure I knew who was boss.

This was the same charade we had to play if we wanted to do anything outside of the house. Asking to do any typical childhood event was this big production and was always wrought with trepidation on our part. That's clearly what he, and she, wanted.

Somewhere in my teen years I became tired of being forced to play by his rules. I got grounded once again, but this time I refused to ask to be ungrounded. I refused to kneel to the king. I remained homebound. I went nowhere because I didn't want to give him the satisfaction of watching me plead. After a year of punishment, I finally broke down because boys had piqued my interest, and I wanted to go to a school dance. It was tough to ultimately concede to his rule, and my ego took a beating, but there was just no way around it. It truly incensed me that he won that round.

Their domineering behaviors were mixed with the physical and sexual traumas to create an insufferable atmosphere. It was a maddening place to be because any time their behaviors came into question I was the silly, naïve child. A favorite saying they had was, "I've been to the mountain." As if stating this explained everything and bestowed upon them some type of wisdom far beyond the comprehension of my childish mind. There was simply no escape. I felt trapped in my own home, surrounded by those that feigned sanity. I saw Edvard Munch's painting, The Scream, and felt as if someone finally understood what I felt inside.

Perhaps on that mountain they suffered oxygen deprivation. As for me, I could only bide my time.


## Nowhere to Run, Nowhere to Hide

What time did show me was the fact that dangers existed not just in the home, but lurked wherever I might travel. My aunt was the one to introduce me to this fact of life early on.

I would see her quite frequently at the family gatherings at my grandmother's house. I found her to be humorous, and I enjoyed her rather boisterous nature. Whenever we all got together, she made a point of engaging us kids in conversation, and I felt as though I mattered. I was fascinated with both her and my uncle because it seemed as though they dressed and presented themselves with a casual air of refinement. In stark contrast to my own home, visiting their well-manicured house felt to me like stepping into a fairytale cottage, a sense of otherworldly magic filling my childish imaginings.

So when my aunt offered to take me to a local public pool, I was delighted and relished the undivided attention. I felt like I was hob knobbing to be able to go to a pool with her. I wasn't a strong swimmer, but loved the idea of being part of the summer excitement a pool seemed to offer.

Because she was an adult and I was child, my aunt clearly had the height advantage and used that in a game she would play with me. She would stand beside me as I squatted in the water, place her hands on my head and then proceed to hold my head below the water. When she felt like I'd reached my limit for being held under, she would let me up. There I would stand sputtering and gasping for air while she howled with laughter.

How or why this was funny is still lost on me. I was already very intimate with danger, and this only reinforced that I could never fully trust anyone with my safety, anywhere.

As per usual, no one came to my defense, although I shared the incidents with my mother. I simply stopped going, as though I had lost interest and had not been in fear for my life–again.

Soon enough I got the message loud and clear that there were bogeymen everywhere. In fact, one tried to abduct me.

I was outside enjoying a summer day break from grade school. I was racing around our maple tree, the veteran sentry that stood watch in our front yard, with the kids that attended my mother's daycare. I noticed a car pull off the road in front of our house and stop at the end of the driveway. I rushed over to the car, happy to assume the authoritative role of the oldest child in the mix.

A man wearing a beanie sat inside. He stared straight ahead and never made eye contact with me, giving me full view of his pale pock-marked right cheek. He mumbled something about wanting to know where someone lived. I couldn't hear him so I asked him to repeat himself, as I leaned into his open car window. "Do you mean Barry?" I asked. He grumbled a response that I couldn't discern, so I pulled myself further into the vehicle. "I can't hear you. Can you talk louder?" Again, I inched further into his car. When this happened for the third time, I began to feel annoyed with the man for clearly making no effort to help me understand him. The realization that he wasn't taking any steps to help me hear him set off an emergency flare inside me. In a mental flash I saw that he was intentionally trying to get me deeper into his car so that he could easily pull me in.

In the next instant, I pulled myself back out of the window and hurriedly said, "Hold on. I'll go get my mom." I began sprinting to the back of house to tell my mother, and the stranger sped away within seconds.

My mother was clearly shaken, even tearful, and it solidified for me that I had just dodged another bullet. As pitiful as it may seem, I recall feeling elated that my mother was so upset and worried about what had happened. In my mind, I took it as an odd confirmation that she really did love me as much as I loved her, as this was the first time she demonstrated an outward concern for my physical safety despite many previous incidents where I was in harm's way. Somehow, I believed it cemented our bond and commitment to one another.

Threats to my safety and life followed me into middle school as well. While riding the school bus home one of the older teens, Biggy, would smoke pot in the backseat. The bus driver never confronted him, even though I complained to her that I was getting headaches and dizziness from the smell. I became irked by her impotence; it reminded me of my mother. Fed up with being sick every day after school, I decided to take care of the situation myself and told someone at school about the events in the back of the bus, having no concept of the potential consequences. The repercussions weren't pleasant.

Shortly after the school bus incident, I went for a walk to the local playground with some of the older kids my mother cared for during the day. As we were nearing the park, I noticed a car heading towards us. Not just toward us, but aiming directly at us. I shouted for the others to hurry and follow me as I tried to out run the car that was pointed straight at me. I was able to escape being hit by running into the park, where the car could not safely travel. A glance towards the driver's seat revealed it was Biggy. In an act of revenge, he had intentionally tried to hit me or, at the very least, lead me to believe that was his intention.

We raced to my grandmother's house, which was perhaps five minutes from the park, hearts pounding. All the while, I frantically looked over my shoulder and tried to stay on peoples' lawns to avoid the road, knowing that he most likely wouldn't drive in peoples' yards. My lungs burned from the physical effort, and my legs grew numb from the strain.

The children and I shared the unbelievable scare we had just experienced once we returned to my home. I was petrified for days that Biggy would try again to kill me, because by this time I trusted in the power of others' evil intentions, but there was a plan I was not privy to until after its completion.

Pine trees grew next to my parent's house. I would often spend my time meandering amongst the lot. My father and brother joined me one afternoon. Their attention, and soon our conversation, turned to the events surrounding Biggy. My father shared with me that he had instructed my brother to dole out a beating to Biggy for his actions, and that the mission was met with success.

The world felt frozen as I stood gazing up at my big brother. My heart swelled with awe and loving gratitude that someone had *finally* fought for me. The fear I felt about further retaliation vanished in a puff of smoke and the enormous relief that followed it was so very welcome. An instant later a tidal wave of shame sickened me at the realization that my brother had been forced into violence, the one thing that wreaked untold havoc in our home, for me–a kid he barely tolerated. And there I stood, looking at both sides of that same dirty coin.

In the years to come, there were more threats hiding around corners, but this time I had to go it alone. While in middle school I was the victim of bullying.

Jane was the ringleader, and she and her two closest friends, Nila and Cassy, went on an intimidation mission. When we would walk down the hall between classes, they would purposefully crowd me until I was jammed up against the wall or lockers, all the while casting a hateful stare my way. Becoming invisible was my goal, but always they spotted me, and if they could reach me in time they would sometimes ram their shoulder into mine as they walked past. Other times they would follow me into the locker room, even though we did not share gym class, their mere presence enough to send me into yet another round of fight or flight as I anticipated a potential attack. I was petrified to go into the bathroom and would risk going only with the direst need, all the while peeking through the crack by the stall door to see if they had come into the lavatory, and fruitlessly willing my body to speed up the process.

School became an unwelcome place for me at that point as I was always searching for them, waiting for them to harm me in some way. Prior to being bullied, school was my respite, the one place I could be safe and distance myself from the chaos that was my home, where I could laugh with the silly and carefree nature of a teenage girl. They stripped me of even the one place I could seek emotional solace, and often times I felt I was at my breaking point as I endured their menacing operation. I was getting no relief, the sense of being hunted and the pressure of threats looming over me followed me in every moment of my day and life's activities. My anxiety never ceased to thrash about my insides like a rabid beast, and my feelings of isolation were a cancerous mass that continually weighed me down.

But I endured, for that was all I ever knew how to do. Relief would only come after they went into high school, and I remained in middle school for another year. Finally, there was some space to breathe, and to this day I still tear up recalling that emotional reprieve.

# Monkey See, Monkey Do

Not only was I a victim of violence, but I was its perpetrator as well. My victims were two brothers named Carter and Alex, our home theirs during the day while their parents were at work.

Alex was the nervous one of the two and became easily rattled if he got into trouble. I saw an easy mark and decided to set him up to get yelled at by my mother. I went to the thermostat for the heater and turned it to its highest setting. I then told my mother that I had seen Alex commit the act. She hollered at him, "You're going to blow up the heater! What were you thinking?! Keep your fingers off of that!" Alex stood there crying and shaking as he took the punishment that wasn't his.

The adrenaline rush of what I had just done gave me a high. I felt so very powerful for having masterminded the successful ruse. In fact, I enjoyed it so much that I decided to do it again and another time after that. It was then my mother became suspicious because I was always the one catching him in the act, and Alex was not the type of child to blatantly defy authority. The jig was up and wanting to save my own hide, I stopped setting up poor Alex.

Carter was also preyed upon by me when I was young. I ran into him when I was an adult and he shared with me how he clearly remembered me intentionally shoving him down the basement steps. I have no memory of doing this, but it was evident by the look on his face that he wasn't making this up. Why would he? I shamefully apologized for my childhood maliciousness, wondering about my sadistic tendencies as I slunk away.

Now I can look back and see I was obviously acting out violently and viciously due to my chaotic and aggressive environment. I wanted to hurt another weaker person the way I too had been hurt. I had become desperate in my attempts to gain some power back and the only way that was accomplished in my house was to abuse someone. It was what I knew.

Another memory I hold in my mind regarding Carter was my insistence that we explore one another's private parts. I obsessed about finding a hiding place where we could touch each other. I arranged the meetings and recall feeling quite forceful about what we were meant to do. Looking back, I can say I felt like a predator of sorts.

I relished the command I possessed in our encounters. True, this was child to child; I believe he was one year older than me, and many may see it as a normal part of growing up, but I'm here to tell you there was nothing normal about it for me. This wasn't an innocent curiosity on my part, but was instead a dominating and controlling behavior where I would not take his "no" for an answer, despite his obvious fear and resistance. I demanded, and he caved.

Suspicions arose when we were routinely discovered alone in the shed behind our house. I quickly changed our meetings to the basement, behind a pile of pink insulation. It just so happened that my mother mentioned I should steer clear of the insulation because the fiberglass might embed splinters in my skin. I recalled her caution while Carter and I stood with our pants down, envisioning my lack of explanation as to how fiberglass splinters had gotten "there." Knowing I could only get caught if I continued, I called off our encounters.

Some might call me a monster; in fact, I viewed myself as just that for quite some time, but I learned that I was a little girl simply doing what had been done to her. My actions were not a reflection of me, but were instead mirroring how I had been instructed. I had been taught the fine art of abuse and I had become an "A" student.

There are times I wonder if there was some other lewd or abusive actions I may have taken part in but can't recall. I suppose it's a real possibility, and if this is so, I apologize to anyone I may have hurt.

## Sticky Fingers

I acted out in other ways, too. I began stealing while I was in elementary school. Initially I stole things that belonged to my sister. I already believed she was the one who was loved best, and if I couldn't have what I felt she got emotionally, I would take the objects she possessed.

I couldn't do anything with the items I stole other than periodically and secretly hold and stare at them, for then my family would know for sure what they had suspected: I was the thief. My sister would accuse me of taking her belongings, my most treasured grab her aquamarine colored birthstone earrings. I always denied it. Again, I felt a sense of pleasure and -you guessed it–power, this time at seeing her distress because she couldn't prove her accusations.

Eventually, I dared to steal outside the home, things that seemed unique and somehow held a magical appeal for me. They didn't have to be of great value; in fact, most were part of everyday life, but in my mind they held some type of wonder. While visiting my paternal grandmother, I became mesmerized with the newest toothpaste on the market, Aquafresh. A tube of it hung by her bathroom sink, and at first I was content to simply smell it, but I would soon find myself making frequent trips to the bathroom so that I could squeeze it out of the tube for a taste, fascinated by its tri-color technology. Temptation grew, and next I stole the whole tube. My grandmother knew who was to blame for her missing toothpaste and alerted my parents. I was made to return the stolen goods, and my embarrassment was far greater than the excitement of its possession.

I wasn't finished quite yet, however, as I still felt a strong compulsion to steal. What I realize now is that I was seeking an adrenaline rush. While at the local pharmacy, several goods caught my eye on different occasions. I was well aware there were cameras that might capture my illegal acts, but that only added to the thrill of seeing if I could get away with it. In the store I was never caught, but at home my parents would often question how I had obtained my mystery objects, things they had never paid for.

The last item I swiped was bath beads, the newest bath paraphernalia to hit the stores. I found their creamy pearlescent color a tempting treasure and proceeded to free several from the hard plastic tube that contained them, the industrial tape providing me with an added challenge. I made the mistake of holding and admiring them one night in the living room, my parents questioning once again how I happened to have found them in my coat pocket. I assured them that one of my middle school friends had given them to me, because all teenage girls routinely gift one another with random bath beads. No, obviously not. I felt as ridiculously foolish as I sounded, and this time the shame I bore far outweighed the pleasure. I was done with my petty thief career.

Several years later my sister declared, "You were always a weird kid." I resented that comment at the time. I suppose to the untrained eye that may well have been the case, but the reality of what I was doing spoke volumes, if only there had been someone who would listen.

## A Glimmer of Hope

I didn't realize it, for I never laid eyes on them, but someone had been listening, and soon I would know this truth to the very depths of my soul.

I always felt a special connection to the small lot of pines that stood next to our house. Being amongst them always left me feeling loved and cherished, as though they created a sacred space to hold me. I would spend my time with them, gently testing the soft pad of cinnamon-hued pine needles sprinkled upon the ground. I savored and repeatedly inhaled the telltale pine scent, my fingers tacky with resin. My goal was to discover the freshly fallen pinecones, which proved to have the most satisfyingly loud crunch, as I hopped about the lot, intentionally stomping on them.

My age was somewhere in the single digits when I found myself staring out at the pines through the living room window. At that time, I lacked the vocabulary to put into words the depth of my anguish around my life. I could have only told you that I hurt. But it was much more than that, and as I look back, I can tell you that an emotional grim reaper had come to call. The shadow it cast as it loomed over me darkened my days, and its fingers tapped the fading rhythm of my heart. These are the words now that I didn't know then for the feelings I had always felt.

I felt so completely overwhelmed and heavy hearted about my life. I didn't believe I could bear anymore of the senselessness and horror that surrounded me. It seemed as though I was sinking fast. Dread of the days, and I feared years, to come seemed utterly unbearable. I could only beg for mercy from someone and anywhere.

That someone must have heard my desperate pleas because in my moments of despair a gift was bestowed upon me. I sensed a sudden, deep inner knowing that I would make it out of my hell, but first I had to withstand some more, in fact a lot more. It was made clear to me that my situation certainly would not change, but that I would, someday, be free. Oddly, it left me with a greater calm despite the knowledge that the chaos would not be ending any time soon. I could literally feel the relief that awaited somewhere in the future.

I was given a sense of hope that day, a rare and precious gift that would carry me through the rest of my life. With this communication I was left feeling less alone in my struggles. Somebody or something had heard my pleas, and although they wouldn't intervene to change my circumstances, there was a witness that confirmed my experiences. "This is bad," I mentally whispered to the presence I sensed.

"Yes. It is," was the hushed response offered by my most gentle visitor, "but I promise you, one day it will end."

I can offer you no logical explanations, but I will tell you that I had the utmost love for and trust in my guardian that had come to call, and the glorious radiance of the love they had for me pierced my veil of pain. And so I made an internal resolve to put my head down and just keep plowing through to the light at the end of my very long tunnel.

Somewhere around that same timeframe, two angels were to appear on my path, this time in human form, and both threw me a much-needed lifeline.

Mrs. Alexander was my second grade teacher, and she gave to me a gift that I've cherished ever since. Like most little girls, I wanted nothing more than to please my teacher. I would eagerly volunteer to help in each and every way she allowed us.

One particular afternoon I completed some task. Whether it was required school work or something I had completed for her, I can't say. What I do remember is looking up at her while she stated with an honest

Kellie Springer, RN

enthusiasm, "You must be so proud of yourself!" Her exclamation left me glowing on the inside and feeling a bit giddy. I was mesmerized with what she had said and rolled the sentence over and over in my mind. I had never had this thought or concept, that I could be proud of myself. The awe it birthed in me was as if she had shared one of the wonders of the universe. I tucked her simple, kind words deep inside. I shared them with no one lest they be taken from me. They became a treasure that I've touched in memory an untold number of times, and each time I do they never fail to touch my heart.

In third grade I was blessed to have Miss Flannery as my teacher. I always felt warmly welcomed and loved while in her class. Every day she would give each one of us a hug that I would come to look forward to, and she seemed genuinely pleased to see us walk into her classroom. I felt important to her, and there was nothing she wanted back from me, nothing I had to do to earn or keep her love. It was safe to be me in her room where I was unconditionally accepted and her affection was pure. I believe those hugs gave me the chance to know physical connection and expression in a way that I hungered for and had never truly known before.

When I was about thirty years old, I found these two remarkable teachers and shared my appreciation with them as best as my words allowed. Both women fed my soul when I was starving and provided my faith in love with a much-needed jumpstart. While they never knew of the desperate circumstances I faced at home, I would like to believe their kindness was a doorstop that kept my heart from forever closing completely.

## First, Make No Assumptions

Unfortunately, third grade also brings with it some painful memories and messages that remained embedded in my being. It was during that year that I was told I was to be tested for our school's gifted program. I was beyond excited, an electrical storm of delight. My excitement was based in facts.

40

Fact: My brother was getting in trouble at home year after year for poor grades.

Fact: My father, who had struggled in school as well, would yell a blue streak at my brother after every poor report card.

So, my logic went, my parents would be over the moon with me for getting tested for this program. I soon learned there was no logic in dealing with them.

I raced home to tell my mother. She stood at the kitchen stove stirring the chicken intended for supper that night. She made no eye contact, and I could tell by looking at her that her state of depression was too deep. She was consumed with herself and had no room for me or my exuberance. The most she could muster was a slight nod in response to me. I was slightly disheartened, but I had grown accustomed to her dulled affect and continued to hold out hope because I *knew* my father would be pleased with me.

After I finished eating supper that night, I stood by my father's kitchen chair, where he still sat eating his meal. I was barely able to stop myself from jumping up and down as my enthusiasm and joy began to brim over. I told him about my scheduled testing. He turned to me, looked me right in the eyes, pointed his finger at me, and yelled, "Don't you ever think you're special or better than anyone else!"

My eyes flew open in alarm; this was not what I had expected, and I was truly baffled by his response. I don't recall feeling better than anyone; I was just ecstatic because I finally felt seen. I couldn't understand his reaction, and I was left feeling absolutely deflated as I sullenly slipped away. What an idiot I had been, to showcase my foolish pride and think that he would be elated.

I took the tests as planned, filled with apprehension the entire time. Was it better to pass or fail? I couldn't decide. I failed. I think it may have been by three questions. The test results only seemed to confirm my father's message, I was not special, and it was there in black and white for all to see. I was humiliated and saw myself as completely inferior to my peers who had taken the tests and passed.

The message I received was delivered to me with such ferocity that I would never dare run the risk of feeling there might be something special about me on any level. Simply put, there was nothing to celebrate about me.

What was conveyed in unspoken terms was that by letting your light shine you were somehow diminishing another's. It was not okay to feel pleased with yourself because then someone else would feel inferior.

As an adult, I was left wondering what would have happened if I had passed my tests and also how my stress from my father's reaction impacted my abilities. Questions I'll never have an answer to, and ultimately they don't matter today, but it feels as if some part of me was ripped from my grasp before I ever had a chance to know it or explore how it fit into that which is me.

## Freak Show

My internal world was just as chaotic as my external one. The vision I had of myself, and held for much of my life, was as skewed as my "normal" childhood day.

I've always had a poor tolerance for hot weather, and so somewhere around fourth grade I opted to get my hair cut short to try to prevent the heat rash that creeped across the back of my neck. This was an emotional decision for me to make because my father made it very clear that he liked long hair; he was possessive about wanting us to keep our hair long. I felt as though I was letting my father down, and most assuredly he would find me ugly with my chopped locks.

The world at large seemed to reflect my fears in a very clear way. On several occasions, a well-intentioned adult would say to my parents, "Oh, what a little cute boy," as I sported my shorter hairdo. I couldn't muster the courage to look at these people let alone tell them I was truly a girl. In truth, I believed they saw me as I knew myself to be. This homely girl was the image of myself that pervaded my mind throughout my life. Even as I got older, I didn't realize that I had grown and become something different. I felt shamefully ugly.

Then there was my sister. She kept her long hair, a desirable length compared to mine. My father often sang a song to her about her beautiful, beautiful brown eyes. I hated that song; the words still flow readily through my mind, and the memory of my jealousy that the color of my eyes were not song worthy. My conclusion? She was the pretty one, not me. It didn't seem to be a far stretch.

As I approached my teens and adulthood, I would notice people looking at me, staring. My above average height was a beacon that drew many comments, and repeatedly I would hear, "You're a big girl." My translation: "You look like and are built like a man." Obviously, I wasn't flattered.

My humiliation and shame about my looks grew to great proportions, for I figured people were looking at me because I was so horrid to behold, an unsightly, masculine mess. I was a freak. My identity as emanating anything feminine was completely lost to me, and I came to believe that any attention that was shown to me was out of pity, or perhaps I was a genetic train wreck that didn't allow others to break their gaze. Around that same time the boys in middle school nicknamed me Hotsy Totsy, a play on my maiden name. I could never quite figure out if it was meant to be a compliment or a sarcastic joke, and was afraid to risk believing the former.

The notion that I was worthy of love was a foreign concept to me. I saw no reason anyone would want to be with me, but my father cleared that up too. As is typical of many teenage girls, I was verbally swooning to my parents over some boy in my school, showing an extreme hormonal lapse of judgment in trusting this part of myself with them. My father listened as I talked about my most intense crush and the hopes I had that he liked me too. A smirk crossed his lips as he then shared his poetic words of wisdom, "He only wants to get in your pants."

My face fell and I felt like a buffoon for daring to dream that this boy would be smitten with me. Clearly I had nothing to offer other than spreading my legs. I took this message to heart, believing there was nothing, *nothing*, to love about me. I had nothing to offer another other than sex; that's all I was good for. I wasn't kind, pretty, funny, or smart. I was a pussy to be fucked; my father told me so.

I wasn't wanted from conception. My looks were offensive. Something felt innately wrong with me. My parents drummed it into my head repeatedly that there was nothing wrong with them or the way they behaved; it was me, *silly* child. My behaviors proved oft times to be frustrating to my parents as I frequently challenged their authority, I the problem child. My mother went so far as to say, "I pity the man you marry." And I grew to pity him too. To think of the burden he would have to deal with by sharing his life with me.

The culmination of all these factors left me feeling as though I lacked any importance in this world. I was a plight to be dealt with, and people simply put up with me. I equated it to being kind of like a housefly. No one truly appreciates anything about them, but we accept that they are an annoying presence in our world. That was me.

Bzzzz...

## Counting on It

I had to come up with a way to soothe myself. My method was to silently count so that the numbers might drown out my disturbing external and internal world. If there was nothing repetitive to count, like stairs, cars, or lockers, I would count by fives, then tens, and finally I rounded off the hundreds until I reached 1,000. I never liked to say single digits once I was past 100 because saying, "One hundred and one..," etc. felt choppy, and I was attempting to create a calmness in my life. Still waters was what I needed.

When insomnia made its nightly visits, I lay awake hoping to accurately count the seconds until the tile on my new alarm clock would make a simultaneous click and flip, marking the passing of another minute. The clock usually won round after round of that game, but it gave me a fun challenge to help pass the night and an opportunity to distract myself from heavier thoughts.

My coping skills seemed to advance along with technology. Eventually I owned a cassette player and one tape, *Get the Knack*. My nightly competition with my alarm clock soon became obsolete as the songs on that tape became the lullabies that played non-stop throughout my nights. They temporarily took me to another place, and there was nothing I needed more than that escape.

## Everything Has a Season

When I was perhaps around the age of twelve, it seemed I might not be in need of a great escape after all. A surprise was in store for me as my father's violence toward my mother abruptly ended.

My mother required dental surgery for infected cysts. Prior to her arrival home from the procedure, I sensed my sister and father were quite worried, but they shared nothing as to the source of their concern.

When my mother came home, she explained why they had been upset, "Because of him [my father], I almost died," she stated with a bit of flair. For reasons unknown to me, and not explained by her, the medical staff struggled to wake my mother. An all-too familiar feeling arose within me; I was petrified because once again she went knocking on death's door, only this time she was nowhere near the safety net I cast for her.

I failed to understand how my father could be involved in her surgical close call. We remained standing in the opening between the kitchen and living room as I asked, "What do you mean?"

She smugly explained that her dental issues were a direct result of his strangling her. Without the damage done by him, the surgery wouldn't have been necessary, and she wouldn't have undergone anesthesia and struggled to recover from it. Thus it led back to, "Because of him, I almost died."

She smirked as she shared that this sequence of events had frightened him, to think she may not have lived and that it was his abusive hands that created the cascade of events. She glowed with a sense of victory and self-righteousness. With great confidence she declared, "He's going to stop." And he did. I never saw my father lay a hand on my mother ever again. It was over.

I don't know how or why he was unable to see how close she was to death every time he strangled her and not come to the same conclusion about his need to stop. It was a shining example of the dysfunctional mindset that was their operating system.

The sadistic demon that resided in my father wasn't finished with his work yet, however. He would make his next appearance the following year. There was more to come, and this time I was in the line of fire.

## Tag, You're It

I looked over my left shoulder, and I saw him barreling towards me in the hallway leading to my bedroom. He thrust me against my bedroom door. My head slammed into a poster that bore a picture of the sun and told me to live for today and dream of tomorrow, as my father proceeded to strangle me.

What led to this moment, I can't say; it is hidden in some deep recess of my psycho that has since remained untouched. I had guesses, but did it really matter? My father had strangled me. How I had gotten there didn't seem to be the key issue, but I still found myself searching the caverns of my mind for how this came to be. As if by witnessing the events that led up to it, it would somehow make sense. The memories that did remain were devastating and intense.

I had a brief recollection of the animosity and hate on his face as he stood with his hands wrapped around my throat. My next memory was standing behind him and watching him as he continued to strangle me. I had once again gone out of body as a means of coping with the terror. Then blackness. I was pulled back into consciousness by the sensation of something warm running down my leg and saturating my jeans. It took a few moments to understand that I had urinated on myself. I couldn't glance down because he was still strangling me.

After the initial confusion as to how this could have happened, I became consumed with shame. I had peed myself, not like the teenager I was, but like a little baby. This was all in a matter of seconds, and it was just then that he too became aware of what I had done. His response was to sneer, shove me to the other side of my room, and give a snide chuckle to say, "Look at you. You pissed yourself." His face read as though I was the most disgusting creature he had ever encountered. Internally, I agreed with him.

He left me to sit alone on my bedroom floor, trying desperately to understand how any of it had happened, embarrassed to my very core. I felt so physically weak afterwards, but I forced myself to get up and clean myself before my mother got home. I managed to keep the whole incident to myself, taking care that my mother wouldn't come across my soiled jeans. As the day's events began to register more fully, I was left with yet more resentment towards my body. Again, it didn't hold strong in the face of his abuse when it dumped the contents of my bladder. My body had given him an obvious victory, and, with no intention of being funny, I was pissed.

It became another dark secret between my father and me, and he took any chance he could get to keep the wound fresh by giving me a knowing, self-satisfied glare. He had won a battle that I was ill prepared for, but I would not be left unaware again.

## Humpty Dumpty

A few years before, I had begun taking flute lessons with Saxy, so named because he played the saxophone. I hated speaking the name because it was too close to sexy, which he was not, and because it only seemed to shine a beacon on the events occurring behind his closed office door.

I had my lessons with him at a music store not far from where we lived. Although the lesson room could have easily held ten or more of the sturdy black music stands, he and I shared just one. Our metal chairs sat side by side, our knees within inches of each other.

I found him to be physically repulsive. His rotund belly strained against the polyester pants that he hiked up to a perceived waist level. His fingers were fat, hairy sausage links primed to explode. Sickened, I would stare at the white hairs that protruded out of his nostrils. Playing an instrument was akin to an aerobic workout for him, his breathing loud and labored as the air forced its way in and out, in and out, of his nostrils. His eyes peered at me like large watery saucers behind the lenses of his glasses, giving him an air of innocence that was incongruous to his actions.

I can't recall exactly when it all began, the tickling, but it was in relation to my budding body. He would start at my knee with a little squeeze and slowly work his way to the top of my thigh, my panic mounting the higher he climbed. In a honeyed and playful tone, his head held in an innocent tilt and lips pursed, he would ask me to kiss his stubble ridden cheeks, as though the sweetness of his voice negated his sinister intent.

I would try to protest, but he would become livid with me, his face turning a crimson red. My quiet tears only angered him all the more. If I didn't cooperate, he would start spewing about how terribly I was playing the flute, spittle flying from his mouth, and at the end of those lessons he insisted to my parents that I needed to practice more. I was confused because I did indeed practice and knew my parents had heard me. In an effort to manage the situation, I would practice even harder, but the charade always continued.

But it seemed that Saxy was in my bedroom, too. I had a Humpty Dumpty light in my bedroom which would leave me feeling vulnerable because its egg shape, big eyes, and the high rise of Humpty's red pants reminded me of Saxy. It felt as if he was in my bedroom watching me.

I would lie awake many hours a night with my heart racing, the similarity to Saxy creating hysteria in me. I was tortured over whether I should turn the light off or leave it on. If I left it on, it felt as if "he" could see more readily as I lay exposed to his lewd stare. Turning off the light left me vulnerable as well because now *I* couldn't see *him*, and the darkness seemed to work in his favor. Leaving the light on usually won out because at the very least I wanted to have the advantage of seeing and preparing for an attack. My solution was to turn the light away so that "he" didn't face me as I checked the light throughout the night to be sure the plastic wasn't getting too hot, fire safety becoming a concern to add to the mix.

The dread of anticipating his advances before I would enter his room for my weekly lesson skyrocketed off the charts. Every week I had a private appointment to be molested. I simply didn't know how to make it stop, his advances only becoming more frequent and insistent the older I got.

Fast forward to my emotional breaking point sometime in my middle school years… I finally told my parents about what was going on during my lessons. This proved to be a very grave mistake, as you will see.

## Round Two

Almost a year after my father's first strangling lesson, he strangled me again. This time I knew what had happened to precipitate this attack: my father supposedly protecting me from Saxy. Once I had finally shared with my parents what he was doing to me at each of my flute lessons, their solution was for my father to go with me to my next lesson. I felt a bit uneasy at having to sit with Saxy again, but was also naively confident in my father's ability to stand up to this man. I believed my father would protect me.

It seems a bit illogical as I re-read that last sentence, based on all of his behaviors throughout my life, but at that time I was still under the effects of their brainwashing to a large degree. In truth I needed to be in order that I might psychologically survive. Although I knew he had hurt me, I was still gullible enough to trust that he would not allow others to do the same. That, and I was blinded by my frantic need to be rescued and so would take whoever I could get.

On the evening of my scheduled appointment, my father sat in the hall as I went about my lesson as usual. He knowingly sent me into a room with a man who was abusing me. He didn't confront my teacher. I guess the assumption was that just the mere presence of my father would stop the assault. It didn't. Saxy proceeded to brazenly fondle me in the same ways he had every other lesson.

I left the room with a cascade of tears streaming down my face as I rushed to tell my father what had just transpired. I was in hysterics, the emotions from the years of abuse erupting out of me. I was sure a battle would ensue as I knew my father was a seasoned warrior. Instead, my father began yelling at me to stop crying and get back in the room to finish my lesson. Betrayal and confusion made my head spin like a twister.

I wasn't capable of completing my lesson because I couldn't stop sobbing or maintain any focus. Without any word to Saxy, we headed for home. My father continued to scream at me throughout the fifteen-minute ride home. I sat as far away from him as possible, smashing my body against the pickup truck's passenger door, brimming with explosive rage and disbelief. I didn't dare utter a word but periodically stole a sideways glimpse of his face, trying to comprehend if this was truly happening or just some demonic, shocking hallucination.

His rant continued even as we made our way into the house. I tried to escape to my bedroom, but he followed me. Once there, he threw me down onto the side of my bed, and while standing over top of me, strangled me with his hands. He was no longer yelling, but his silence felt much more deadly.

My hatred and savage fury were so massive that I lost all concern for my life. With extreme willfulness and defiance I made the choice to open my eyes and bore them right into his, challenging him. My eyes spoke what I could not, "Go ahead, you think you got the balls to do it? Kill me, you *mother fucker*. I dare you." I had absolutely no fear of death. I refused to stand down. My stare unnerved him. I saw the flicker of self-doubt flash through his eyes as I held his gaze, and I knew I was the victor. I've never known a power greater than what coursed through me that night. It was only then that he released me and ceased his attack.

This time I told my mother the details of his abuse and all that had transpired at my flute lesson when she returned home that evening. There was no grand outrage or discussion to be had, only a silent acknowledgement on her part.

For the rest of that evening my mind was in a perpetual state of venomous revenge. I was livid with my sister, while she sat at the kitchen table doing homework, and not coming to my rescue. And I had nothing but vile contempt for my father. My thoughts became consumed with how to kill him. I could and would take no more.

Several scenarios played out in my mind as to how I could murder him. Should I shoot him with the gun that stood in their bedroom? Or would I have better success hitting him over the head with a heavy, foreign object? What object? Was there some other way? My main concern was that no matter how I planned to do it, it had to be a way where he wouldn't be able to physically overpower me, and one that would be a success as I would have only one shot. If I couldn't kill him, I felt surely he would then kill me.

What stopped me wasn't some moral dogma. What stopped me was the fact that I knew I most likely would be caught and punished for killing him, and this to me felt like he would win in the end and get the last laugh. I also played out in my mind how my family would react. I believed their level of denial ran so deep that they would never be able to understand what had caused me to go to such extreme measures. I also imagined their pain as they suffered the loss of my father, and more than anything I felt the agony of their abandonment as they blamed me for that pain. I was certain I would be left standing alone, and the anguish of having no one felt far more unbearable than continuing to tolerate my father. In the end, I made no attempts to try to kill him.

The next morning, and for a few days afterwards, there was a slight hoarseness to my voice, tenderness in my neck, and a clicking sensation each time I swallowed. Each click made me want to burst out crying, because there was no distancing myself from the event. It felt as if he was there tormenting me with each click, poking his finger into my emotional and physical wound. It was agony. Instead I buried the tears deep within and allowed no one to know of my physical or emotional torment.

The following afternoon I was standing outside, right below our front porch, as my mother began to walk by me. She stopped short after looking at me. "You have black and blue marks on your neck," she said.

"I *told* you he choked me," was my bitter reply. If I could have, I would have added, "...you stupid bitch."

With utter amazement, she responded, "But he said he didn't."

Why would his denial surprise her? Why would she believe him after all the years he had done the same to her? If she indeed did believe him, then why didn't she confront her daughter who had supposedly made up this horrendous lie about her father? True insanity.

Did she ever go back to him to confront him with the obvious evidence that he was most certainly lying? I've not a clue. That was the end of our discussion about any of it, and, as per the unwritten rules, we never addressed it again.

But personally, I wasn't willing to let it slide into the great abyss this time. I refused to pretend that something extremely horrific hadn't happened. If we weren't going to address it verbally, then I would use the only tool available to me, a frigid silence.

My act of revenge was to refuse to talk to him for a month. Nothing. I wouldn't even glance his way. The energy in the house was caustic with rancor, and I could care less that I was the cause. I spoke not a word to him until my mother approached me shortly before my fourteenth birthday and pleaded with me to speak to him. "He's upset that you're not talking to him." Interesting that he had somehow become the victim.

"Can you please stop ignoring him so that we can celebrate your birthday?" she begged. And I did, for her. Always, for her. She was distraught that he was supposedly hurting, and thus I broke my silent protest. I remember how his eyes flew open in surprise, and his whole body sighed with relief the first time I spoke to him again. It's odd, but I wish I could recall the words I said. Most likely, they were unimportant in their true context, but his face glowed like a new father. He seemed to think that I had forgiven him. That was far from the truth.

As I review those sequences of events, I still have difficulty understanding it all. At the time, I could never have predicted that outcome, nor could I comprehend the strange twist of events. Looking back, I surmised that the actions of Saxy and my ensuing emotional meltdown triggered something in my father. In my desperate attempt to make sense of the senselessness, I guessed that he must have felt powerless in dealing with his emotions and so lashed out in a fit of rage, his main coping mechanism.

I never returned to flute lessons after that. My mother remembers that they ended the lessons. Of course I have a different version of what transpired, and it's permanently embedded in my brain because at the time it took all my will to swallow my pride and tell them I was quitting.

When I first started flute lessons, I received a lecture about the amount of money they were spending on my flute and was told that this had better not be a passing fancy. Always looking for a chance to get a dig at me, my brother snidely declared I would indeed quit and certainly waste their money. I became determined that I would never ask to stop my lessons, as every ounce of me wanted to prove my brother wrong.

My brother lay in wait for years. He got his chance to rub his victory in my face a few days after my father's attack.

I was putting dishes in the dishwasher after supper; the rest of my family was still sitting around the kitchen table. My mother brought up the fact that I would no longer be taking flute lessons. My brother crowed with a self-righteous, "I told you so."

My stone cold retort to my brother: "I have no choice because the person who was supposed to protect me decided to attack and strangle me instead."

A strained hush filled the room as my entire family remained eerily silent. My siblings and my mother sat frozen in their chairs, their eyes wide and darting as they fearfully anticipated my father's reaction. I had broken a cardinal rule: we never talked about my father's rage after one of his episodes, and we never blatantly challenged him. I had thrown down the gauntlet, and I was so crazed with hatred and fury that I silently dared him to come at me again. I would have fought back at my most primal level and to my very death. In fact, I fully expected an attack as I had never seen him back down from an opportunity to assert his power over any of us. Surprisingly, he chose to remain silent and act as though I had said not a thing, pretending that I had not outwardly and directly provoked him. I counted that as one more significant triumph in a battle I was not respon-sible for creating.

My mother's version of the events doesn't ring true, but I'm sure they make her feel as though she was the protective parent in some way. Seems to me she failed terribly, many times over.

## Just a Babe in the Woods

While my life at home felt intolerable and isolated, I spent my days at school creating the connection I ached for, and sex seemed to be the only answer.

While in the midst of my silent protest towards my father, my rebel-lion running rampant, I did not lack the words to express my desire to be with Mitch, as I wrote him sexually explicit letters. Like many of the other girls in my grade, I had developed a crush on him and fell victim to his flirtatious nature. My school was smack dab in the middle of white bread farm country, and he was the bad boy with an ethnic variable that broke that mold. Sports and the interest of the opposite sex were part of his regular curriculum. He had my attention, and I was willing to give him more, the only thing I thought I had to offer, to capture his attention in return. It worked.

I had turned fourteen just the week before and had a second date scheduled to meet Mitch for our tryst. Our first planned rendezvous fell through, and I tried to assuage the shame I felt for what I had agreed to by noting that on our first attempt I was still thirteen, and at least now I would sound slightly less whorish with one more year come to pass–never mind that it was only a matter of days difference between those years.

We met at the annual fair that showcased livestock, fruits and veg-etables, homemade baked goods, and displays of flower arrangements and artwork. What was to occur across the street from the fair was not nearly as wholesome, as later that afternoon Mitch and I made our way to the woods behind the school. The Bunny Trail, quite aptly named, was the not-so-romantic spot where we lay to do the not-so-romantic deed.

We were not alone, however, for our brief encounter because soon we were joined by my chemistry teacher, who was also Mitch's track coach. He bumbled passed us with that crooked grin of his and asked only, "Hey, uh, what are you guys doing on the Bunny Trail?" He gave a soft chuckle, and left us alone to awkwardly gather ourselves, and we soon made our way back to the fair.

What waited for us there was Mitch's posse and my further humiliation. It soon became very clear that for him it was not about connection, but a different "c" word further along in the dictionary–"conquest." He handled our time together with the maturity of a fifteen-year-old male high on himself–meaning he spilled every detail to anyone who would listen, and there were plenty of ears available.

In the days and weeks that followed, those ears grew a mouth and began spouting and shouting degrading comments to me down the halls of school. I was fodder for many a joke while he received high fives. Mortifying? Embarrassing? Yeah, and then some. The words to Phil Collins' song "I Don't Care Anymore" became the grit I mentally employed so that I could make it through a school day. But the attention span of those teen boys was thankfully short, though not short enough for my liking, and eventually they moved on to the next drama that fueled their hormonal surges and fantasies.

To his credit, Mitch did talk with me after many months had passed in order to apologize for his behavior and my pain. The heart that I had initially believed he possessed saw its way passed his ego, albeit a bit too late for me and what might have been a budding relationship.

The next school year brought another bad boy to town, Matthew, and soon enough I found myself vying for his much-sought-after attention. While Mitch and Matthew shared the same lack of propensity for academic success, Matthew proved to be capable of using discretion and, surprisingly to me, respect for me.

Despite my many attempts to lure him under the covers, he would protest, "No, you're not like that. I don't want to do that to you. You're different."

Had he not read the script I knew by heart, the one where my value was in direct proportion to the hole between my legs? I was thrown for a loop. If he would not accept that from me, then I was truly meaningless. That thought was more than I could handle. I saw no other option but to push and shove until he saw things my way.

He resisted with great chivalry, but my stubborn nature and need to matter far outweighed the kindness of his heart. One afternoon, after pinning him to the bed, I succeeded in what I had set out to accomplish.

We dated for a few short weeks, but soon enough he told me that he wanted to continue dating other people. I could not appreciate his honesty and only used it to fuel my sense of deep rejection.

Revenge was soon on my mind. I knew how to exact some pain on him and strike a blow to his ego. I decided to have sex with his closest friend, Carl. Carl was ready, willing, and able. But as we were entwined in the act, it suddenly struck me that my behaviors were absurd and unacceptable in my own rule book. That I had put myself in that position, both figuratively and literally, was a place I needed to escape quickly. I asked Carl to stop, explaining I changed my mind, and he gave me no quarrel.

I won't say I didn't have a choice, because ultimately I did, but I will suggest that my choice was made immeasurably more difficult because the long arm of the past had given me a not so gentle nudge. My sexual escapades were most certainly following the trail of beliefs I held about myself. I was learning the hard way, however, that my actions were not in line with my values, and soon I ceased intentionally throwing myself at boys with the desperation and longing for love that kept a steady thrum in the hive of my heart.

## Biting the Hand that Fed You

My already weakened heart was to take another shocking blow in what seemed to becoming a troublesome annual event for me, Strangle Kellie Day. To change things up, this time my mother played the starring role.

We both were standing by the kitchen sink, and I'm not clear what words transpired between us. Chances are I had been committing my infamous crime of "talking back" and was complaining about making the mashed potatoes, yet again, as they sat in a pot on the counter in front of us. After our very brief and angry exchange, she turned to me and began strangling me, screaming at me all the while.

By that age, I was taller than she and was able to fend her off. As I turned to get away from her, I caught a glimpse of the daycare children watching what was going on, and I felt fear for them. I knew the horror of watching someone being attacked, and I also felt humiliated that they should see me being treated that way.

I continued to make my way across the kitchen, cowering and covering my head, as she pummeled my back with her fists. Once I got to their bedroom, I tried to close the door on her, but she kept trying to push her way in and continued to strike out at me through the opening. Her face looked maniacal, possessed.

She had gone too far, my limits pushed way beyond reason. While giving her a cold, dark stare, I very calmly stated, "If you hit me again, I'm going to hit you back." It was if I had given her a verbal slap; her eyes registered shock, and she simply froze. I had given her something never afforded me, a warning.

I very cautiously opened the door, wanting to be sure I was safe but internally hoping she would attack me again because at that point I wanted to unleash all my years of fury onto her right then and there. I knew if I started to hit her, there would be no stopping me, and it would have felt glorious.

As I opened the door I said to her, "I can't believe you of all people would do that to me. You know how that *[being strangled]* feels." She gave no response and simply turned to walk back into the kitchen.

Those events were never talked about again after that; the *Nothing Happened Here Rule* was strictly enforced once more. I don't think she told my father because if she had, she would have to confess she was a hypocrite.

The disbelief I felt because she tried to strangle me, the little kid who had tried to rescue her when my father was doing the very same to her, was astronomically heartbreaking. She had betrayed my trust in many ways over the years, but none compared to that day. It remains the greatest betrayal of my life. The last emotional thread that tentatively connected us had been violently severed with an arrow to my heart, and I had to finally admit what I had always secretly known: I stood alone.

My father never physically abused me again after the incident surrounding my flute teacher. My mother also remained hands off after I threatened her. I wondered what caused them to suddenly stop. Why were they now able to control themselves? Why couldn't they have controlled themselves sooner? Was it because both times I defiantly held my ground and refused to hand over my power to them? It's a riddle in my mind that I've turned over many times, never finding the answers I seek.

## Just Say No

That slogan was no riddle to me though. I heard the message, but I chose not to give it much meaning. One of my closest high school friends offered me cocaine. It sounded like a bad idea I was willing to try. For me the question as to why I would do such a thing was far less relevant than a limp, apathetic, "Why not?" We made a plan to experiment with the drug in the kitchen of my parents' home while they were out.

I had no idea what to expect, but I was not disappointed. Not long after I snorted the tiny white chunks (we were not experts at cutting), I felt as though a firework of euphoria exploded in my brain. That I could feel so very happy, when only seconds before I had been swimming in misery, was astounding to me. Unfortunately, my new-found friend was lacking as well; the bitter taste that dripped down the back of my throat was rather unpleasant, and soon enough it dropped me back to the bottom after we had just risen to the top.

I wanted more. I needed to get back up to where I had just been blissfully floating. That was an issue, because we had no more. My girlfriend left our house, and I became obsessed for weeks afterwards with thoughts of how I could get more of the drug, finding more happiness my true goal.

First, I knew I would need someone to supply the cocaine, and the notion that this would not remain my little secret did not sit well with me. I did not want to be seen as a drug addict and become part of the rumor mill; I had ridden the train of public humiliation once before and did not find the ride a comfortable one. Secondly, money was an obvious necessity, and I didn't think my babysitting or restaurant work would bring enough cash to keep me supplied. I toyed with many ways to get more cash, but only came up with stealing and prostitution as reliable means of getting an increased cash flow. That thought was more depressing to me than the state I was already in, and I concluded that cocaine and I were, thankfully, never to meet again.

## There's No Place like Home

I had been searching for an earthly great escape from what seemed like a hell-hole most days. I knew where I wanted to be, but it seemed I was only meant to stand outside its gates and longingly gaze upon its splendor, like a shopper with her face plastered against a store's display window.

I had been there once before, and I knew I was going back, just not soon enough for me. *Home* is a truth I've carried with me always. I have never not known of its existence. It's more of a feeling for me, one of utter bliss, peace, and love, but even those words do little to capture its essence. I'm safe there. There I know I am precious, as is everyone and everything. It's a glorious and addictive place I visited often in my day-dreams. The grandest of all escapes. There's no drama, no pain, and no humanity. Just purity and spirit. My truest level of being exists there with no body to misuse or abuse.

But I wasn't there yet.

Having a physical form left me vulnerable and in harm's way at any moment; I had learned that lesson well. My body had become a walking memorial to all I had endured physically and emotionally. My body and my brain housed all my pain, and remaining present in its confines overwhelmed and petrified me. The only relief I had was to disconnect and dissociate from my physical being.

My body became numb to me, so numb that I didn't realize that I was. Rarely was I aware of actually feeling my body. I moved and walked and talked, but the best description of it what it felt like was to say it was robotic. Touch to me wasn't something I relished. My sensory experience of touch was similar to when a dentist gives Novocain for a procedure. You can feel the pressure of them doing the work, but the sensation is dulled. That's how I experienced touch.

I longed to go to my true home and leave this plane, to be released. I'm not talking about suicide. Suicide had never been an option for me, no matter what was happening. Not because I thought of it as a sin or a moral issue, but instead I saw it as creating more hardships for my soul. It was a knowing I've had all my life–that cutting my life short this go-round would only amplify the intensity of those same lessons in another life. Perhaps somewhere in another time I had already gone that route? There were no shortcuts. It was just that I didn't mind if I shed this physicality and all that came with it. I would willing and gladly go at any point because I knew better things awaited me there.

In some ways it felt like a cruel joke that my father never did kill me while strangling me. Killing me felt like it would have been an act of mercy, but he had proven not to be a merciful man, taking me physically and mentally to the precipice of death time and time again, but always holding me captive in his refusal to set me free.

## My Gospel Music

I was still under my parents' lock and key, and a new romance seemed a pleasant distraction. If at first you don't succeed...

I knew the truth of Pat Benatar's words as she sang of the darkness that was childhood abuse in "Hell is for Children" or the conflicts of love in "Love is a Battlefield." I belted out these songs loud and proud because she so poignantly shared what I could not. This should be no stunning revelation, but based on my role model of relationships and love, I continued to make poor choices in the area of love.

I've said my parents were extremely controlling, and they were, but by this time in my life my radar was honed to break every boundary they set for me. Often times, I succeeded.

Boys my age held little interest for me following my prior unsuccessful engagements with them. Soon enough, I took my risky behaviors up a notch by sneaking out and planning sleepovers with my much older boyfriend, Gary. He was twenty to my fifteen. I was working various positions at the restaurant next to my parents' house, and he had become a regular at the bar. Once I captured the eye of a much older man, the rest was pre-ordained, for failure of course, but I had not a clue as to how far down I would be taken.

For about two years he became the reason for my every breath. He was extremely possessive of me, something I now know is another face of domestic abuse, but at the time I understood it to be the love and attention I was dying to feel. Someone cared about my every move; he didn't even want me getting the mail across the street lest someone notice me. I basked in what I believed to be the purest adoration. There was nothing I wouldn't have done for him, because that's love, right?

The fact that he too had suffered beatings as a child and as a result struggled with his own anger, frequently getting in fights, or being the hired hand to rough up someone, only endeared him more to me. He was a kindred soul, so I needed to believe. For the first time, I didn't feel alone.

My naiveté didn't allow me to see his alcohol use as a concern, nor was I wise to the fact that he frequently used the drug known as crank. I had vague knowledge that he might have been involved in the selling of drugs but allowed myself no serious concern about that.

True to all stereotypes of a dysfunctional relationship, I had suspected he was cheating on me many months prior to his eventual confession, but he had vehemently denied it all. Each time he assured me he was faithful to me, I was left to feel that I was the mental one, the same role I had played in my family at that time as everyone around me denied any and all wrongdoing.

It all came to a screeching halt. He was having an affair with his niece, who was a year younger than he, and she had become intentionally pregnant with their child.

I of course begged and pleaded, a classic picture of desperation for the one I thought I loved. In the end, he left me to live his life with her and their daughter, while I proceeded to emotionally collapse.

I had no appetite. I lost weight rapidly, and my sister became concerned about me. In an effort to allay some of her fear and attention, I would force myself to eat something in her full view, literally gagging on the food each time I tried to swallow. She alluded to the fact that she was wise to my not-so-secret relationship and its tragic ending, which only added to my mountain of humiliation. I was ashamed that she was aware of my deceptions and embarrassed that she could see that he had chosen another over me.

That was the first of several abusive relationships. Interspersed in those destructive romances were a few kind souls who honored me, but they were short lived because I still sought the fix of the bad boy. Taming the wild stallions, comforting them, and healing them with my love became my passion and challenge.

My most sick relationship also happened to be one of my significant turning points. Once again, I was dating an older man, Jim, about seven years my senior. He fit the bill for being controlling and jealous. I was warned that Jim had a track record of swiftly ditching his current girlfriend for someone much younger; this time I was the trade-in model. Of course, I saw myself as the special one, not the flavor of the month. We happened to work together in a bar, and we bonded and enjoyed one another's company, drinking after hours and smoking pot. Marijuana served me in that it allowed me to laugh freely in a way that was not familiar to me anymore. In time, it robbed me of my stellar short-term memory, one thing I did take pride in, and I realized my relationship with it, and the late night gorging on Cheetos and Domino's Pizza topped with green olives, must come to an end.

Things turned sour with the relationship I had with Jim as well when he began cheating on me for another woman who was two years younger than my twenty-one.

Part of me saw it as a karmic debt for a time when I had briefly dated another man, all the while knowing he had a girlfriend. I felt skanky during that period, having fallen short once more of my personal values, as though I should make my home amongst the cockroaches in the putrid alleys of New York. And every time the rightful girlfriend caught a glimpse of me at the gym, her eyes confirmed my self-assessment.

So when I was on the receiving end of the back stab this time, I initially took it with a sense of relief that I was finally paying my penance for having knowingly hurt another woman once before, but time would reveal that my payback would be tenfold.

The script was always the same; the cheater refutes the infidelity charges. His denial fueled my madness and obsession. He began to treat me as though my accusations were delusional; same old same old, that I was ever the sick-minded one. One afternoon we were standing outside on the sidewalk by his apartment in a heated argument, continuing the dance between accuser and denier, and he spit in my face. I had been through a lot, but that felt like the most degrading thing anyone had ever done to me simply because that was his exact and only intention. There was no thought on my part; I just instantaneously slapped him hard across the face. His glasses flew off, and the next day he lamented about the $200 it cost for a new pair, blaming me for acting the lunatic and taking no responsibility for decorating my face with a hocker.

I then went on the hunt, and on one particular evening I intentionally drove past his apartment and found what I had been looking for, proof. There sat the other woman's car. He refused to answer the door despite my repeated attempts at the doorbell. Never one to roll over, I found a ladder in the alley and proceeded to climb into his second floor apartment window as he tried to push me back out. A physical fight ensued between the two of us while his newest love interest hid. He had me pinned to the ground. In an attempt to free myself, I grabbed him in the crotch and twisted as hard as I could. I thought the pain would be so great that he would stop. I was wrong; instead, my actions only enraged him further, and he cracked me across the side of the head.

Neighbors below heard the fighting and wisely called the police. I quickly covered my ass, telling the authorities that he refused to give me my glasses, and I simply wanted to wear them so that I could see to drive. The glasses were still sitting in his bedroom, my last possession left in his home. The police had him get my glasses. One officer happened to notice the mark on my cheek and asked if my boyfriend had struck me. I was more than happy to confirm that he indeed had hit me, as he attempted to justify his actions to the officers. After receiving my glasses, I was sent on my way. I was sure to put on my glasses lest my deception be discovered, that I was already wearing contacts, and their addition actually made my vision blurry.

The following day at work he limped about, making a point of telling me how uncomfortable his genitals felt. He also claimed the police beat him up for attacking me, declaring unfairness. I saw no evidence of this, but couldn't disprove it either.

As for me, I sported a pitchfork-shaped pink bruise on my right cheekbone. It became my scarlett letter, and it seemed to tell the story of my utter worthlessness; what had once been inside was now visible for all to see. It felt as though I had been branded with the words, "She's a piece of shit." I couldn't look people in the eye for fear that I might see their pity or judgement. The theme song of my soul was the chorus to the Allman Brothers' "Whipping Post."

My hearing took a hit as well and remained muffled in my right ear for a several months afterwards. I made every effort to avoid seeing my family, making sure I was gone whenever they were home. One day my sister happened to catch me at the house and noticed the mark on my cheek. Later she told me that she shared this with my mother and that they were concerned for me. Her genuine worry felt awkward and embarrassing to me. I mumbled a very vague response to her, hopped into my car, and sped away. My mother, however, never mentioned anything to me. I must say during that period it was the one time I was grateful for our familial pattern of avoidance and denial, but in retrospect, I find it disturbing that a mother never tried to help her daughter who had been abused. Once again, she failed to protect me.

The scene at work was straight from high school. My ex and his new girl began to spread lies and rumors about me amongst the other staff, who would often painfully avoid eye contact with me. Many times the two of them would spy me and proceed to whisper and giggle as I would approach. While I had become the brunt of many a joke, he apparently believed she was to be admired and shared her latest modeling photos with anyone in sight.

Their actions only served to fuel my roiling enmity, and I began to bully my rival. I refused to get out of her way any time we had to be in the same vicinity, purposefully bumping into her. Her discomfort was apparent, and I thrived on that.

I had sunk to a new low. My behaviors were out of control. I was a bomb primed to explode. I was deeply disappointed in myself for crawling through that window and for my intimidation tactics that followed. I knew at the time that it wasn't a wise choice, but the louder voice wanted vengeance and, ironically, to prove I wasn't crazy: that I hadn't imagined anything and that he was indeed spouting lies. His denials and betrayals were reminiscent of the same mental manipulations my parents embraced, and as it ripped at my festering wounds, I reacted like a wounded animal.

Soon enough his new romantic interest became pregnant with their son, which just seemed to solidify their life together and my meaninglessness.

Keeping in line with the theme of the whole scenario, it all came to quite a theatrical end at work. I was asked to leave about four months after our altercation. I did question the reasons for the restaurant manager's request. I had stopped playing the bully after a few incidents; I was never confronted on those behaviors by management, as I had been the one to turn myself around and from that point forward had concentrated only on holding my head high. It was a set up for sure, as my ex stood by the manager's side, a snide smile of satisfaction spread across his face to reveal the wide gap between his two front teeth. What he had told management about me I could only imagine. The only answer I received was for my manager to say, "We just think it's best." I was done fighting; it was time for me to leave.

The realization that I was heading down the same path as my mother sent me into a state of shock and a profoundly deep depression. I was beginning to live just as she had, playing out the drama of abuse, and I knew its ending all too well. It was in that moment that I made a very clear and conscious decision: I would live my life alone before I allowed myself to be abused again or act in an abusive way myself. Her life would not become mine. I felt at absolute and total peace with never having another relationship again.

And then, I met Craig.

## Trust No One

I understood very early on that no one was to be completely trusted, and I proceeded with that guiding principle. My operating manual was to be ever on alert for betrayal and deception. It became a self-fulfilling prophecy many times over, of course, because no one is perfect, and I took any and every digression as a sign that indeed the only one to rely on was me, plain and simple. I was on my very own covert spy missions, watching and weighing the actions and intentions of all.

When confirmations finally came, I took it all very personally. Everything became a marker for my worth, or, more accurately, my worthlessness. They had finally seen me for what I was, nothing. They had seen me for what my parents always knew me to be.

Of course, it didn't help that romantically I was always drawn to those with gaping emotional wounds. I saw and felt their pain and more than anything else, I could relate to it. Typically, I set about trying to heal the wounded with my love, or what I thought was love. I should more correctly call it enmeshment as my every action and intention was about them and how to bring endless happiness into their lives. My pleasure was only important in that it was inextricably tied to seeing theirs. My needs? I didn't know there was such a thing, only that others needed.

All of my efforts to make them feel loved and content also fed into the internal, and eternal, tape that played in my mind: I had to offer proof that I was worth having around. Remember, I had no redeeming qualities, so I had to "do" for others so that they might want me in their world. If I didn't prove myself invaluable, I should and would be kicked to the curb. When I landed face first on that curb, I knew it was because they found someone much more beautiful and glorious than me, and what I had to offer was low rate.

As I mentioned earlier, dispersed amongst all those I was trying to fix were some very few who tried to treat me with reverence. They would tell me of my special qualities, honestly share the commitment they were willing to make to me, and always treated me with respect. I didn't trust the longevity of their intentions and was even able to warp their kindnesses to fit the definition I had of myself: these individuals were simply trying to be nice, treating me with the kid gloves you don for those with special needs. They saw me for the sorry rubbish I was; they were just too big hearted to say so. They were doing me a favor.

Today, I like to think of those souls as planting a seed for things to come. They were the universe's way of giving me an inkling of my worthiness. I wasn't quite ready to grasp the full concept, nor did I know of their importance at that time, but now I see it was the very infant stages of my healing journey, like trailer flashes for a movie preview, the movie of my journey into my own light.

No one faced a challenge bigger than Craig, however. We both worked at a chain Mexican restaurant. He was a short-order cook and made the appetizers for my customers in the lounge, when I still worked as a cocktail waitress with my bartender ex-boyfriend Jim, before being fired. A bright light, similar to that of a camera's flash, appeared in front of my eyes the first time I saw him standing behind the cook's line. I then heard the words, "This is the guy I'm going to marry." I felt it and knew it to be true, but I still was not an easy catch.

He was simply too nice. He was kind and considerate, and not abusive in any fashion. There was nothing that should have kept me at a distance other than the fact that I didn't know what to do with someone that possessed such qualities.

When we first began to date, I pushed him away as best I could emotionally, remaining somewhat aloof to him. Being the smart guy that he is, he soon realized my heart wasn't in it to the level that his was. At the time I mistook his open heart as a weakness, not as a source of power, and so I didn't honor him in the way that he deserved. Ultimately, he began to feel rejected and pulled away from me as well. His pulling away only confirmed the truths I had been toying with all along: he was too good to be true.

## Green with Envy

But I stayed. And he did too. I had used my strong will many times over and eventually decided this time I would commit it to loving someone who obviously deserved it. Those old habits though… they do die hard.

The Hulk from the old TV show *The Incredible Hulk* felt like my childhood soul mate. He knew how I felt and, better yet, was able to act it out. His violent releases became my envy.

His fury transformed an average man into another being all together. I had a Hulk living inside me, pounding about within in an effort to get out and unleash my sense of injustice and hatred. I recognized the intensity of the Hulk's rage as my own. Its ferocity made me feel alive and all powerful, a path of destruction lying in my wake. My body knew the transformation that releasing this madness could bring; adrenalin fanning the flames of indestructibility.

It brought a smile to my face as I watched the Hulk wreak havoc. I cheered on his wrath. But never, never was I allowed to voice any degree of anger, let alone my own Hulk. I only got to be the victim many times over of my parents' insanity and spewing venom. This daily, and in time yearly, diet of unfairness only fed the Hulk within.

I had attended college as a nursing major, and right after I graduated I made a beeline out of my parents' house, a moment I had dreamt about for an eternity. It was the promise of that moment that had allowed me to continually plod forward in my day-to-day emotional drudgery. What I didn't realize as I walked out of their house and into an apartment was that Craig wasn't going to be my only roommate. The Hulk had packed his bags, and he was coming to stay. I was no longer the one in control.

## Speak No Evil

About two years into my relationship with Craig, things began to unravel again and further this time, in direct proportion to the chaos of my inner world. I feared I was becoming my father. I felt explosive, the Hulk transformation no longer containable. I wanted to hurt someone, badly. Anyone and for no reason at all. I now had become Hulk.

My first job as a Registered Nurse was at a drug and alcohol recovery center. The stories of others' pain and abuse had come too close to home. I knew their hurt and frustrations. Naively, I thought I had escaped mine when I moved out of my parent's house, but while working there, the culmination of all I had withstood was staring me down, digging into every festering emotional wound my battered being possessed. "Triggers" was a new term to me, but that didn't stop them from impacting me as the pressure of all that I had held in for twenty-some years began popping like the rivets of an old steel ship.

I panicked that I too would become a raving rage-aholic, that I was no better than my father. I feared he had won, that the cesspool of emotions and events that had been my life had taken me to a place that I could never return. It seemed I was still his emotional puppet, that he pulled those strings even from a physical distance. Trapped, just like when I was a child.

Interestingly enough, people would look at me during this period of my life and say, "Why do you look so miserable? It can't be that bad!" Apparently, I modeled the constant scowl my father donned, as well as the tumultuous nature of my own mind. Complete strangers would continually offer their two cents on my state of being. Their comments did nothing to alleviate my struggle and only made me seethe more. They had no idea; it was that bad and even worse than they could have imagined. I wished at the time I had had the courage to say this to these folks, but I only allowed their words to fuel my resentment and feed the shame that seeped out of my pores. I feared they could see what my parents had always known, that I was the obstinate one, making much ado about nothing.

The gravity of my choice was apparent. I could live the life of my father, and the one that had been unconsciously plotted out for me by them, or I could seek healing. Healing became my choice if for no other reason than at that time I didn't want him to win, defiant as always. I had spent my life battling; I would not go down this easily and live their legacy.

That legacy included messages from my year spent in kindergarten. Apparently, I shared some personal information about our home with my teacher, Miss Kanner. She in turn sent a hand written note home to my mother. I sat on the bus studying the pink paper, which was faintly stamped with strawberries, and my stomach churned. I knew what was written in the note didn't bode well for me. I racked my brain trying to figure out what I had done wrong, but nothing came to mind. I struggled as to whether I should hand over the letter. In the end, I decided the wisest choice was to give the note to my mother. She was not pleased with me. She said in no uncertain terms, "Don't you ever share what goes on in this house!" I still have no clue what my transgressions entailed but for twenty-two years I held true to her command, I told no one. The time had come for me break that rule.

The yellow pages were my first step on a path that has since wound its way through the course of my life for over twenty years. I picked up the phone book and intuitively picked a therapist for myself. I had a knowing when I spoke with Andrea on the phone that she was the person I could trust with this dark side of me.

Before meeting with her, I had never spoken in depth to anyone about my life as a young child, other than to try to explain to Craig why I felt I needed to see a therapist. I was embarrassed to tell him of my childhood and even more humiliated that I required help. Surely, he would see me as I saw myself, weak and bothersome. But I was desperate to not live from the place of an all-consuming inner storm. And I jumped, taking my first leap of faith. Faith in what, I had no idea.

*"Re-examine all that you have been told...*
*dismiss that which insults your soul."*
—WALT WHITMAN

# Therapy 101

Of course my first days of therapy were filled with the telling of my then-present struggles, and soon enough, the story of my past. Ironically, I was going to therapy because *I* was the issue. I wanted to know how to fix what was obviously wrong with *me*.

I vented and fumed about my parents, but still lacked the insight to understand that this wasn't about me being crazy but instead were my reactions to a crazy-making situation. For the first time, someone heard about my family and affirmed what a very small part of me knew to be true: something was terribly wrong in that house, and I wasn't the problem, despite what my parents wanted me to believe.

My parents invested many years and a lot of energy in maintaining the façade that all their abuses were simply normal behavior. They said it with such conviction and authority, so many times over, that I couldn't help but question my own sanity. They convinced me, to a very large degree, that I was the troubled one.

To have another confirm the insanity that I had been railing against was somewhat of a shock to my system. I had been alone in that battle for so long that to have someone else by my side, seeing the depths of the dysfunction, was a cataclysmic event for me. The voice within asked, "You mean I was right? I'm not deranged?"

It was during many of these sessions that my boiling stew of contempt exploded. Finally, finally I was able to give a voice to all that I had endured both physically and mentally. I began to crave my therapy because it became the validation and release I had longed to realize all my live long days.

## You Are Getting Sleepy...

While the bitterness freely flowed from me, the wide range of other emotions escaped my slippery grasp. Like many other victims of child abuse, I struggled to share my tale with any inkling of the trauma that roiled about in my psyche. Each time I caught a glimpse of the sheer terror, panic, or anxiety that was attached to a memory, my mind would instantly slam shut that door. I had a vague sense that I had those feelings, but I just couldn't bring expression to them or feel them to their full depth.

Just as with trauma victims, it was the way my mind had sought to protect me all those years. Rage was my only friend. It allowed me to feel powerful in an impossibly powerless situation. With rage as my nourishment, I became a warrior. As a child, to have a constant awareness of my seemingly bottomless sorrow and abandonment would have left me psychologically debilitated and paralyzed. Instead I allowed hostility to fuel me.

It's no mistake that I picked rage as my go-to emotion, though not consciously, of course. The message in our home was that rage dominated the house; those in power used it to rule the roost. Wisely, I picked the emotion that appeared to wield the biggest sword as a means of navigating my life. I found that most people are scared of you when you're enraged. Incensed individuals often seem to control people and situations everywhere; most people cower and the raving lunatic gets their way because others simply want to shut them up and calm the beast. Projecting a fierceness also kept others at a safe emotional distance and fed beautifully into my need to not allow another to get too close to me.

The issue was that while I may have had some justifiable venom flowing through me, there was also a conglomerate of other feelings that sought to be heard, and in fact needed a voice if I was to heal to more fully. The problem? I couldn't readily access them. As I would recount incidents that occurred in my childhood home, I often felt removed from the events, as if I was reporting on someone else's life.

Enter, hypnosis.

Andrea suggested hypnosis, and my initial reaction was one of fear. I was more than concerned that I would be too exposed and at her mercy, and I had never found others' level of mercy to be topnotch. With gentle coaching, she allayed my worries, and we gradually began to utilize hypnosis as a means to communicate with the plethora of other emotions that had taken up residence within my being.

It was then that I could cry and sense the deep levels of betrayal, disbelief and grief. I remembered and, more importantly, I *felt*. There were times that I would be so deeply in the thralls of a silent scream that the strain would break the tiniest capillaries in my face and neck, leaving me covered in a freckle of pink dots. I wanted to throw up, the emotional pain was so deep and intense. My insides felt as if a giant had torn me apart and begun to veraciously knead my guts. I would double over on the sofa as I relived my most intense feelings. I fought the strongest desire to claw my face and rip at my hair. It was utterly exhausting, and sleep was my great escape.

I would fantasize about my next opportunity to take a nap. I always fulfilled my daily obligations, but it was not without great fatigue and mental fog. I found my greatest relief in my moments of slumber. Sleep, and more sleep, became my great and only escape.

## Hitting New Bottom(s)

Of course, reality did not allow for me to remain in bed perpetually, despite my longing to do just that. I had a job to attend, everyday life to live, and a relationship to nurture, but my tank was running low. It was my relationship that would receive the fallout as I wrangled with my past and its vast sea of emotions. The hopes and promises of Craig and me living together in our first apartment began to sour as my stressors seethed within, only to eventually make themselves known in our home life.

I became obsessed with the placement of the bathroom towels, tissue boxes, and the answering machine. At first, I would simply go about and realign all these things that may have gotten skewed from their normal use. I felt calm when these objects were in their "right" place, as if there was order and predictability to the world, and I was in control, despite the chaos that threatened to escape from me personally.

Craig, of course, didn't feel the compulsion I did about these matters, and so when he did not make an effort to straighten these objects to their correct alignment after he was through with them, I began to see this as intentional disrespect. His actions felt as though he was purposefully try- ing to aggravate me by not adhering to my needs. I had lived far too long with my needs not being met, and I deeply felt this compulsion for order as a necessity that created calm for me.

As my anxiety and anger rose, our relationship plummeted even more. I heightened my skills at weeding out deception and was ever on alert for cheating on his part. The more critical my eye, the further and faster he ran from me.

He ran so far that I eventually decided to move out, while he moved on and sought the comfort and an ego boost from another. We had offi- cially crashed.

Oddly enough, moving out was one of the first healthy choices I made for myself. He truly wasn't treating me very well by that point, excluding me more and more from all aspects of his life. Even hurting, I was able to see that his pulling away was a direct result of my own behaviors. I can't say I felt to blame for his actions, but I could understand that he was just as overwhelmed as me at that time, and his acting out simply looked dif- ferent than mine. He was fearful of me and didn't trust that I could and would change. I felt the same with regard to him.

Despite all of our ups and downs, there was a part of me that knew without a doubt that a real love remained and in time I would reach out and share my feelings with him. We both had a lot at stake, our hearts, but after a time, we renewed our commitment to one another, and with that, we took tentative steps forward to re-establish our romance.

We both felt overcome with uncertainty. I had immersed him in a world he could not fathom or begin to comprehend; he was going in blind. Where I was headed on this healing journey was unknown to me, and that was unsettling as I could make very few promises. Through various conversations I attempted to share my issues, and witnessing the effects of those on me caused him some degree of panic. I know he felt ill-equipped to handle what I put down in front of him, and his brain went automatically to the fear that I was going to lose it, go certifiably insane in my attempts to heal all of this. He often suggested that maybe I should slow down or take breaks in my process of healing when he would see me at my emotional worst. I approached my healing as I had approached every challenge in my life. I was on a mission, and I refused to be thwarted.

What I failed to see most times was that he was offering me the observation that I might be gentler with myself. Compassion was not offered to me as a child, and I didn't know it was an option. I had survived by sheer force, and so I believed that a strong will would carry me through this as well, and so I pushed myself further and deeper.

Andrea saw my bottom before I did. She understood the depths of my trauma better than I based on her years of training. To me, it was simply my life, and I had little else with which to compare it. I had taken the very first steps of what would prove to be an expansive journey and had just begun to unearth what remains lay hidden. She recommended at some point in my therapy that I should consider an antidepressant.

I balked at the idea. An antidepressant equated to the utmost failure in my mind, a surrender, and I was a born fighter. I panicked because I felt it provided the proof for Craig that I most definitely **was** crazy.

I knew the signs of depression, as I worked as a psychiatric nurse, and so I made conscious efforts to avoid any behaviors on the diagnostic checklist of depression. Notice I said "conscious efforts." I had to *think* about avoiding the signs of depression. I knew the game I was playing with myself, but I was a creature that endured. I spent years proving "I can take it", and I would just take some more. Until one day I couldn't.

I remember sitting on the pale blue loveseat in our second apartment, and I just couldn't push myself anymore. I couldn't find the emotional energy to avoid those signs and symptoms on the checklist. I didn't even have enough left in my reserves to stand. I was sinking, had sunk, and I needed to wave the white flag. With great effort, I picked up the phone, called Andrea, and arranged for myself to get a prescription. I was in sheer terror of having to confess to Craig that I wasn't strong enough to deal with it all. Again, I saw him leaving as his worst fears began to play out before his eyes.

I think this time was the scariest to him; in his mind he honestly saw me institutionalized. I know he was petrified of me and what I might become. So was I. Perhaps they had won?

I took the medicine, and what I found was myself lifting from the depths of a despair that had become my norm. I remember sobbing when the medicine began to work because cheerfulness was coming in a steady stream instead of in spurts. The many years of cloud cover was slowly lifted, whereas in my wildest dreams I couldn't have imagined that the sun still shined, or that it shined on me.

I stayed on the medicine for a period of time, how long I can't recall, but I do remember my reasons for quitting didn't come from a place of healthy choices. The medication gave me a common sexual side effect, and that side effect caused strain in my love life and another hurdle to face. It was the one time that Craig couldn't hide his frustration with me and my quest to heal.

I saw him pulling away as his patience faded. I also saw my inability to perform the way I thought I had to sexually. I explained to Craig that what I was experiencing was a direct result of the antidepressant. I had no control over what was happening, or more accurately, not happening.

Truthfully, he didn't seem to care about the reasons. Resentment was the only emotion that registered on his face. I was bitter at what felt like his selfishness and lack of support, but I remained tight-lipped about those feelings, as fear assured me that they might be the final piece that sent the Jenga Tower of our relationship crashing.

What I did instead was dig deep for understanding. It was there that I found that he was ill-prepared for all I had been going through and what might yet come. I was familiar with the beast, having ridden its back all my life, and I was struggling to manage it. He too was on unstable ground after having entered the ring blindfolded. He was a young man who just wanted to be carefree and have some degree of normalcy somewhere in his relationship, not harsh realities.

I fell into one of my old belief patterns. *The only thing I'm good for is sex. That's all I'm good for. I've nothing else to offer. If I can't do that right, he'll leave.* Sadly, I felt I owed him something for putting up with all the chaos that was attached to me. So, I held true to my self-sacrificial script and stopped the medication in order to save my relationship. He never asked me to do this, but at the time it was the only way I knew to resolve the conflict we had. The truth was that we were actually on some common ground because I too longed to appear normal at least somewhere in my world.

I knew that what I was doing wasn't the smartest option, but I made the choice anyway because I saw his ill temper as coming from a place of fear. This was a situation he didn't know how to fix, and he lashed out. I in turn felt guilty, guilty for creating the mess. I put before him a situation that he had to deal with, one he had no responsibility in creating, but one in which he was now being victimized too. I rescued him, and us, the only way I knew how to at the time.

The actual victim in child abuse isn't the only one victimized. The web of abuse reaches far and wide. The partners in the abuseds' lives often suffer from the repercussions of their pasts. Craig voiced his feelings that he had become a victim on some level as well. Obviously, not to the depths that I had, but being with me was being with my past and the healing of it. The relationship dynamics were tested again and again, and only keen awareness of the origin of the conflict, the past, would carry us through.

# Have I Mentioned I'm Angry?

I believed one of the most unattractive parts of me and my past was the unrelenting cacophonous din of my angry thoughts. The bitterness only seemed to highlight the miserable, disagreeable person I thought that I was.

There was no pause button when it came to these thoughts, only a button stuck on repeat as I was consumed with my litany of angry rants: *I'm angry. I feel angry that no one cared for me, only for themselves. Angry that no one knows how tortured I feel inside, both then and now. Angry that I have to endure and pretend. Angry that there's no one to soothe and cradle me. Angry that I can't stand the thought of someone soothing and cradling me. Angry that I never knew the comfort of a mom's gentle and steadfast love. Angry that I was never allowed the sense of protection that the word "dad" embodies. So angry I could kill them. So angry I hate to even write the word "dad" and "mom." Fuck him. Fuck her. I want to kill them and watch them suffer just like they made me suffer. Angry because killing them isn't an option.*

*No more torture. No more.*

*Please, no more. I have nothing left to give. Someone, please make it stop. Can anyone hear me?*

# Funeral for a Friend

If it seemed as though no one could hear me; I was left to my own devices once again. I had to bring an awareness and listening ear to my inner voices that had been squelched and contained in the caverns of my mind.

One of the most integral parts of my therapy was creating different parts of me that embodied different ages and emotions. No, I don't have multiple personalities. I was always quite aware that these sequestered parts of myself were indeed part of my whole self, but this method made, and makes, the baggage and needs that come with each component more manageable in my mind. I dealt, and deal, with them on an individual basis if need be, addressing one issue at a time versus feeling barraged with the intensity of my wounds. It's like the inner child concept, except I had many of them.

The traits of each little girl or teenager led me to a different level of awareness about myself. Each held specific lessons and memories. They each embodied something of importance for my healing. I began to talk to them in my mind, assessing their thoughts and needs. It felt safer to have them communicate their experiences at times. It allowed me some space to take care of them when my innate reaction would be to emotionally freeze if I were dealing more directly with myself.

By utilizing this method, I was able to step outside of myself and address them as I would any other child that needed love, support, and nurturing. I had to become my own mom in this regard and tend to my kids' needs. Just like any other mom, I often felt overwhelmed with the needs and desires of this brood to I which tended. These were some severely marred little girls, and I initially lacked the empathy necessary to even want to support and nurture them. I lacked a tenderness in dealing with myself, and so I had very little to share with them. I desperately wanted someone else to swoop in and rescue them and me, but my search came up empty. The task lay solidly in my hands. At first I faked it, went through the motions of what I needed to say and do. I wasn't fooling them, but the beauty of it was that they saw and knew my intentions; they understood that I meant them no harm and only wanted them to feel loved.

The relationships remained very tepid as we all took the tiniest of steps toward one another. I had to gain their trust, as they had no experience in trusting their caregivers or the world at large. They always expected to be abandoned and left to deal with matters on their own. Time was the one thing we had on our side in order that some reassurance might manifest that they could trust me, and we would need a lot of it. For one of us, time had run out.

## Down the Rabbit Hole

When I was growing up, my father raised rabbits for us to eat. Little brown or white, fluffy balls of purity manifest. I loved watching the gentle twitch of their noses as they smelled their surroundings. Part of my chores was to feed the rabbits. I felt as if I was intentionally deceiving them. I was feeding them and caring for them only to turn around and eat them. I was disgusted with myself. I sensed they were wise to my game and hated me just as much as I hated myself. Every time I would try to hold and cuddle them, I would get scratched. I believed this was my retribution for my deceptions. I felt a relief that on some level they were able to hurt me too; it assuaged some of the guilt.

Listening to them die was heart wrenching. The squeal as they met their fate would nauseate me. A few hours later, there they would sit on our dinner table, crispy-fried body parts that were slick with butter. Internally I struggled with more guilt and self-loathing as I proceeded to gobble them down for dinner.

I was so relieved when we finally stopped breeding the rabbits. My betrayals of these sweet, innocent beings could stop. I hoped their death squeals might cease to reverberate in my mind.

As I progressed through my therapy, part of me identified with those rabbits. I too was a nervous, trapped, and betrayed innocent creature. I sensed their terror as they sat frozen and wide eyed in their cage, because I knew that type of terror as well. I still heard the last noise they made before they met their death and I too squealed inside, with panic and dread as I watched and felt the abuse around me. In those moments of hysteria, I also wanted to scratch and claw to get away.

She is one part of me I named: Rabbit. I even hesitate to share her name because she is so very fragile and precious to me. I want to keep her tucked away, safely hidden from the world.

I had to lay her to rest. It was too painful to ask her to endure any more in this world, and so in my mind's eye, I performed a burial for her. This frail child finally collapsed in my outstretched arms, nothing but a wasted body remained of her tormented being. She could endure no more. My burying her was the only mercy and tenderness she'd ever known in this world. In passing she found the peace she sought and had always deserved.

My body was consumed with grief at yet another loss. There was nothing left to do but weep for my suffering little girl that never made it out alive.

## Role Reversal

Putting part of me to rest didn't negate the necessity to tend to those parts of me that remained and continued to impact my days.

For most of my teenage years, I felt like competition to my mother. I sensed a sexual tension from my father, sometimes in the way his eyes rested on me. I didn't want the attention and felt responsible for his actions, actions I feared left my mother feeling jealous and less than. It all added to my limitless supply of guilt.

Swirling amongst the guilt was bitterness, a by-product of watching my mother become embattled with her weight all her adult life. Seeing her weight issues and feeling victim to my father's attentions, I became resentful. Just like my father, I judged her for being overweight. In my resentment I blamed her for his trespasses. *Perhaps if she wasn't so fat and unattractive, he wouldn't be leering at me*, or so my irrational thoughts went, and then, greater guilt for having such unkind notions.

Emotionally, I was often in competition with my mother's role as a wife as well. I became the marital counselor for them. Listening to their arguments, I could see and hear all the garbage they were slinging at one another. Days were spent in silence as they punished one another for perceived hurts; it was then that I would go to them individually and offer insights on how to resolve the problem. I relayed messages from one to the other so that the silent war might end as it made the air in the house oppressive with tension. Any time my mother wanted or needed my father to do something, she would say, "You tell him. He'll listen to you." And he would. Ironically, the two people with whom I was in a constant power struggle had given me more power than a child should ever be allowed.

This role model of being irate and refusing to talk to the "offender" was how I then handled conflict in a relationship. I didn't know you could have a discussion while disagreeing; I thought adrenaline-pulsing scream-ing had to be involved and must immediately be followed by turning a cold shoulder. It was about pummeling the other emotionally in order to feel more powerful and prove you're right. The silence afterwards pun-ished them, left them ostracized, and showed them what a terrible thing they had done. Forgiveness wasn't an option; you simply held onto the hurt in order to fuel the next fight.

This wasn't a working model Craig was familiar with, and in fact the first time I went into full combat mode, I saw his eyes fly open with alarm. He avoided conflict; I felt at home in its tumult and fervor. In that moment I understood part of my father's motivation for all his years of fury. I felt supremely wicked in that state and even enjoyed the look of panic I created in him.

In the next instant, I felt deeply ashamed. This was not how I wanted to treat someone I loved. It was through Craig's eyes that I saw how wild and out of control I was behaving. It was nothing he consciously said to me, just his reaction that let me know something needed to change because I was truly scary in that state. I must admit though: even today if I feel cornered or wrongly accused, my instantaneous reaction is-to use Craig's description—"come out swinging." That hair-trigger still exists deep within the workings of my brain. Thankfully, incidents such as these are few and far between but exist as a reminder that I could easily bring out the ranting and raving if I don't stop to think, listen, and breathe, rather than react.

## Choose Your Words Wisely

In reaction mode I wasn't physically aggressive, but verbally I could sever someone limb by limb. I sensed the weak spots in another's psyche and wielded my weapon with extreme relish because I knew full well the capacity of words to harm or heal.

My favorite word is "hallelujah." When I hear that word sung, and I feel instantly connected to The Source and as if transported to my beloved homeland. I am flooded with an ancient knowing and memory of who and what I truly am. I become the knowing as there is nothing to separate me from the ethereal truth. My tears tell the tale of the love from which I came. The gates to my heart vanish, and the most pristine rapture fills every crevice of this magical world. It is then that I can sense the ancient sounds of the angels' melodic chorus, found in the deepest memories and recesses of my soul.

"Sooty." That was a word I despised, and I wanted to gag just saying it or even typing it. That was the nickname my parents used for my genitals.

I mean, what the hell is that? It made and makes me feel disgusting and sexually vile and violated. It caused a darkness to creep into all that is me. I wanted to crawl up in a ball and hide, apologizing for having something as foul as a sooty. That word was shameful and embarrassing for me.

Even a single word has power and can either feed our soul or strip it bare.

## Perfect Role Models

The word "apologize" is one that holds great potential, depending on its absence or presence. In my childhood it was never present.

Actually, one of the greatest lessons my parents taught me was to apologize. Not because I can recall them apologizing, but because they didn't. Ever. They were just as capable of flying as they were apologizing. It seemed humanly impossible for them to admit they may have been wrong about something, no matter how trivial or blatant the evidence to prove it. It left me seething. I understood the power and importance of an apology, even if they couldn't. Lack of ownership of one's wrongdoings erodes away at a relationship, and the foundation of my relationship with my parents had disintegrated because there was never any validation of their errors or resultant damage.

As an adult I make it a point to own my mistakes when I am aware of my errors. A saint I am not. I can't say I reveled in taking ownership–my pride has been known to rear its ugly head–but I did savor the look that crossed another's face when I validated them. I've discovered that most people are willing to forgive if there is sincerity in an apology. Our greatest trespasses come not from our mistakes, but from not owning them. I've found apologizing often brings the relationship back to one of mutual respect and allows for new levels of trust and understanding.

My parents were also great role models for parenting in general. Based on their style of parenting, I clearly knew what I did not want to do as a parent. I made it my cause to not follow in their footsteps. I understood all too well the disastrous outcome of the choices they so unconsciously made; my children would not suffer the same. That meant my work was cut out for me, processing the old so that I might create anew. It felt as though I was starting from scratch and not with the healthiest of stock.

## Like Father, Like Daughter

There was a lot to be discarded from my stock room, and in cleaning house I began to make some space for other people.

For a fair amount of my adult life, I barely tolerated other people. I was very particular and calculated in my socializations. I had no time for what I deemed stupidity or listening to others who just wanted to hear their own voices. There seemed to be no point in the words of others; most were dishonest and calculating in their delivery. I made no efforts to hide my disdain. My face communicated nothing other than annoyance, and I would sit in a barely disguised bitter silence as another sought my connection and conversation.

I had embodied my father on some level, my own version of antisocial. Not a diagnostic antisocial, just one where people were not for me, and instead I found them draining and childish.

I had a lot of shame about the side of me that appeared cold and distant. This was so reminiscent of my father's icy persona that I judged myself cruelly. Throughout my entire childhood, my family would say, "You're just like him". The theory went that he and I were in such conflict with one another because our personalities were so similar, never mind that he was an abusive behemoth.

While it is true that my father and I share many similar traits, I railed against the notion that I fell into the same category as he. I was not wielding my wounds to repeatedly physically and sexually harm others. While I had my own inner demons, I was working valiantly to lay them to rest while gaining insight and understanding. That doesn't seem to be the path he chose.

Trying to understand myself in retrospect, I believe it was similar to having a bad day, just on a larger scale. You have a rough day at work, and when you get home, suddenly everything about your family and pet is grating. I had had a rough first twenty years, and I in turn took it out on the world. There was no space or desire for anything other than going through the motions and returning to dwell in the safety of my own personal cave.

Oh, how I loved that cave. Cocooned inside, I could escape everything and everyone. I didn't know or see the value in engaging with the outside world; I knew it simply as a necessity.

Craig became my role model for how to behave and engage with the world. I spent a lot of time observing and feeling his interactions with others and opened my mind to the possibility that it could be a pleasant thing, a desirable one perhaps. He brought an innocence to his socializations that I had lost long ago.

While I was tending to my wounds, I was also very, very gradually opening the door to allow others one step closer. I tested the water, ever on alert for the gifts that others shared with me because I had begun to allow them that space.

In the process, I discovered discernment; not everyone could be held to the same standard or depth of connection. I grew up in a household where boundaries were hazy and were trampled upon continually, so discernment was about learning and re-establishing healthy, no longer rigid, boundaries for me. But I also began to grasp that even those that weren't safe for my inner sanctum had something to offer me, if nothing other than a polite conversation. Politeness became important to me because it gave another the chance to feel as if they mattered; I could see it in the softened expression of their glowing faces. As I painstakingly learned I mattered, I afforded others the same.

## An Excision

Cutting my father out of my life was to be my first monumental step in proving to myself that I did matter, but it came only after I fell victim to him yet again.

While in the midst of therapy with Andrea, I made it my goal to explain to them the depth of my hurt and arranged a meeting at their house. I returned to the scene of my trauma alone and ill-equipped.

I stood before the both of them in the living room, feeling small and intimidated by my task. I failed miserably in my mission as I couldn't find the words to convey the extent of my turmoil, nor did I have the courage to address the sexual abuses. Instead, I offered a watered down rendition of my woes as my head swirled in its attempts to take me far, far away. I received a nod of the head as my father casually stated, "I shouldn't have done those things." He smiled and reached out a hand to me, which I reluctantly took, and pulled me down to sit on his lap. Time seemed to have suddenly been warped into slow- motion.

It felt terribly wrong and sick, yet I allowed myself to be coaxed into his waiting lap. He continued to beam at me and seemed so pleased with the outcome of our talk, hugging me while I sat stiffly planted where he had placed me. In that moment, I understood that the dysfunction of my family unit was far greater and bigger than me. That I would be able to heal myself and still remain a part of their life began to seem like an impossibility. What they saw as a healing moment, I knew to be the beginning of the end.

One year later, my father and I would meet that end. For Christmas he had carved a wizard especially for me. He eyes were alight with pride as I opened my gift. I was touched that he made something with just me in mind, but I was also dreading the fact that now I was obliged to give him a hug, my mind doing an emotional tap dance. He sat in his recliner as I leaned over to embrace him. As I stood bent over he reached his arms upward and rested his hand on my right breast, very nonchalant.

Internally, I recall tensing up and feeling very confused about what to do. I instantly doubted my experience, internally questioning the energetically charged sensation that seemed to remain from where his hand had lain. Shocked and bewildered, I pretended as though nothing had happened and attempted to slam a mental door shut on what had just occurred. I remained silent and continued with the festivities.

Later that night I found myself lashing out at Craig. There was nothing he had done to warrant my hostility; it was confusing to me and, I can only assume, to him as well. I was able to take a step back, do an internal inventory and realize the resentment I was wielding towards Craig had nothing to do with him but instead was a reaction to my father's groping hand earlier that day.

Once I understood the cascade of events, I shouted at him like some kook, "My father grabbed my boob when we were at their house, and now I'm taking it all out on you!" For his part, he stood in shock because he was completely unaware of what had transpired earlier and was baffled as to how to handle the situation I had just thrust in his hands. After a few moments, I was able to explain that I was feeling violated and needed to protect myself. The result was that I had pushed back at the person closest to me, but not the person responsible.

My next and only possible step became crystal clear; I needed to sever all ties with my father. I saw how easily I fell into the learned pattern of submission when it came to being sexually violated and how I became lost in confusion.

Oddly enough, what made me end my contact with my father wasn't fear of him, but the fear that I could no longer rely on myself. Experience had taught me that my body was not a reliable source of protection, but mentally I was tenacious, and that had become the backbone of my survival pack. But therapy was showing me a fresh perspective, and with that I was able to see that in situations where I was sexually challenged, I seemed to be rendered helpless, at least temporarily. That was not someplace I was willing to go anymore. It came down to choosing him or me, and I chose me.

I did muster the courage to tell my mother what happened as she floundered for an understanding of what possessed me to cease speaking with my father. This was a huge emotional risk on my part, and she stayed true to form. Her response was to be perturbed with me as she disdainfully asked, "Why didn't you just slap him?!" There was no concern or empathy for the painful position I was in, only the suggestion that I'd handled it like a fool. I also found it interesting that she didn't question the fact that he might do such a thing, just that I had handled it poorly.

"You know," she continued, "you can't run and hide from him forever." Again, she labeled me a coward. But I had stood up to that man on many levels throughout my life, and I had nothing left to prove to myself or them. It took more courage to walk away than it would have taken to stay.

Staying implied I was accepting our dynamics. Saying goodbye called our entire system into question and made me the target and perceived source of their stress and hurt. When I was a child, I had no choice but to orchestrate my way through their perverse labyrinth, but that was the beauty of being an adult; I could walk away and refuse to engage in the drama.

Periodically in the first few years I'd find myself wondering if there would be a letter in the mail from him, my little girl's eyes alight with hope as I approached the mailbox. Hope that I mattered. Had he even thought of me or considered reaching out? The answer was a resounding, "No." I've never heard from him since.

He refused to validate and honor me for twenty plus years; it was time to listen to the message he was clearly projecting. For the first time in my life, I was listening to him without protest. I hope that made him happy.

## Survivor's Guilt

Walking away from my father came with an unexpected price.

Who was I to whine and cry like a little baby because my mommy and daddy weren't nice to me? Perhaps this entire process was fraught with self-pity and was a shining example of self-indulgence. I could have had it worse, I know. There are others that suffered far greater trespasses and torments.

*I live a blessed life today, yet I wallow in what it is I never received and the void that remains. What type of ungrateful bitch am I? Just move on already. You got out; isn't that enough?*

My answer? No, it didn't seem to be enough. And worse yet, I felt guilty because I did make it out. Grace had afforded me the people and situations to attempt to mend my heartbreak. There are many that still sit in the throes of their past, never able to cut any of the ties that bind them to that time and place.

I didn't know how to help them. I searched high and low for the magical concoctions that might bring them the chance to free themselves. "Here," I wanted to say to them, "take this and do that." Why have I been fortunate enough to be led down this path, surely I was no more deserving than they? I wanted to bring them all along with me, a parade out of the darkness. I couldn't turn and look back, because knowing that they're still standing where they were once planted was like a dagger to my heart. Without them, I trudged forward.

I'm sorry that I was not strong enough to carry you, too. So very sorry.

## Good Riddance

While I can't save everyone touched by the vile hands of abuse, I did my part in an effort to eliminate any further victims of Saxy.

Perhaps a year or so into my therapy, I had a startling revelation: Saxy might still be teaching. If that was the case, there was a chance he was still abusing children. Instantly, I thought, Someone needs to tell. A horrifying jolt shot through my body as I had the realization that that someone was me.

I felt utterly bewildered as to how I was going to do this. I tried to backpedal, thinking to myself, What are the chances that he is still working? He must have retired by now. A guilty conscience next took me to, Who do I even call and what exactly am I going to say to them once I have their attention? I was consumed with fear that no one would believe me, and I would instead be made the villain, forced to defend and protect myself once more.

In my mind's eye I could picture another young girl sitting with him in his room, all alone as she endured what had once been my fate. I understood that if I never tried to make that phone call, then I too was responsible, on some level, for the abuse he committed in the future. There was absolutely no way I would take part in that. I then made the only decision I could. I placed the call.

I still had no plan nor any clue as to what words would tumble from my mouth. My first step was to simply find the number to my high school and dial. I recognized the woman that answered the phone; she was a mom of another student who was one year younger than I. Her daughter had been in band as well when we were in school and I felt my chest tighten as I realized she might know Saxy, and worse, remember me. I would no longer be anonymous, and she might feel the need to protect him once I told her my story.

I made a point not to mention my name and choked out my point of business, "I was calling to ask if Saxy still teaches at the school."

"Oh no," she said with a gentle air of condolence, "he passed."

I stumbled in my response to her because I had begun to shout, "Yes!" and quickly realized that was not the most socially appropriate thing to say. Instead, I hastily thanked her for her time and hung up because I felt myself wanting to explain to her what had happened to me, and I wanted to ask her if he had taught her daughter. Thankfully wisdom prevailed as I realized my mission was accomplished; he was no longer a threat. The only thing left to do was end the call.

After hanging up the phone, I exploded with a giddiness. Relief washed over me because all was complete, meaning I didn't have to pursue continued efforts to protect other children. I leapt about my house laughing out loud, punching the air and so very, very ecstatic that he was d-e-a-d, dead. I loved the sound of that. Dead and gone, no longer a danger ever again. I wondered where he might exist in death, and if he was witnessing me as I reveled in his ending, and what he might think of that. I paused a moment to also consider that somewhere in time someone may have grieved for him, or perhaps still missed him. Did they know the side of him that I knew? I felt a fleeting flash of compassion for whoever "they" might be, but then my celebration continued because I felt nothing but pure jubilation that his end had finally come.

Many years later, I came to know of at least one other girl he had molested as his music student. A high school friend I later encountered thought my experiences of his abuse might be a possible explanation for her sister abruptly quitting her lessons with him years earlier without offering a clear explanation. How many more of us existed in this club that I had never wanted to join? I sent a prayer to my sisters to whom I am silently connected, hoping that they too might find healing.

## Upholstered Pachyderm

The angst I felt about placing a phone call to out Saxy's predation was paltry compared to what next lay on my plate, spilling my long-held tale of sexual molestation at the hands of someone much closer to home.

While in therapy with Andrea, I made the grueling decision to share with my mother the memories I have of my father molesting me. I invited my mother to one of my sessions and said to her, "I need to tell you something about Dad."

She gave an almost imperceptible nod of her head, and for that millisecond I thought I was going to get the validation I was so desperate to feel, see, hear, and taste. Instead she said, "He cheated on me."

It seemed as though she had reached over, violently wrenched the validation from my hands and proceeded to greedily consume it for herself. I was momentarily stunned because I was not there to confirm or deny anything about his infidelities and their marriage. That moment was to be about me, and as reality set in, I understood that she had once again made things about *her*, and *her* pain and *her* needs. I had gotten my validation, but not the one that I sought.

Gaining my composure I said, "No, I wanted to tell you that I have memories of him molesting me." She didn't appear to be stunned, nor was she defensive.

She began to ask questions, mainly directed at Andrea, and one of them was to inquire if I was mentally ill, perhaps suffering from the same issues as her father. I laughed out loud in utter disbelief. Andrea shot me a look with her eyes that sternly said, *"Stop that."*

For a moment, that pissed me off a bit as it felt as though she was taking my mother's side in this insane exchange. Intellectually I understood her role was to not appear contentious or hostile to my mother, but emotionally, I needed to know her loyalty belonged to me. I soon set my annoyance with Andrea to the side, knowing full well she was doing what I had asked of her, her job.

But that is not to say that my animosity was vanquished because I was then fighting the urge to shout at my mother, "You've *got* to be fucking kidding me! You're asking if *I'm* the crazy one?! Oh my god, it's just like when I was a kid. 'What's wrong with Kellie?' Here we go again. Nothing ever fucking changes with you." I quickly gained my footing, however, as I realized that for my mother this was a natural question coming from a woman whose own childhood entailed having a parent with mental health issues. Perhaps, she imagined, I had inherited what plagued him.

Andrea assured her that no, I was not suffering from mental illness and that this was very real for me. I contained myself, but I truly wanted to victoriously whoop, "Hah! I told you!" I think it would have been easier for her to hear I was mentally ill because it would have been a much simpler explanation for the havoc I seemed to create in their world, and they would remain scot-free from any foul play or responsibility.

In a follow-up phone call, my mother told me she had confronted my father about sexually abusing me. "I asked him," she said, "but I could tell by his reaction and the look on his face that he didn't do it."

That was such a ridiculous statement that I couldn't find a fitting response, I just sat on the other end of the line as my shoulders fell, my body heavy with a familiar anguish as I realized she had chosen him over me–again. And then I felt the bitterness awaken, the thought occurring to me that it must have been the same convincing look he had donned when he denied strangling me, despite the bruising on my throat that told another story. Their degree of dysfunction was a mind-blowing spectacle each and every fucking time, they certainly were reliable in that aspect.

I then took one more step into my private and hellish ring of fire; I made the choice to address my estranged father directly about his abuses. I knew I would not feel emotionally safe doing it face-to-face and that I would need support so, I opted to call him during one of my sessions with Andrea. He has always answered the phone with an atypical and disgruntled, "Yeah," instead of the common greeting, "Hello." Just that one word took me back to feeling like a frightened little girl, but with Andrea's presence I was able to stumble through my words as I confronted him and his behaviors.

Not shockingly, he denied anything and everything. He shouted at me and was so incensed that each word sounded painfully strained. I feared I was going to give him a heart attack and considered ending the call. But as his rantings continued, I found the fight that remained in me, and I began to scream back in my own defense. Andrea saw the futility and felt the mounting absurdity in the exchange and encouraged me to hang up. I was grateful that she intervened because I was fully caught up in the battle and couldn't see that ending the conversation was the healthiest and wisest choice.

When next I spoke to my mother, she shared their concern that I had taped the call. I had indeed. My intent in taping it was so that I could go back and listen to me confronting my abuser, a token of empowerment for myself. I had no other nefarious intentions or plans for the recording, which she was suggesting. Their paranoia was not new and continued.

I was visiting my mother at some point, and as we went to enter their home, I discovered the door was locked. I pulled out my key to unlock the entrance, but my mother stopped me short saying, "We changed the locks." She made it clear that my siblings had a copy of the key for the new locks. She completely and very intentionally dodged the topic of getting me a key as well, but the message was clear— "We don't trust you. You are an outsider."

The vast chasm between us only continued to grow. My parents had now tossed an upholstery cover over the elephant in the room, but I was not fooled; I knew it still remained, and it bore the weight and enormity of our familial lies because I understood that denial of reality or a truth doesn't make it nonexistent.

## Heart to Heart

It had been years since I lived with my mother, but our connection, and my intuition, were so strong that distance did nothing to hinder our bond and still had the power to create a re-play of the old dramatics.

After taking a run one particular evening, I sat on our living room floor to stretch. A pain shot into my chest, around the area of my heart, and with it an image of my mother appeared. I intuited that she was having chest pains, and fear sent me running to pick up the phone to call her.

"Have you been having chest pains?" I asked.

"Yes," was her hesitant reply.

"Well, I felt them. Have you told anyone or gotten it checked out?"

"No," she said somewhat defensively.

"Mom, you shouldn't just let something like that go. You have to go see a doctor about that. You could have a heart attack!" I sternly advised.

In an annoyed tone she replied, "Alright, Kellie," and we ended our call.

I promptly phoned my sister to tell her what had transpired. We sat on the phone together, crying. That our mom was going to die was our fear, a fear we had known very intimately as kids and one that was making itself known once more. We both were in panic mode, and I could see the connection, though I doubted my sister was able to identify what was transpiring.

Within the next week or so, my sister called me to say that our mother had been taken to the hospital due to chest pains. She reported that while my mother was at work, she began to have chest discomfort again. She called her doctor and was told to call an ambulance. Apparently she was mortified by the scene of an ambulance coming to get her at her work, and my father was mad, at me.

The hospital could find no evidence of a cardiac issue, and it was concluded that a medicine she was taking was the culprit of the chest pain. My parents were annoyed at having to pay an ambulance bill, especially since the result was that she was not in cardiac distress. My sister knew I would want to call my mother to talk to her about the incident but warned, "I don't think you should call the house. Dad is really angry with you."

He was pissed at me for creating a scene, for pushing my mother to get medical treatment for chest pain. "Fuck him," was my response to that information. I had never spoken those words out loud to someone in my family, and I savored them as they melted in my mouth like a dark chocolate delicacy. My sister remained silent.

I imagined it was the same anger he felt when I was a little girl trying to save my mother's life as he strangled her. My "drama" and involvement were a thorn in his side then as well. I found his reaction to be on the verge of insanity once more, and it solidified my reasons for having cut him out of my life. I could only shake my head and think to myself, *He's a fucking ass.*

# Humanity Versus Spirituality

As I sought to mend my pain, I often found myself struggling to create a balance between my human and spiritual side. In spirit, I felt a familiarity and safety, while my human interactions and reactions haunted me.

Anything connected with spirit drew me in and away. Books, meditation, workshops, healing circles, psychics, mediums, and spiritual expos fed my need to connect with spirit and disconnect with humanity. That world was where I felt at ease, content and alive.

Behaving "human" left me feeling deeply ashamed, for I felt I was somehow disappointing spirit by not expressing the purest form of myself. The deep-seated emotions of rage and hatred that consumed me most of my existence caused me to harshly judge myself as unworthy yet again.

Judgment of others came easily as well, for their drama and superficial conversations left me drained and overwhelmed with their lack of insight. People were irritants, like rubbing sandpaper over my skin. Talking in an honest fashion about personal growth and spirit was where I wanted to go. Instead, I was left with deep feelings of annoyance and had limited tolerance to be around others socially, and then I judged myself further for less than loving thoughts and observations.

My body proved to be my greatest nemesis. I was trapped in this shell. This body, the clearest expression of what it meant to be human, had betrayed me. It wasn't strong enough to protect me from the hurt inflicted by others. My spirit felt invincible, but this sack of bones proved to have its limitations, its power nothing in comparison to my soul. Everything about it seemed paltry in comparison to all things spirit, and I resented taking care of it. This body wasn't my true home, instead it felt like prison. I was living in the enemy, not just with it, and it was a lifetime sentence.

To embrace my humanity was one of my greatest challenges. To say I too behaved human, and what I perceived as less than my true self, left me hanging my head in mortification many times. I didn't want to be in these trenches. I wanted to fly high and free. I felt duped, abandoned in this foreign land. But here I remained, and so I've had to become the observer.

Craig was my greatest teacher of the splendors of humanity. While closely watching him, I could see him delight in every moment of his physicality and that of our surroundings. He didn't want to go anywhere but was content in being fully present in his body. As thoroughly satisfied as I was in anything deemed spiritual, he was equally enthralled with humanity. Since I had a very poor frame of reference for this, I utilized my empathic abilities to get a sense of what it actually felt like. I tapped into his feelings to understand the many physical pleasures of this earthly plane.

My body continued to challenge me at every turn, from my earliest years, and only managed to become more debilitating over time. Not only was I on a mission to attend to my mental and emotional scars, I was also intent on rehabilitating the flesh and bones that my spirit inhabited. My physical essence had endured many traumatic events, and each and every one of those assaults had become embedded in my body. My body knew and remembered, the energies never having had the opportunity to pass through, but instead were contained in the very cells that created my form. There had never been a time for processing, only surviving.

The task seemed monumental, but I persevered. I did all the "right" things: exercised, meditated, ate organic food and not meat, drank my daily quota of water, sought many alternative healers and various schools of thought, fed the economy with the vast multitude of supplements I ingested, but the one thing I couldn't give my body—which was absolutely free—was mercy. I pushed and drove my body for years using sheer force. Ever the authoritative parent, I refused to listen to its messages. I was treating my body as my parents had treated me, and just like me, there came a day when it would take no more.

## Invisible Tattoos and Missing Parts

The rest of me did not walk away unscathed, and it seemed I'd been branded. In my mind, my wounds felt similar to the tattooed numbers on Holocaust victims. Although invisible to the naked eye, what was left behind was a constant reminder of the past, ever present and with no escape. It was not over when it was over.

Embracing my wounds caused me to cringe internally. I had to continually coax my brain to embrace all the parts of me. This was who I am; I bore the scars of war just as any soldier would who has seen battle. I *knew* this, yet my mind revolted at the suggestion that I accept those remnants, that I accept me.

Like a bull, I've charged my way through the wastelands of my childhood, examining all that presented itself to me and staring straight into the eye of my deepest horrors. I've worked tirelessly at redubbing those outdated tapes that looped over and over in my mind, implanted by their hands, with new healthy and healing truths.

Yet there I was, still with a limp in my gait. At times, I still stumbled over that old circuitry, its pathways through my brain ceaseless. Tears of frustration welled in my eyes because no matter how hard I tried, they were still there, my own phantom limbs. And that, I didn't know how to embrace and accept.

To be free of them and this torment was all I've ever wanted, only to find that I can never be totally free, just in remission. Remission may last several days or many months, but always I will be given a chance to sift through and confront yet another layer of this rubble under which they buried me.

Something was missing. I was missing the connection that simply allowed me to luxuriate in this resplendent life without first stopping to repeatedly open the doorways of my heart and my soul. I was forced to think about accepting love and bliss. I had to talk myself into allowing love through this filter they seemed to have installed within me, this filter that blocks my natural proclivity to pleasure and love. If I looked only through the lens of the filter, I saw with my wounds, in truth, their wounds. Every day it was necessary to transplant the lens with the clarity of spirit and remove the filtration system that only allowed a muted version of my love-filled life. Every day. Many times a day.

Time and again I called, *Is there anyone out there that can mend this inner circuitry?* I didn't want to accept that my parents had impacted me so greatly and in such ways that I'd never completely recover. To me, it felt as if I accepted the remains, I was somehow openly accepting my parents. I couldn't accept them; it hurt too much.

I couldn't accept them as part of me. My imagination wouldn't allow it; it was too terrifying a concept, having my parents so very near to me again. For the first time since I'd begun this odyssey, I was at a true loss as to how to proceed. There was a solid brick wall that blocked my sight from seeing the other side of this obstacle. I could see no way around but every day I returned to examine the wall, hoping to find a loose brick or perhaps a crack that would allow me to see beyond its limits. There was nothing to be found.

# Powerfully Powerless

The only thing I could find on my treks toward healing was more pain. One of the harshest things in this physicality for me to endure was the incessant worry that surged in my entire body, like a fire hose turned to full blast. I did not go in search of it, but instead it found me. I didn't have to look far to discover that this was not a safe place, this planet Earth. Everywhere I turned, I saw a system wrought with hazards and harm. It was not the Earth's fault, but instead we humans who cause the systems to run amuck.

It kept me awake some nights, the litany of abuse and harm we cause the Earth and one another. I possessed a mental catalog of all our evils, the list a ticker tape that forever ran through the background of my mind. I continued to make every effort to minimize my personal impact on our environment, this planet we inhabit and my fellow humans, but the responsibility and tension I've felt for my wrongdoings told me it was never enough. It was reminiscent of my childhood, and the anxiety I felt at watching all the pain and destruction that swirled around with the abuse. I felt responsible and overwhelmed then too.

Responsible to fix it. Responsible because my mere presence caused it. And just like before, I couldn't stop it all from happening and was in fact powerless over some components simply because I did exist on this Earth and certain consequences were, are, a direct result of my day-to-day life. No matter how diligent my efforts, my actions were entangled with imperfection. Most assuredly, I was still powerless over others and their choices.

The irony was that as a child, my power was intentionally stripped from me, yet I was consumed with a monstrous sense of responsibility, which conversely meant I was extremely powerful. What a mind-bending dichotomy.

The fear and oppressive sense of duty could've paralyzed me, but I didn't lay down then, nor will I today, or the day after. I did and will do what I wasn't able to do all those years ago: I comforted myself. I consoled myself with the knowledge that I've continually strived to make conscious and kind choices to the best of my ability. I reminded myself that this human play is intended for all types of roles and experiences to be played out, for both me and others. I've always reached once more to remember that this is a world of opposites, and we wouldn't know love if we didn't know its lacking too.

This was what got me through and this was the only way I knew how to not collapse under the weight of my actions, my family's, and those of my fellow man.

# All Good Things Must Come to an End

Reclaiming my true power, the orchestration of my own life, required my utmost dedication. For approximately two years, I faithfully attended my weekly purging sessions with Andrea, and then it occurred to me that our time together was over. My heart ached at the thought of ending our relationship because I felt a deep bond of trust and love for all that she had offered me. For her part, she strongly recommended that I continue my time with her. She was certain I had a lot more work ahead of me. I told her I agreed with her; it was far from over, but my intuition had led me to her and now it was telling me our relationship had run its course.

She had served me well. She was my first sounding board and the very first person to validate me, filling my desperate need to be heard. I believed in her intentions and truly felt the compassion she conveyed, a first for me. I was full of gratitude for the support and guidance she shared in the terrifyingly dark nights of my soul. I could only move tentatively and intentionally forward because, metaphorically, she held my hand.

At this point, I sensed we had done together what we came here to accomplish and next I needed to seek energy healing. Where that would come from and how that looked I had no idea, but I trusted that sitting on her sofa each week was no longer where I needed to remain. I bid her a fond farewell and allowed the universe to guide me on the next leg of my quest.

Phase 3

*"If you're going through hell, keep going."*
–WINSTON CHURCHILL

# A Broken Wedding Vow

As I stepped out into the world, ever on alert for the next turn I was to take, time passed, and I found myself holding my own as I returned to what our society defines as normal.

Craig and I had been focused on building our life together, and we bought our first home. Soon thereafter we were married, but not before I had to dodge the monkey wrench my mother threw into our day.

Months prior to our wedding, I had a very frank discussion with her. My father would not be walking me down the aisle, a close male friend would play that part. I had no relationship with my father any longer, and this was to be one of the many realistically sad fallouts of my childhood, no father at my wedding. I phoned her to ask if she, however, would be attending our wedding.

"I don't know, Kellie," was her first response. She didn't say it, but I knew she was torn as to which side she should support, me or him. "Do you want me to come?" she asked.

"Yes, that's why I'm calling you. But if you're coming I need to know so that I can order your flowers. If you're going to be there, I want you to have flowers to represent the fact that you're the mother of the bride. If you can't come, just tell me, but I don't want any surprises. That means if you tell me you're not coming to the wedding, I won't buy you flowers, and I don't want you to show up unexpected. There's no changing your mind once you give me your decision. I don't want surprises on my wedding day."

She mulled over her decision for perhaps a week or more and decided she would not come. That stung a bit, but I had already prepared myself for that outcome. That meant the only person who would represent my family would be my sister. This was the inevitable result of having no contact or stable relationship with my parents or relatives. Once my mother rendered her choice, I reinforced that I did not want her to make an unexpected appearance; that her decision was to be final.

What did she do? Well, she came to the wedding, of course. Surprise, surprise, surprise. As I walked down the aisle towards Craig, I noticed a look of alarm on his face. Once I stood beside him at the front of the church, he whispered to me, "Your mom's here."

I couldn't fucking believe it, yet I could. Stomping all over the boundaries and my needs was status quo for her. Why was I foolish enough to hope for anything different on one of the most important days of my life?

Craig was sure I was going to lose my mind and go off on her right then and there at the altar. I chose to stifle my anger, like I had done many times before, and instead focused on our vows and our day. I did not want to give her the power to ruin that for us. At the end of the ceremony, I said to her quite matter-of-factly, "What are you doing here? I asked you not to surprise me."

She seemed confused and hurt that I wasn't thrilled to see her. I was confused by her confusion and hurt. After that exchange, she left to go home while the rest of us proceeded to enjoy the celebration at our reception.

In a later conversation, I called her out for her selfishness. She was quite baffled that I wasn't grateful to her for coming to the wedding. I responded with, "You didn't come for me; you came there for yourself. I specifically told you that I wanted you there and you decided not to come. Then I clearly asked you to stay away from our wedding once you made that choice, but instead you ignored my request and did whatever *you* wanted. You were concerned with your feelings, not mine."

She remained befuddled as I remained firm.

## Treading Water

Despite the potentially explosive beginning to our marriage, Craig and I continued on a steady and blissful course.

Several years into marriage a precious soul graced our life with their presence; our first son was born. Being a mother was a miracle to me and left me even more bewildered by my parents' ability to disregard that wonder. When our son was two years old, we moved from our townhouse into a newly-constructed single family home.

Three more years passed, and we were to be blessed yet again with another treasure, our second son. After his birth I left the world of nursing completely, where I had still been working a couple of nights per week, to stay at home full time.

My focus, time, and attention went to creating a life for them that was abundant with love, stability, safety, and an innocent happiness. Being a devoted mom and a conscious parent was my deepest devotion. I had very little reserves left to tend to my needs despite inner rumblings of warning.

Life was going "as it should," but still my emotional struggles pulled at me, seeking my attention so that they might know further expression and release. I heard their calls and felt the continual gnawing, like a mouse that had taken up residence in my mental attic. The phone book held the answers for me the first time I went searching; this time it was an actual phone that was to ring in my next round of healing.

## Healing Hands and Supportive Friends

Several years after completing my therapy with Andrea, I searched for an energy healer who might help me in furthering my process. I had not a clue as to what type of healer I needed, but I was being called to work with an energetic guide. I realized I had put that call on hold for too long as my inner world swirled and twisted about without reason. I felt myself losing control again.

It was at a play group gathering for my oldest son that I shared with the hostess mom my desire to find a healer. Just as I was expressing my need, the phone at her house rang. She rushed to answer it. As fate would have it, it was a male friend of hers who was versed in energetic healing. I needed no clearer sign than that and promptly began what was to be another passage in the voyage of earnest efforts to mend my inner world.

Initially, my sessions were one-on-one and could best be described as hands-on healing. It was through the energy that traveled from his hands and into my body that I began to free more layers of the residue I held within. I cried, and cried some more. I screamed, and then again. My body flailed and convulsed with random movements of release. The energy and the emotions that came with it were at once explosive and completely depleting, but it felt like the first time that I was able to let go of some of the trauma held within my physical body.

Through my time spent in these sessions, I also began to attend a Healing Circle. Every Sunday night I gathered with a group of like-minded souls to share our struggles and our joys. Our evenings spent together always ended in a group hands-on healing, where each person received energetic support from the group as a whole. Always, I was supported and nurtured by this group of soul friends. They allowed me to be just as I was, only wanting the best for me.

These folks saw my ugliest uglies and loved me anyway. Perhaps even more importantly, they saw and spoke of the richness that was my soul, applauding and honoring my truest essence. They gave me permission to come more fully into my power, to own and shine my light. They have my deepest gratitude.

As with everything, our time together came to a close, but the bond that we shared during those years is eternal.

# Body of Evidence

While I was traversing an emotional and psychological journey and cleansing of mass proportions, my body had also been along for the ride. The mind-body connection has become commonplace now, but in my youth there wasn't much thought as to how one impacted the other and vice versa. Today, we know they're intimately intertwined and influential in our functioning. This ride of self-awareness and growth was also about understanding how my body had been impacted by my past and advocating for its healing as well. Not only was I being called to leave no stone unturned as I sought health and balance, but I was to examine and polish each and every one.

Physically, I had struggled since I was a young teen. My symptoms were mild at first and gradually increased in intensity and number as I aged. I won't list every symptom I've experienced, but I will list a few to bring home the point that my body was struggling.

In my early years, I started with muscle aches, insomnia, fatigue, sensitivity to heat, and low blood sugar episodes. In my early twenties I continued with those same symptoms but with an increase in the intensity of some as the fatigue and insomnia began to ramp up. By my late twenties, my menstrual cycles were even heavier and longer and of course, always the fatigue. Spotting then became a part of my normal cycles, difficulty losing weight, acne, and let's not forget the fatigue. Next, were infertility issues followed by hypertension, tremors, lightheadedness, hypothyroidism, adrenal fatigue, light, heat and noise sensitivity, poor exercise tolerance, nausea and vomiting, and forever and always, insomnia and fatigue. Those were the days when I could have one drink and end up puking in my bathroom as if I had just downed a bottle of vodka. Someone simply tapping their foot felt like an assault to my system, as if they were wielding a jackhammer. By the time I was in my late thirties, I had to stop and rest whenever I needed to walk up the steps in my house as my heart would race, I'd be out of breath and lightheaded, and my legs too weak to handle their load. The act of standing could make my legs tremble with exhaustion. Anyone looking at me would have seen none of this, only a picture of health.

It's important to note that during all this time, I lived a healthy lifestyle. I pushed myself through exercise, the intensity of what I was capable of decreased drastically, but I naively thought exercise was supposed to be that difficult, and so I pushed my body. I wasn't obese, and I ate a healthy diet of no meat and lots of fruits and veggies. I didn't drink coffee or alcohol in excess, but instead nourished my body with eight glasses of water each day. I was not a smoker. I didn't use drugs. My lifestyle choices in no way matched the struggles of my body. I did "everything you're supposed to do" to live healthfully.

"WTF?!" I screamed, to myself and later to my poor husband, as my patience for my body reached its all-time low. I felt at war with my body, and I was feeling truly crushed by the competition.

Throughout all that time I researched every symptom and condition I was labeled with. I invested a small fortune in health practitioners, both alternative and traditional, as well as natural herbs and supplements. As time went on I was drawn more and more to the nontraditional methods of healing: acupuncture, Reiki, Ayurveda, color puncture therapy, Rolfing, and various elimination diets and detoxes.

Each approach I took was never THE answer, but would provide me, at times, with some minor and temporary alleviation of my symptoms. I could never get to the root cause of all of my symptoms, until I met my cardiologist. I made an appointment with him as a concession to the battle with my body. I saw it as an act of surrender. I felt I had been annihilated.

I had sought treatment a year prior from another cardiologist, but his treatment was to prescribe pills that left me bloated and still hypertensive. Intuitively, I knew he didn't have the answers for me, and so I went on a mission to find what was truly going on with my body.

My new cardiologist seemed to know instantly what I'd spent twenty years trying to figure out. I had dysautonmia. Many mainstream cardiologists were still in the dark about this systemically complex issue. I honestly wept as he explained to me what the diagnosis entailed. Finally, someone got it, and I was left with this huge mystery solved.

And then he spoke these kind words, "It's not your fault."

I felt a burden lift from me as I realized this wasn't something that I had dreamed up (at one point a neurologist actually accused me of being an addict, faking symptoms and seeking drugs), nor was it something I had manifested through my poor lifestyle choices. His words, while referencing my new diagnosis, had a direct correlation energetically to my childhood abuse. Those were the words I had longed to hear my entire life, that none of the events that transpired were my fault, nor had I made it up. Unbeknownst to him, he was offering me healing on another level as well.

Simply put, dysautonomia meant my autonomic nervous system was haywire. The system that was meant to keep my body in balance had none. There are two parts to the autonomic nervous system, the sympathetic and parasympathetic. The sympathetic prepares us for danger and responds with fight, flight, or freeze. The parasympathetic performs just the opposite and relaxes our system when any perceived threat vanishes. My body's check and balance system had short–circuited, and it seemed my body had no off switch. For years, really all my life, I'd been operating full steam ahead, emotionally that is, and my glands, hormones and nervous system were simply fried. I was short circuiting, everywhere.

I was prescribed various prescriptions to manage my blood pressure and insomnia with the expectation given to me that it would take time to get some of the varying symptoms under control. The hope was that once my nervous system relaxed, some of the other symptoms would dissipate. I wasn't amused that this wouldn't be a quick fix, nor did I relish the thirty-pound weight gain and additional fatigue caused by the medicine. How I could get any more tired I couldn't imagine. But I had enough energy to devote to my next mission, getting off the medicine.

## Following the Trail

I was determined not to live the remainder of my years a slave to prescription pills. While I understood the importance of managing some of my symptoms immediately, I also knew this wasn't what my body required to fully heal. The pills were only masking the symptoms, not treating the cause.

I felt physically and emotionally tense and uptight, rageful, and impatient. I knew it was time to reinvest in traditional therapy because I sensed there was more healing to be done with my past. If my mind and brain still lived in a world of constant threat, there was no way my nervous system could ever power down.

The first thing I needed to do was clean house of the intense leeching emotions that continued to suck the life out of me. This was part two of therapy. I wasn't able to see passed the flood of intense feelings because once again they were all-consuming. It took quite some time to muster the courage to tell Craig I wanted to go back to therapy. I didn't want to appear weak or troubled, a mental mantra that could do nothing but keep me stuck. I felt like I had to explain why I wasn't "over it" yet, and I felt guilty about spending the money on me yet again. The pressure I felt emotionally and physically grew too great to tolerate, and I confessed my need for help.

While sharing my frustrations and feelings of impotence, a friend mentioned a treatment modality called EMDR, *Eye Movement and Desensitization and Reprocessing* therapy. She shared that it was helpful for the processing of traumatic experiences, dampening the emotional charge associated with those memories.

I needed to hear nothing more and proceeded to scour the Internet for information on EMDR, hoping to find a local therapist. I had no luck finding someone locally on a web search, but I was soon to be led in the right direction.

I received an invitation to attend a networking group with various healers sharing information about their work. One of the attendees shared that she was a therapist in my area, and part of her practice was to utilize EMDR. I wanted to leap right out of my chair, but instead I sat impatiently waiting as the others took their turn at sharing their different modalities. Once that portion of the night was complete, I made a beeline straight to her to introduce myself.

I discovered her name was Hailey, and she became the one who would sit opposite me in a therapy setting where I would once again emotionally and verbally vomit all that had been putrefying within my mind, body, and soul.

It was the same story; nothing had changed there, but this time I was much more in tune to what it was that I was laboriously dragging through my life. Venting the chaos in my mind and utilizing EMDR at different points took me to yet another layer of healing, which was initially never quick enough for me. Hailey had her job cut out for her as she gingerly pumped the brakes on my continual drive, always pushing myself for more, deeper, faster.

Sometimes that healing came with a high price as I was left in the midst of my suffering for many days, its presence seeping out of me in an effort to be released. Despite the taxing nature of my therapy, I looked forward to my time in therapy as I found it so very soothing to be validated and supported in a non-judgmental space. She grasped the nuances of trauma and its impact on the brain; her deep understanding allowed me to tentatively peel away the layers of self-judgment.

Hailey challenged some of the dysfunctional beliefs and programming that I clung to, but just as importantly, she slowly and gently fostered in me my ability to see myself as a the powerful person I am. I came to rely heavily on my courage as I was stripped of my unhealthy defenses, only to expose and discover parts of myself that had remained lying in wait for their day to come.

## Delicate Balance

On more days than I can count my body often felt pressured and ready for any incoming dangers. This was what happened when I processed the events of my childhood, all systems ready. It was draining and maddening. Balancing the teeter-totter between releasing and healing without over-whelming all aspects of my being was a very fine art.

Some levels of my essence needed to release in order to heal, but I'd been programmed for so long with the operating system of height-ened awareness and panic that my body knew no different, believing I was still in a fight for my life. It had become my body's owner's manual, one that was terribly destructive to my overall health and wellbeing, but was a result of living the formative years of my life in dysfunction and chaos. That's what's important to understand here: these were the formative years of my life, the first twenty-two to be exact. People who experience a one-time traumatic event, rape being an example, react similarly to the violence. Imagine the horror of that one-time event, and the storm of emotions created, spanning over twenty years.

Complex Post Traumatic Stress Disorder (CPTSD) is the official term, but I call it hell. The name simply implies that the traumas were many and enduring. It was a personal tsunami on all levels of my being, and it has threatened to swallow me whole more times than I am able to recall. I had my "home" demolished in the storm and was forever in the process of creating a new and updated blueprint, having started all the way at the foundation.

When I was a little girl, there was no one to tell. No one. I had fallen into the bottomless well of loneliness. The days went on externally as if nothing ever happened, and so I held on with no sense of relief or release in those days gone by. The memories had the power to rip the breath from my chest, and with that, I was easily swept into the scenes of my abuse as my mind and body readily played out the full-length feature film, yet again. Nothing had been forgotten, and if I allowed it, the reel of my personal horror movie would loop repeatedly as my mind tirelessly sought to make sense of what had occurred. But time had taught me that the ending remained the same, and there were no answers to be found in the credits.

So when I felt my faculties spiraling out of control into the dark and dismal abyss of my past, I practiced simplicity. I came to rely on the basics of my body, my senses. I would instead ask my brain and body to bring attention to what it was I that heard, saw, and felt–a trick Hailey taught me. It took superhero strength to will my mind away from my theatre seat for one as I purposefully recounted the description of what stood before me in the present: "I see the blue sky. I see the red sign. I see the pink flowers. I hear the wind chimes. I hear the rustling of the leaves. I feel the wind on my skin. I feel my pants brush against my leg. I hear..." On and on I would go until eventually I sensed greater equilibrium and an easing of the tension.

The story is old and has finally been revealed. I've since chosen a script that invites safety and acceptance, and it is a choice I will have to make a million times over.

## Faulty Wiring

In the process of therapy I came to a realization: I never learned the feeling of safety or ultimate calm. No, I didn't skip that day in school. It was never on my lesson plan. You might as well have asked me to describe living life on Jupiter, that's how far out of my frame of reference it was. I've heard descriptions of what it might be or how it should feel, but I can't even imagine it. It was a foreign concept to my being, from before birth, I believe. As a fetus, I was energetically exposed to my family's rage and violence. I swam in the sea of stress hormones pulsing through my mother's body, her nervous system fully alert. My nervous system has its roots from a place of continual alarm, and the goings on in our household kept it engaged in that alarm mode.

In one particular instance, while receiving a technique called Colorpuncture Therapy, I unwittingly traveled back to an infant stage. As I lay in my crib, listening to my parents arguing, I felt my limbs fly outward in a startle response typical of young babies. I felt scared and desperately alone. This vision, real or not, allowed me a glimpse of the intense stress and strain I endured from my very beginnings. I began to understand my struggles in finding calmness within myself, and self-compassion awoke, painfully blinking its crusted eyes in the light that offered some healing.

I came to comprehend that, for me, the past would always attempt to highjack the present. I became more sensitive to my symptoms and patterns. Thus, I saw that as an adult, my fear continued to manifest in my body as a feeling of acute tension, my body straining to contain the many emotional detonations. My speech escaped me in rapid fire. My mind sped along its personal autobahn. I was ever alert, reading everyone and every situation with the finesse of the most well-trained Navy SEAL. I lived in no world of innocent illusion. I knew and believed everyone was capable of harming me or anyone else for that matter. I lived it; I saw it. I knew what people are capable of; we all have different limits, but a malevolent side lives within all of us.

Don't be mistaken: I don't live in a constant state of fear of others; I just accept that at any point, given the right circumstance, a situation can lead to violence. This may sound at odds to what I just shared, but I believe in our core all of us are loving spirits, that that is our true essence.

But it has been my experience that we don't always act from that place and can very easily be swayed if our own personal triggers are activated. World and community violence ceased to shock me. Instead events saddened, sometimes disheartened me, and sometimes triggered my own inner traumas. But surprise me? No.

I didn't fear foreign terrorists because I lived with one. I knew the enemy could live in my own home and yes, my own heart. He's my father; I longed to love him as a child. I do what I can to protect myself and accept that if someone truly intended to do me harm, no amount of planning or laws will provide protection. Oddly, there was some level of calm in that acceptance.

What I learned over the years I spent with Hailey was to have an internal measure of my anxiety. If it was extremely high, I did an "adult check" of the situation that was alerting my watchman. Often times, it was my child that was in a state of alarm. Someone or something had reminded me of "then." It was up to me as an adult to take a step back and reassure that child that my intention was to always to protect her. Protect her in a way that no one else ever did.

# A New Awakening

My path in healing was always intentional and focused, though not always in my control.

One particular morning I was awoken from a dream by the ringing telephone, the disturbing dream I had been having still alive and very real. In the nightmare, I was under water about to go exploring a rare, natural site, but first the tour guide asked me to adjust to the intense pressure of the depth and water. I decided to not go on the excursion, feeling in the dream that the pressure and work it took to breathe under-water was triggering my memories of struggling to breathe while I was being strangled.

After being startled into reality by the phone, I was left with a lingering sense of pressure in my chest. This was new to me. The physical memory of being strangled had always surrounded my neck and throat. This was a new sensation, one I'd never consciously recalled; the pressure mounting as my lungs fought to expand. The pressure building in intensity with each millisecond, along with my panic.

It was these dream remnants that lingered with me throughout the day, like emotional lint. I remained on the verge of tears all day long, sometimes allowing a few to overflow from the well of torment, as sadness took a wire brush to my heart. Its enormity was too vast to be contained in the boundaries of words.

I walked about nauseous and saturated by the waterfall of ache. But I trudged about my day: taking the dog to the vet, making minestrone soup, folding laundry, helping my son with homework. All the while, my mind yanked me back to remember and relive the pressure that denied me a breath, like some medieval torture device that was a corset on each lung. The frantic horror and heavy despair tossed me about from one energetic extreme to the other but both threatened to be my demise. It left me feeling isolated and alone; no one knew. No one could see my anguish, my inner despondency. This was what abuse looked like, a stay-at-home mom doing her chores.

For my part, I tried to coax my brain out of the pitch black tunnel of terror, begging for some relief. I tried to console that part of me that was grieving, assuring her it was only a memory, but a terrible one at that. I repeatedly forced my senses to focus on the present, and I strained to concentrate on the love in my life. But it was hard, so unbearably hard because the pain washed over me again, and again, and again – there was no pity to be taken upon me. "I can't breathe," my mind and body reminded me. It felt never-ending, an inescapable hell that left my insides raw from my emotional fleshing.

But everyday life would move on with or without me. I had to carry on.

## Support from Strangers

It was times like these that an unseen hand from the universe would lift me and carry me forward until I could once again find my footing. Quite often, my life preserver would come disguised as a song.

I wish I could reach out to each and every artist and musician who has held my hand on this voyage. Music buoyed me when the siren of despair called me into its murky waters. Verses spoke of my deep resentment and unending sorrow.

It was also through music that I was able to tap into a great and unhampered bliss that eluded me on a daily basis, its energy constrained by my struggles. Triumph's song "Hold On" expresses this magic of music divinely.

The words were written by another, but they conveyed my truths, and song gave expression to emotions that I wasn't permitted to express. Whatever words I needed to hear were on their way to me through the radio waves from people I'll never meet. Their songs allowed me to feel seen and heard; the universe was listening and offered me some solace in their work. I believe it may be the only gift of love that I was able to receive without the filter of fear and undeservedness.

"Sunshine (Go Away Today)" by Jonathan Edwards is the first song I can recall connecting with as a child on a very deep level. For me, his words expressed the emotional energy I lacked because all the energy I had was already being used to carry my heavy shroud of darkness. The thought of the sun shining only seemed to cast a glaring contrast to emotions I was denied.

This song also allowed me to vocalize my deep animosity and rebellion toward my father as Jonathan Edwards sung about the man in authority who wanted to control the lives of others, yet demonstrated no control over his own.

When I was in middle school I used my library time to listen to the Beatles' *Sgt. Pepper's Lonely Hearts Club Band* album each and every period we were there. I would feel exceedingly anxious waiting to get to the library, the fear that someone had checked out the album weighing heavily. I needed that album.

The album had become therapy for me, although I had no conscious awareness of it at that time. I'd put on those uncomfortable, oversized earphones, hide my face in my folded arms and escape from everyone. As I lay hidden from the world, I'd weep, most especially to the song "She's Leaving Home." I'd pick up the arm of the record player to reposition the needle so I could listen to that same song over and over again. The words plucked at my heartstrings and allowed my sorrow a temporary escape. Shortly before the period would end, I'd put on a more upbeat song so I could stop crying and be ready for the next class.

As I write this the irony strikes me: the parallel to the title of the song, its lyrics, and where I stand today in my life. It was a prediction of things to come, and its poignancy is not lost on me. I'd never connected those dots before. I left home, just like the girl in the song, and my parents couldn't understand why for they felt they sacrificed so much for me, and in return I abandoned them. I cried for the girl that I was, her parents, and the heartbreaking choice I was forced to make in order to find what my family could never give me.

Most especially today I feel Melissa Etheridge and Alanis Morissette express beautifully for me what it has been like to specifically walk this path of recovery from abuse with their songs: "Precious Pain" and "Silent Legacy" by Melissa and "Precious Illusions" and "Guardian" by Alanis. I carry these songs within my heart and call on them to feel inspired and understood, words of grace and comfort from a complete stranger who somehow knew the verses of my life.

# A Not-So-Great Discovery

While the universe was funneling its support from those various souls, I continued to valiantly attempt to receive and process with Hailey. As the anger found its release in our sessions, I was left examining what appeared to be an entirely new species. I spent many years of my life living in and processing what seemed to be my endless supply of fury, but when I finally got to the bottom of that well, a surprise awaited me. What lay beneath my spewing and venomous feelings was a pitiful discovery and I was left to feel annoyed at myself for what I perceived as a personal weakness.

Anxiety has oft times been described as butterflies in your stomach. Butterflies seemed too docile for my anxiety; mine felt like scampering, squealing, neurotic guinea pigs that were clawing in a desperate attempt to escape their confines.

Years ago if you had asked me if I was an anxious person I would have quite confidently have told you, "No." In fact I told Hailey just that and she very kindly attempted to hide her surprise that I was shocked to meet what I thought was a stranger. Clearly my anger had allowed me to feel bigger, stronger and definitely masked the incessant internal alarm system that seemed to run in the background of my days. It had become so normal to me that I hadn't realized its abnormality.

As the years gradually passed, I was able to bring conscious awareness to my anxiety—and I hated it. I abhorred, despised, detested, and loathed its presence, each and every one of those words and all of them combined. I could see why I had (unconsciously) chosen to detach from the ever-present unwelcome guest that resided in my lower abdomen. If I checked in with the feeling, I heard, "I'm scared" and "I've got to get it right" repeatedly. Incessantly. When I deepened my focus, I saw myself as a young girl, eyes wide and darting while I searched the pitch black for clues of what was to come, but the details of how, when, and where were lost in the dark and the anticipation mounted. I tried my hardest to see my way clear, but I was alone with nothing and no one to guide me; all I was left with was the knowledge that something horrific was about to happen. The guinea pigs sensed it too.

This feeling came upon me anywhere, as I stood in my kitchen putting trash in the trashcan or as I drove down the road. There was no rhyme or reason to its sudden presence, not always a specific trigger that activated it. It seemed my mere existence was cause enough for alarm, and it battled on, demanding my awareness to its omnipresence. It would not be forgotten and almost felt like a possession of some sort. I wished there was someone who could exorcise it from me.

I felt enraged at its assertion into my otherwise peaceful days. *Why must it linger?* I wondered. I never found the answer to that. Perhaps it was similar to an appendage left over from our cavemen ancestors, one that no longer served me today but was part of my makeup nonetheless. The history in this case was not someone else's spanning millions of years ago but was instead my own and rested right over my shoulder: tap, tap, tapping. I dared not look back, only straight ahead, because that's what I chose to give my attention to and was the only weapon I could wield against the disquiet that threatened to destroy the healing and tranquility I'd worked so hard to amass.

*I see you. I hear you. And there's no doubt I physically feel you, anxiety, but I will not feed you.*

It's precisely due to this heightened state of fearful anticipation that I was not a thrill seeker. Amusement parks with their wild and adrenal pumping rides were not for me. I lived that feeling of sitting at the top of the roller coaster for my entire childhood. I only seek calm and a sense of safety today. Some might call it boring, but for me safety remains as basic a need as food.

Likewise, I was unable to tolerate any type of playful or controlled physical combat, like martial arts or wrestling. My body endured too much of the real thing all those years ago. Internally, I didn't experience it as play, but instead was left to feel physically assaulted; my sense of aggression mounted, and I wanted to attack. My boys, who enjoyed the typical rough housing of most males, knew Dad was the one to go to get this need met. I truly could not bear the contact and simply had to describe it to my children as, "It doesn't feel good to me."

The best thing for me was to honor my need for safety and calm and not push myself to be part of something that society saw as a norm but I experienced as trauma. Today, I say no to anything that sends me into flight or fight mode. I've been there, done that. No more; please, and thank you.

## Mystery Solved

While I may not have held the exact combination to the lock that would release my guinea pigs, I did hold a key that would set some part of my mother free.

Back when I was eleven or so, my father shared a most honest part of himself and his pain with me. We were driving home, and somehow our conversation steered towards his mother. He began recanting some of the hurtful things he remembered from his childhood that he held her responsible for. The last thing he said before we pulled into our driveway was, "…and I decided then that I would never let any woman treat me the way she did."

I sat in silence as I absorbed what he had just revealed. I could feel and see the wounded teen that was speaking to me. Compassion filled me, and comprehension soon followed. Every abusive thing he had done was because of that one sentence. We were paying for her sins, and I knew he would never call it even.

It was about twenty years after that conversation that I found myself driving with my mother, and we were having a discussion about my father's abusiveness. As unlikely and bizarre as it seems, we were at the same spot on the road where my father had shared his story with me.

The coincidence was too large to ignore, and I decided I was meant to tell her about that day so many years ago. When I recounted his last sentence to her, she said, "Oh, so that's what that was about." A curious look crossed her face, as though this understanding had given her some relief and answers to long-held questions. It was painful for me to know that for all those years she had still been trying to figure out how it all had come to pass. Sorrow filled me as I soon realized that I shouldn't have been the one to tell her this; it could have and should have been a discussion for them as a married couple. But even sadder to me was the knowing that there was probably never a chance that she would have the courage to ask him her question, nor he the ability to answer. No doubt they were partners in all of this, committed to denial as strongly as they were to one another.

## Bits and Pieces

While I had completed a piece of my mother's personal puzzle, I discovered a method of completing my own jigsaw as well.

It is said that when we go through a trauma, such as abuse, that while we may feel irreparably broken, we are indeed whole. Was it wishful thinking? Wasn't I at the very least bent? I wrestled with this idea many times.

Initially, it felt as though through these words of supposed wisdom my wounds were being swept under the rug. Truly, I felt as though chunks of my being had been violently blasted to smithereens. *How was this to be denied?* I wondered. No, *demanded* is a more accurate statement.

When I allowed myself the visual of my maimed spirit and body, I was flooded with the sense that they, my parents, were still with me. I saw the holes that remained. Somehow the damage would forever link me to them, and with that came the feeling that they still had power over me, that they were inescapable. That was far from comforting.

I decided to construct my own version of these two truths: I am whole, but my parts are now rearranged due to all I've withstood. This brought me some level of comfort and power. They may have caused damage, but I still walk whole and completely functional, just in a new configuration.

Does it make sense? Probably not, but it was more rational than many things they did. It allowed me to feel as though I was not irreparably damaged goods and at the same time not deny that I'd seen my share of shit.

## Newsflash(backs)

My shit had a way of flying in my face at unforeseen times and places, and once again I was left to clean up a mess I never made.

What does a grown woman living in Pennsylvania have in common with victims of an elementary shooting in New England? Nothing it would seem, but my brain told me differently as I lay awake night after night. My mind revisited the pictures that played in the media: the suffering on the faces of the parents, one woman screaming out, and the look of her unbridled horror. All of it slammed into my being as if by physical force. I was reminded. Reminded of my countless screams that were never released and never witnessed by another, but instead became as frozen as those images on the TV screen. Memories of the distraught witness in me as I helplessly watched the abuse of my mother, dog, brother, and that of my own self. That woman was screaming my scream; she knew the sensation of being gutted alive. She understood what it felt like to have someone torture you and emotionally kill you, but never allow you the moment of exhaling the last breath that is death's physical release.

The children, as they waited in their classrooms. The merciless waiting that kept them and me tethered to the massive weight of our impotence. Waiting to be killed. Again, the panic and anticipation of what was to come. Nowhere to run, trapped. Emotional claustrophobia setting in. I knew that too. It was a horrific feeling waiting, waiting for your life to violently end, the apprehension a smothering blanket. Knowing you were at another's mercy, and knowing their intentions were nothing close to that. The power lay completely outside of oneself and rested instead in someone else's menacing hands.

It was events like this that triggered the haunted corners of my mind. I had a choice to make. Give in, give in to the memories and the obsession to replay it in an attempt to gain what is a false sense of control over the events, or feel it, acknowledge it's a trigger, but not my reality. While I held compassion and an understanding for what they may have endured, it was not my story, just a familiar reminder. I proceeded to coach my brain. Parented that little girl within me who remembered and was so sure it was happening *now*. *Again!* Reassured her it's not in the present but the past, comforted her all the while demonstrating to her that we do now have the power. The power was in our hands to shift our focus, use our brain to give attention to the safety in our life now, not the terror in our world then.

Just a "simple" example of how a victim of abuse might get tossed about like the wind if one was not aware and diligent in understanding the past and keys to healing.

## How Ironic

In a strange universal twist, my healing path crossed that of my father several years after we had last spoken, and I was the one intended to offer the gift to him.

My father's mom made her passing at a ripe old age in her early nineties. All of my life she lived with her younger sister, an arrangement that occurred after my grandfather passed while in his late fifties. It was a bit like having two grandmothers in one house, but my heart belonged to my great aunt, Helen, who remained unmarried and without a family of her own for her entire life.

For the last several years of their lives they had been living in a nursing home. While visiting them, I decided to ask them some more personal questions, something that we never did as a family. My first question: "Do you have any regrets?"

Aunt Helen became a bit misty eyed as she shared her answer, looking more than a bit shamefaced. My grandmother heard her sister's response, but made no acknowledgement of what had been said. "So what about you, Mom-mom?" I inquired.

She simply stared straight ahead, making no eye contact and said in a deadpan voice, "That I was mean sometimes." My great aunt sat slightly behind her, nodding her head in vehement agreement.

"To who, your kids?" I asked.

"Yeah," was her emotionally devoid response.

"Well, why don't you tell them, apologize?"

"Nah, they know," was her way of ending the conversation.

I can't say that I was shocked that she couldn't or wouldn't offer an apology as that did not seem to be a dominant trait in our family DNA. A couple of years went by, her sister passing before she did, and then her time came to exit this life. Because I had limited contact with my family at the time, only connecting with my mother and sister, and virtually none at all with my other relatives, I sat by myself at her services.

It was uncomfortable and awkward, but I knew and accepted that the day would progress that way and would only be a reflection of the choices I had made. At one point the gentleman conducting the service asked if anyone had anything they wanted to share about my grandmother. The conversation I had had with her regarding her regrets came slamming into my awareness. I sat there shaky and sweating as I debated in those few seconds whether I should go to the front of the room and relay what we had discussed. I felt as though I was being pulled to a stand, although my mind was screaming its protests and straining to keep me firmly planted in my seat.

*Oh fuck,* was my last thought as I made my way up the aisle to stand behind the podium. My father and his siblings sat in the front row; he had his forehead down and resting in his right hand, which I could only presume was to avoid looking at me. I had not a clue as to how anything I said would be received. I stood before everyone and explained that I had no prior plan to speak but instead felt compelled to share with them what I had learned a couple of years ago. I replayed the conversation, stumbling over my words, and finished by saying, "You would know better than me what kind of mother she was, but I thought it was important to tell you what she couldn't say–she was sorry." The room remained silent and I walked quietly back to my seat, where I attempted to regain my composure and a normal heart rate.

How was it received? In the same fashion I watched all matters be dealt with before, avoidance. Everyone just pretended I had said absolutely nothing. There was no outcry that I was inappropriate nor acknowledgement that I had offered any sort of appreciated gift. For all intents and purposes, it appeared to be a non-issue. I believed otherwise, at least for one person in the audience, my father.

As my emotions began to settle, I found it absolutely ironic that I would be the one chosen to present a potential moment of healing for him. Me, the one person he confided in when he shared his somewhat unconscious motivation to totally dominate and control any woman in his life. Me, the one person who railed against his every effort to do just that. Me, the one person that dared to say, "No more, because you've already hurt me way beyond measure." Me, the one person who craved his apology as though my life depended on it, handed one to him from the person he felt had caused him so much harm. Me, the one person who wanted more than anything to close my heart to him, stood vulnerable and open-hearted as I spoke my grandmother's words so that his heart might know a peace he would never offer me in return.

It had to be me, and I was so very grateful and honored that I was capable of rising to the occasion for my grandmother, my father and my true self.

## Reliving and Releasing

The longer and deeper I connected to the healing process and who I knew myself to be, the more internal garbage would bob to the surface and demand its time in my mental spotlight.

Yet again, I would wake to feelings tied to a traumatic event, the heaviness and mourning tugging at me to sleep, so that I might shut out the world and the feeling. When I tapped into its source, I knew there was nothing in my present day to warrant that depth of sorrow. I realized the grief I felt surrounding Charlie was surfacing, a new level to be healed and released. I cried and shook.

Charlie consumed my thoughts. I longed to say to him, "I know you were hurting too, and that's why you did what you did. I forgive you. But please know... I feel so heartbroken." But he was gone, no longer a part of my life.

Allowing the release of the emotions left me feeling a bit lighter in the days that followed, but soon I would come to a new realization: I was angry at Charlie. He had betrayed my trust. Obviously, not with intention or consciously, but I had believed that he deeply loved me, and I felt a personal treason had been committed. I had been abruptly and shockingly abandoned. On some level laden with naiveté, I had believed he was on my team, because he too was a child, but soon enough I realized it was every man for himself, and I was low man on the totem pole.

The anger soon matured into my familiar friend, rage, which proceeded to play out in my dreams. Just like every other dream I've had, there was nothing sweet about it.

I woke from the nightmare with a vision of myself as a young girl kicking Charlie. I was kicking him with the intent to hurt him. To the outside world, I would most likely look like a little girl having a tantrum, but in truth I was in the throes of a deep wounding. I could still hear the words I screamed, *"You lied! I hate you! I'm never going to trust you again for the rest of my life!"* And I never did.

Quickly my mind conjured the image of my parents. Like attracts like, rage attracting rage. I felt the storm swell inside me like some emotional form of the black plague. I then saw in my mind's eye my unleashing of all the resentments of my childhood.

I saw myself stab them with the unexpressed hatred I felt growing up. The unvented frustration at having to follow their insane dogma and sense that they knew better. My anger that they repeatedly muted and its big brother, rage–a commodity only afforded to them. Always the victim to their garbage heap of emotions. It was forever about them demonstrating their dominance and control. *Take it, take it!* Swallow it down until it became embedded within the cells that I am, the air that I breathed and the story of my life.

I felt the uncontrollable need to let it out. Once again, I saw myself stabbing them. Stabbing them with the force of my own inner explosion. In the vision, I stabbed and stabbed with an unending and fiery vengeance. I quickly realized that my body needed actual physical movement to release the energy. Just punching a pillow with this force would be like squeaking out an "Ow" after someone cut off your limb.

I shared my thoughts with Craig, and he asked the question I'd been thinking, "Would it help you to physically stab them?" Not go to them and literally attack them, but get a pillow or something with their picture on that I could stab. I knew this would help relieve the pressure.

I also realized I needed a witness. I needed someone I loved to witness the magnitude of the madness that was lying within me. I was never permitted to show this side of me, and it felt as if he was willing to be there with me, to allow me to go there, then it was a way to be seen, heard and honored – my experience and its aftermath validated. I also needed to be loved despite it all. I needed him to say, "It's okay, let it out. I love you anyway."

I needed him to believe and trust the truth of who I am. I needed him to believe I was still loveable even with the demon that resided within. I needed him to believe I was not the monster, but my rage was simply a symptom of all I'd endured. If I could've seen and witnessed that externally from another, I felt it would be a huge step in releasing the deep festering wounds. I needed acceptance so that I could begin to better accept myself. It was another step to owning who I am, not what they created or programmed me to be.

I didn't fight it, because I knew it would then only grow bigger and deeper. I honored the wound that was never allowed acknowledgement all those years ago. I allowed it all the while knowing that it had no con nection with the now unless I gave it full access. It had run its course, and I had to move on.

It was a very fine balance, to allow the processing without allowing it to consume my present. My children were gifted at keeping me in the present. They did not have the full concept of my experiences. They were preoccupied with their own worlds and needs, with no realization that I had this inner expanse that often threatened to forcefully abduct me from the present as I toiled and strained to make a daily practice of healing. This was one of their many gifts to me; by focusing on them and being their mom, I could retrain my brain to live in the now. Through them I've been given a bliss*full* respite from my past. Their needs were their priority, which is as it should be.

# Beagle Hauntings

Despite my best intentions, there are some days that my children's needs must take a back seat to my own. During those times that the past comes calling I am not always capable of muting its impact on my family. Sometimes, the past wins.

My youngest son wanted a dog of his own. In exploring what breed he would like, he settled on a beagle. I felt a clutching in my heart as he said this because I knew I couldn't do this for him; it was too painful for me.

I wouldn't be able to live with a beagle because every time it howled with that distinct sound of a beagle, I would be instantly transported to my painful memories of Barney. I cried just imagining it; there was no way I could manage actually living with the constant reminder. I also knew this because my neighbors had two beagles, and my insides lurched any time I heard them baying. They're my legal beagle limit.

It was then that I felt even more somber because my young, innocent child was being impacted by my childhood wounds. It seemed as if my father's hands were reaching through time and grabbing him by the shoulder. It unnerved me.

I felt a failure of sorts, that I couldn't fulfill this need for my son. I didn't relay my trigger to him, but instead gently guided him to other breeds and the glories of mutts. I was then left feeling deceptive on some level, although I knew cognitively he was unscathed and that this was something simple but profound that I had to do to take care of myself.

Nevertheless, it was a dismal day when a little boy couldn't dream of the dog he wanted, when the actions of his grandfather cast a long shadow on his childhood because somewhere back in time he had so adeptly destroyed mine.

# Living Corpse

That destruction came with such ferocity, an unfathomable possibility in my young mind, that everything that was me and mine up to that instant was eradicated. There was no defense or weapons I possessed that could prevent the casualty that was to become me.

It's a common experience among sexual abuse victims that they feel as if they've been murdered. It truly feels that the perpetrator killed you. I've tried to put this feeling into words, but it seems to lack definition.

I only know that the violence committed upon me felt so sudden, shocking and vicious. It was beyond any level of comprehension and I was left not knowing. I no longer knew me or innocence. Part of me had still believed in the magic of our world and the wonders that awaited me, but I quickly plummeted from that cloud, slamming into a hard reality without a parachute. My understanding of life vaporized at the speed of my freefall. Where I landed was some alien and alienating place. I had been time warped into another me and another existence all in a matter of minutes, seconds really.

Who I was before no longer existed; she had become as substantial as the wisps of a ghost, and I never got the chance to say goodbye. A cruel trick had been played because surely a murder had been committed but still the body remained, the shell of who I once knew myself to be.

## Scarred

In my new and unwelcoming dimension of cruelty and chaos, no one noticed the scars that wrapped their way around and through me. It proved to be a land of illusion and emotional seclusion. Nobody saw the bruises left on the inside, but I assure you that the tenderness remained and kept me frozen in a time and place that had nothing to offer but a haunting remembrance.

Sexually. One cannot live through sexual abuse and not be affected sexually. My body had been through too much and remembered every bit. It didn't know the difference between an abusive or tender touch. All touch had the potential to feel intrusive and cause for alarm, or caution at the very least.

While writing this book I chose to keep most of the specifics of how I've been affected sexually from the abuse to myself, rather than share it with the world. This was a conscious decision on my part, and it felt as if I was protecting myself by making that choice. Putting out too many details of my sex life was reminiscent of the abuse itself; to me it would feel as if my body and its sexuality would be fodder for voyeurism once more if I shared too many details.

What I do feel comfortable saying is that physical touch for me has been a learning process. I had to, and continue to, learn how to accept loving touch. I must focus a laser beam of concentration on being present to the touch and literally remind myself what love is supposed to feel like, sometimes repeating the mantra in my mind, "This is love." I mentally encourage my body to let go and enjoy itself before some part of me shuts down and off instantly and automatically, without any thought on my part. I easily slip away, a disappearing act from my very self.

I unconsciously learned to dissociate, to remain fully present in my body, my mind's coping skill for the trauma and its way of having safe-guarded me. It was not a choice I made, but a response, learned so very young, and one I've not learned how to completely free myself from uti-lizing. Thus, the intense concentration on my part to override the system that was put in place.

I have to say it was one of the remaining aftereffects I still resented. I used to resent my body for it, but as therapy progressed, I began to just begrudge having to do this strange internal dance in order to connect in one of the most basic human ways.

I longed to truly let go and release my body from these shackles that kept me from ever crossing that threshold into unhindered physical bliss and safety. I crawled and scratched my way toward the brink, but was never allowed full entrance. It has proven to be my personal rendition of the pearly gates to which I am denied access. *What must it be like to have no limits in the pleasures of your body; to have no fears?* I marveled. But it seemed as though it was not to be part of my story. I found it to be the only envy that haunts me. The best I could make of the situation was to again utilize Craig as my role model–this time for enjoying this part of my, our, life. As bizarre as it sounds, I tried to ride on the wave of his pleasure, an act of emotional surfing. I allowed him to be my teacher. The good news is that he's a patient teacher.

Of course, there were certain movements or places on my body that trigger flashbacks. I had to strongly focus on not engaging the flashback(s) and subtly redirect the touch in a way that felt safe to me. In no way did I want pictures of my abuse flashing through my mind as I shared intimate moments with the man I love. If I was not fully aware, an abusive scene would begin playing out in my mind that had nothing to do with the present situation. In fact, it enraged me a bit when it happened, but I've learned not to engage that emotion either as then I'm simply giving the power to my abuser in my very own bedroom, a place supposedly of safety and comfort to me.

I tried to be understanding with myself and the process. I didn't create the situation. I was simply responding in a way that was in correlation to my childhood; no one could do any better or try any harder than me. I continued to learn and reclaim what was stolen from me so long ago, improving as times goes on, and seeking my right to live a loving and joyous physical life.

## Routinely Bad Procedures

The bedroom wasn't the only place my past has come to visit. As long as I remain tied to this body, I am vulnerable to any, and all, everyday events that had the potential to elicit a traumatic memory.

I can't remember ever viewing my body as my friend or a comfortable place to exist. I loathed the responsibility of taking care of it, my carcass of shame and pain. Having a physical expression left me feeling vulnerable, trapped, and exposed, always open for attack. My body wasn't strong enough to protect me and attracted the attentions I longed to escape. My body remembered when all I wanted to do was forget.

Something as common as a visit to the dentist filled me with dread and worry days before my scheduled appointment. The invasion of my mouth felt just like that, an invasion. The tool that they used to shoot air in the mouth has sent me into full panic mode as I reclined in the chair. Sometimes the air would hit this certain spot in the back of my throat, and I instantly remembered. That point in the back of my throat told my brain that "it" was happening again. I've had to will my body to stay planted on the chair, my hands clutched together. As they performed their job on my teeth, I got busy with my brain and told myself repeatedly that I was safe; I was at the dentist's office, and they were trying to help me.

At one appointment, I decided to not force myself to endure what was happening and instead alerted them of my need. I was able to gather the courage to wave my hand to get the dentist's attention. I calmly and briefly relayed that flashbacks of my abuse were being activated and asked if they could make every effort to try to aim that jet of air more precisely onto my tooth. The dentist heard my concern and responded with what he believed to be a witty comeback, saying, "But it's air. That's a good thing, right?"

I failed to see the humor and did not return his smile. "Fuck you," is what I really wanted to say.

Anesthesia dealt me a new challenge. Prior to a surgery several years back they put me into some type of suspended state. As I lay on the gurney, I lost all ability to breathe. The staff was telling me to take a breath, but my muscles wouldn't cooperate; they felt as yielding as stone. I knew the staff were watching my vitals skyrocket and did not understand my crisis. In vain I kept trying to will my chest to rise, but it was the panic that rose instead. Wide eyed, I mouthed to them, "Can't breathe," and they proceeded to put me under complete sedation instantly. Not being able to breathe isn't pleasant for anyone, let alone a strangling victim, and soon I became fearful of the next time anesthesia might be necessary for a medical procedure.

One of my next triggers did not involve anesthesia, but its impact was felt just as deeply. While at my cardiologist, the nurse practitioner checked my carotid pulse, not just on one side, but she used her hand to check both sides at the same time. Picture her holding my trachea with her fingers and applying pressure in order to palpate the pulse. Her position was exactly as if she was trying to strangle me. I was well aware on a conscious level what she was actually attempting, but my body registered a completely different event.

Trying to take care of my needs, I politely asked her to not check my pulse in that fashion, giving a brief explanation of its importance to me. Her face registered horror, as though I had accused her of a heinous act. Sputtering, she assured me she wasn't trying to strangle me. I had to reassure her I was well aware of her intent, but I was simply trying to take care of myself in this situation. The remainder of our time together I sat trembling, but it was I who had to don kid gloves to care for her and calm her fears, as she appeared awkward and rankled by our conversation. Interestingly, I never saw her again at any more of my appointments.

Persistent GI issues are common for abuse victims. I was scheduled for more testing, this time an endoscopy, by my GI doctor. I was nervous about the tube going in my mouth, but reassured myself I wouldn't be conscious for the procedure. Based on my prior experience with anesthesia, I requested they promptly knock me out, thinking I had all bases covered. They listened respectfully and then proceeded to take me to the procedure room.

Once there, a tall woman approached me from my left, and I felt the terror instantly, physically threatened by her looming over me as I lay vulnerable on the gurney. The next thing I saw was her hand approaching my mouth as she explained she was going to put a guard in my mouth so that I wouldn't bite the tubing they would be putting down my throat. Tears sprang from my eyes as I tried to cooperate with her putting in the mouth guard, but when they began to strap and tighten the mouth guard to the back of my head, the gauze pulling at the corners of my mouth, and someone's hand putting pressure on the back of my head as they held it in place... it was simply too much for me. I stopped myself from lashing out and hitting, but mumbled as best I could for them to take it out, which they did. I sobbed. They responded quickly and professionally, knocking me out instantly.

I woke with tears streaming down my face, something I had only read about in books. One of the staff was present as I came to and asked why

I was crying. I very briefly explained to her that I had a flashback from my abuse as they were prepping for my procedure. She coolly disregarded what I shared saying, "The anesthesia does that sometimes," as if what had occurred to me before the procedure was some type of delusional effect of the medicine. She simply turned and walked away, pulling the privacy curtain closed behind her as I was left to weep alone. Once more I remained in the throes of the aftershock, and I required several days to process the emotions and bring my mind back from the unanticipated trigger I was reliving, desperately attempting to relinquish its tenacious hold on me.

It was incidents like these that often left me mired in dread and worry. I never knew when an event may trigger a flashback, throwing me into a tailspin. In days gone by I would suffer in silence. I've tried to prepare myself and staff as best I can for any possible landmines, but as I've experienced several times, I can't always know what is to come. It was a frightening and a lonely place to be. I took care of myself to the best of my ability by asserting my perceived needs, but chaos could still ensue, and when it did I was left with the cumbersome task of wading through the swamplands one more time, all on my own. The trauma never felt less impactful nor the burden to transform it any lighter.

If there was an instance that staff did ask what was wrong and I gave an honest answer, I've gotten everything from fearful looks, to defensive comments and jokes trying to make light of the situation. People seemed unable to deal with the truth and quite frankly I was too busy trying to help myself. They were on their own.

My parents may profess not to remember anything, but my body sure did, and it took concerted and concentrated efforts to pull my brain and body away from the past trauma in order that I might appropriately react to a routine event. I know for certain that I'm not the only one this has happened to and believe it should be part of training for those in the health profession. They're dealing with entire entities and a lifetime of occurrences, not just the body part or procedure they've received training in. At the very least, they should understand that this can happen and can be a very real and terrifying event for the patient. A simple, "What do you need?" or "How can I help?" would go a long way for the client. They're not there to do therapy, but they are there to assure that the time with them goes as smoothly as possible.

## Déjà vu

Once more GI testing was ordered, another tube to snake its way into my stomach. This time I felt prepared because I knew they'd have to use the mouth guard again, but I planned to explain my previous experience. I'd share with them that I understood the need for them to use the mouth piece, but I would simply ask to be knocked out for the process. I had a plan to take care of myself and my needs.

Nevertheless, the day of the test I was nervous. I didn't want to have to share my childhood trauma with anyone. I didn't want to think about it or show anyone my wound; it was like ripping a bandage off, but the situation required a small degree of explanation on my part if they were to understand the significance to me.

I explained my concerns and needs with the first member of the anesthesia team. He was supportive and assured me they could work with me, that all would go smoothly. I felt slightly more relaxed.

The anesthesiologist approached me soon thereafter, and we reviewed the same information. While he seemed to understand I was afraid, he proceeded to explain the importance of the piece of equipment and the need for me to be as awake and as cooperative with them as possible. I assured him I truly understood the reasoning for the offending piece of plastic, but that I simply couldn't do it, I couldn't sit there fully alert and knowingly allow them to trigger sexual abuse flashbacks.

I. Could. Not.

I'm not one to give up, but I felt frantic and knew my extreme fearfulness would only escalate if they tried to make me proceed as usual. Last time I went through the preparation, the flashbacks left me ready to hit someone on the medical team. I had to stop myself from acting on the panic in that instance. I was overwhelmed just thinking about it; actually doing it was out of the question.

The anesthesiologist then reiterated the need to protect the camera, "That camera costs between $5,000 and $6,000. I can get in a lot of trouble if you don't have the mouth guard in place for the doctor."

"Fuck you and your fucking $5,000 camera!" I shouted in my head. It was insulting to me that the value of the camera was of more importance than my pain, or his getting into hot water. Was there always a price I must pay? It seemed that way. I could no longer stop the tears from coming.

I thought I looked the fool now. I was assertive and in control prior, but I soon became certain that I looked like a nut job, and they would see me as just that. I felt so alone sitting there and trying to deal with this that I almost asked them to get my husband from the waiting room so that I might have some help. Almost. I figured that would only add fuel to the "crazy lady" presentation.

It was then that the first member of the anesthesia team returned with a strong sedative in hand. He stopped the conversation between me and his team member and proceeded to inject my IV with a drug. "This is Versed. It will ease your anxiety," he assured me. "Feeling any calmer?" he asked.

"A little," I responded.

"Alright. I'll give you some more." What it did was erase everything from my conscious memory from that point until I awoke post procedure. Apparently the med created a type of amnesia, but I remained aware enough in the procedure room in order to cooperate with the mouth piece.

A part of me was grateful for the staff that pumped me full of the drug that enabled me to proceed without further known trauma. However, I felt as though some control was taken from me in that he didn't prepare me for the full effect of the med; I just went out cold, or so it seemed to me. That left me feeling some resentment because I didn't know what happened, or didn't know what was going to happen to me and my body after the injection. His misleading representation, that I would simply feel calmer, left a bitter taste in my mouth. I would have much preferred the whole truth on how the med would affect me. I was more than capable, intellectually and emotionally, of understanding that information. It felt unsafe to me and demeaning, as though I was a child incapable of understanding such complicated manners and they needed to control my outburst. Once again, someone commandeered my body, and I had no say. *What was the last thing I said or did*, I wondered. It seemed I was always left wondering.

I didn't know what else I could have done differently in that situation. I stated my needs very clearly and understood the medical staff's required equipment. I was simply asking to work with them in order to eliminate my suffering. For a moment, I fantasized a verbal slapping. Perhaps I should've said something along the lines of, "When you put that mouth piece in and tightly strap it to the back of my head, it feels like my tiny child mouth is being stretched open by a dick as a hand grabs the back of my head and forces my mouth to be fucked." Would my message have been clear then? Would they have understood my hesitation?

So, I had a tad bit of irritation as to how the whole thing went down, but I told my brain that we were not going to focus on what went wrong. Instead, I directed my thoughts to the kindnesses of the day. I remembered the male Registered Nurse that was funny and conversational. I sent gratitude to my GI doctor who came up to me as she saw me crying. After I explained my fears following the anesthesiologist's comments, she verbally and genuinely assured me by stating, "Of course, this is hard for you," and for a moment I felt heard. I focused on those acts of connection and caring, those that I received from certain others and those I gave myself. It was the continued compassion towards myself that would ultimately lead me to what had once been far off in the distance, forgiveness.

*"It takes courage to grow up and be who you really are."*
–E.E. CUMMINGS

# A Timeless Tale

Hans Christian Andersen came to lend me a helping hand as I sought to release and rebuild, or at least his story, *The Ugly Duckling*, had.

I kept having flashes of images from the version adapted and illustrated by Jerry Pinkney, one I had read to my boys in years past. I also kept hearing the title over and over again. What I remembered about the times I had read this story was my feelings of sympathy for the sad little duckling that struggled to fit in while enduring the others' cruelties and, of course, the jubilation at his victorious ending.

Next the phrase, "I'm a swan," kept replaying in my mind. At first I scoffed at idea that I was a swan, a seemingly vain proclamation, but it would not cease its incessant trumpeting into my awareness. Obviously, I was meant to listen, not just to the words, but the message itself.

Soon enough, I grasped that what I was being shown was the simple truth that I was the odd bird, the one that could never fit in and fully belong to my family of origin because I was a different breed. That's not to say I was better than they, just that I was not the same. I could never be a duck because I was a swan; there was no changing that core truth. All of my years of trying to fit in to their mold were in vain, and could have only ended in the defeat that had become so familiar to me. I got it. *There was never anything wrong with me!*

Desperate times call for desperate measures, and I openly embraced a children's story as my guide. Perhaps my process sounds quite elementary, but I tell you my shoulders dropped in relief yet another notch as I allowed the understanding to wipe away a bit more of the self-loathing grime that smothered and blanketed my soul.

Perhaps the story was also an omen of things to come, that I might just get my fairytale ending, but only after completing several more chapters of my own life.

## Warped Body Image

My emotional shedding and processing during my time spent with Hailey allowed me to further challenge my old notions surrounding my body, in the most microscopic manner, and to examine their source and truth. While paging once more through the old chapters, I was writing a new one.

In one of those chapters, I recalled how I would sit in our bathtub as I kid; creating and playing with Crazy Foam, I would talk to my left and right side of my body. My left side was the bad side. I believed it was always tripping and intentionally hurting my right side and used all the bruising on my right side as proof. While bathing, I would yell at my left side for being so mean and refuse to share the Crazy Foam with it, or even show care by washing that side of my body. My right side, was gently tended to and coddled. In fact, my yelling got so loud that eventually my mother heard me and questioned who I was talking to during my bath. Feeling embarrassed, I then remained silent, choosing instead to give my left side the silent treatment. In time, I lost compassion for and connection with all parts of my body and loathed everything about its existence.

As I shared earlier, as I grew into adulthood, attention from the opposite sex left me feeling quite uncomfortable because initially it hadn't occurred to me that they might be attracted to me. I assumed they stared in an attempt to figure out the foreign genetic puzzle that was me. Internally, I was mortified, feeling apologetic for my mere presence and for causing such an unpleasantness in our visual world. And if they did make advances toward me? Well, that was because they simply wanted someone, anyone really, to fuck–not love.

Until I was about twenty, I refused to wear makeup. I used to think to myself, *If they don't like the way, I look then they don't have to look at me.* I rebelled against the world, flaunting my ugliness in their face and I also wanted to please my father, who hated makeup.

Through a friend's encouragement, I eventually swayed to the other side of the pendulum and found I liked hiding behind makeup. With makeup, I felt more feminine, ever so slightly, but noticed the double takes didn't stop. It was then, with very gradual steps, that I started to entertain the idea that maybe others found me attractive and not hideous. This was a strange and new concept that I rolled about in my mind, fearful that I was fooling myself. I would stare at myself in the mirror trying to see myself as others might. Maybe I wasn't the Neanderthal-looking woman I perceived?

Then I felt scared. Hunted, just like I felt at home with my father and with my flute teacher. In every look I saw someone willing to harm me, the makeup spotlighting that I was just a piece of ass to be fucked. My father was right. They would seek me out and treat me like the piece of shit I was. I was wrong; the makeup wasn't allowing me to hide, but had instead exposed me. The lessons I learned not so long ago came calling to remind me of my intrinsic value, of which there was none.

Unbeknownst to me, I had some modicum of power when I saw myself in a masculine light. I could, at least partially, identify with those who held power. My father was my first and most influential role model of what a man was, and in our house he had the power. If for a moment you held any power within your grasp, he would rip it from you and beat you over the head with it, just so you didn't forget your place. And so, unconsciously I attempted to identify with the all-powerful male.

But once I had opened the door to my feminine side, I was petrified and resentful. There was nothing I enjoyed about being a woman; it only served to amplify feelings of weakness and helplessness, much like the vision I held of my mother when I was young. She demonstrated to me that women weren't to be trusted, and I adapted by keeping women at an arm's distance. This was a tough spot to be in, for as a developing woman this only added to my overwhelming sense of self-loathing. As a woman, I could be abused; it was a given. I understood that being used was my fate. I was wanted, but no one wanted me. And it was all my fault.

Shame filled me. In the deepest parts of me, places I could not name but only feel, I believed that there was something intrinsically wrong with me that caused others to behave, or want to behave, in this "animalistic" manner. I had no frame of reference for a healthy sexuality. I felt there was something about me that sent others to the dark side of their sexuality. Their reactions weren't all about how I dressed or the looks I gave. In fact, I couldn't and most times still can't, hold the gaze of a man I might catch looking my way. Shame blossomed when I caught their stare. I seemed to have been born tainted and somehow brought out the evil in others. I wanted to apologize for making them "feel that way."

When it came to the same sex, I felt shame too, for my belief that I was somehow making them feel less than by simply being me. If attention was turned to me instead of them, I would feel responsible for stealing the limelight, much the same way I felt like my mother's competition when it came to my father's affections. I felt her sense of lacking. Again, I took the blame for both of my parents' experiences.

Craziness, I know, but not unusual. This isn't about ego, thinking I was some supermodel, but instead an over inflated sense of responsibility for others' actions and feelings. No child can fully accept that there's something wrong with their parent when the parent behaves in some abusive fashion. After all, in a young child's mind, the parents are all-knowing, and we need to believe, in order to survive both physically and psychologically, that our parents' betrayals are ours. "If I wasn't like this, then they wouldn't be like that" is the mantra that molds our body image and misconstrued sense of self. I gradually learned a healthier perception of myself, my responsibility, and my sexuality now.

How? I stopped focusing on trying to look attractive, but instead attempted to express my truth through my physicality. Was how I dressed an expression of me and how I was feeling? That became my goal. If I happened to capture the eye of someone in passing, I made an effort to not look away, but instead smile, despite the gut reaction to glance downward. I told, and keep telling, myself that perhaps what they recognized in me isn't someone to be used, but instead a reflection of spirit to be admired and remembered.

## Breaking Up Is Hard to Do

While plodding along and taking one tentative step after another in my efforts to mend, I began to know a greater sense of worthiness. Despite my drive to propel myself forward, the one area I still clung to with unflinching desperation was a dream that my mother would know and acknowledge my worth as well. That she might finally own her behaviors and apologize for the suffering she caused.

The plea that echoed in my heart remained unchanged: *"Please, Mom, just tell me you're sorry. Tell me you didn't mean it, any of it. Tell me that I'm not a fool for having loved you so deeply because you are just as devoted to me. Please, Mom. Tell me."*

Part of my intentions for the first several years of this journey was to bring my family along with me. I felt desperate to not leave them behind in the emotional squalor. To me, the opportunity to heal and learn from all that had come to pass felt heaven-sent. I wanted them to see and know and understand that things could and should be different. I longed for us to be the openly loving family I dreamed of, and I hoped that we could be free of our demons together. But they refused to follow me, and I had to keep going. Turning back was not an option for me.

As I mentioned earlier, my father was the first person I cut out of my life. I simply faded away. Despite what I intellectually *knew*, I *felt* full of self-doubt at the time. It was the beginning of ostracizing myself and only fed into my sense of never quite fitting into the family unit. I wanted to belong. Who doesn't? For several years part of me held out hope that he might change. I was afraid to walk away and miss that opportunity, but of course this was just another childish fantasy come to light.

It would take me two more decades to discover the resolve to sever ties with my mother. Through all the years leading up to that point, I internally grappled with my choice to keep her in my life while not communicating with my father. She wasn't innocent in any of this, I knew, yet I didn't possess the emotional steel to say good-bye. Somewhere, somehow she was still attached to me, and I couldn't imagine living with the void if she was suddenly gone.

The thought of choosing to be an orphan felt like my worst childhood fear, that my mother was dead, had come to life. In truth, I had been orphaned from the get go, but to make that decision myself to intentionally turn my back on our history, a symbolic death, was a whole new beast. Instead, I did what I had always done as a child; I betrayed myself for any semblance of connection to her.

But there I was over twenty years later, *still* trying to get her to own up to her part in the chaos. Once more, she refused, and we battled. While verbally boxing, she snidely implied that I too abused my children, that I wasn't a perfect mother; simply a hypocrite. Her implication felt as though she had just dragged my children into the very hell I spent years escaping, the one place that I vowed to myself that my children would never know. She had metaphorically locked them into the madhouse I had spent years escaping.

A bomb exploded inside of me and then in my mind's eye, I saw myself slapping her across the face. I saw this, but of course did not act on it. (It was my husband who pointed out later that, unlike them, I didn't attack a more vulnerable person because at this point in her life she was a senior citizen, and I was the one with the physical advantage. It was interesting to me to realize that if I had acted on the urge to hurt her, my family would have demonized me, yet they continued to define their actions as harmless.) Raising children with respect and compassion was science fiction to her, a lie that she believed I lived.

She agreed that even today people are still hurting children, but to her warped logic, it became validation that it was all a normal part of life, not abuse. She couldn't see what all the hubbub was about. She jammed her pointer finger into her puffed-up chest in a proud defiance and proclaimed, "I was hit with a shovel, and I'm still standing!" Clearly she saw this as a victory, but from my vantage point I didn't see this, us, as a success story.

Whack! It was as if *she* had just hit *me* with a shovel, this one comprised of an energetic force and understanding that truly slammed into my level of comprehension. If she couldn't honor her own horrific experience, how would she ever validate mine? There was no way she would or could ever make that leap; the chasm was insurmountable. I saw with crystal clarity the futility of my actions, intentions, and words.

Along with compassion, her memory failed her. She said she had no recollection of my father and then later her strangling me. I then replayed each and every incident in detail for her. She shamefully cast her eyes downward, staring at the kitchen table where she sat. Soon enough she found her self-righteous indignation and declared, "I'm glad you remember such terrible things about your childhood!"

But this time I was ready. I refused to back down and allow her to sink into the black void of denial. I responded with a cutting, "It's hard to forget when someone tries to kill you."

She guffawed, "Like I would do that!"

In turn, I suggested that if she saw one man strangling another right outside her door, she would certainly come to the conclusion one was trying to kill the other. She remained silent, and I walked out her door, never to return. The end had come, and I instantly knew and accepted her for who she was and where she stood.

A myriad of emotions and thoughts raced through me for months to follow. It added insult to injury that my own mother couldn't remember some of the most horrific things that happened to me, acts she had perpetrated. It was as if it only confirmed what their actions showed all that time ago: they were more concerned with themselves than with me. I was of no importance.

It was heartbreaking to know my mother didn't know me at all, to think she saw me as a hypocrite who was simply repeating with my children all that I had been taught. If indeed this had been true, she was doing now what she had done then: she allowed it.

Most glaring in our last encounter was the fact that my vicious mother was just below the surface and ready for war if I dared to challenge her dysfunction. The sweet, chubby, thoughtful mother was present only if I played along with her self-delusions. Once again, the rule was that I had to sacrifice myself for her comfort. Not anymore, I was done playing this game. In a flash, I was no longer enmeshed in my longing for her as a mom; that tiniest of flames died.

I was done begging for recognition and ownership on her part. No longer would I seek an apology or remorse from her. I was done groveling and fighting back. I was simply done. "We" were no longer. She could go her way and I mine, as it was clear our paths together had now come to an end.

## Regret, Reflection, and Gratitude

It had most certainly come to quite the dramatic end because during that last encounter with my mother, tempers flared, and we both yelled with great hostility. My regret: my children were present.

When initially speaking with my mother, I guided the conversation outdoors and away from my boys. Soon my mother became concerned about her neighbor overhearing me, discounting the fact that she was in the midst of shouting as well, and proceeded to go inside. Foolishly, I followed her, despite the brief moment of hesitation that reminded me of my children's presence in the house. I was too triggered in that instant to listen to my rational mind and was instead hell bent on not letting her run away from me or what I had to say.

My boys have never seen me, my mother, or us as a unit behaving in the manner I've described. They remained inside with us two irate women for several minutes. Soon my oldest son wisely chose to take his brother and himself outside, and as far away from the bedlam as possible. They tiptoed out the door, their actions in stark contrast to the stormy discord of my mother and me.

My heart sank as I saw them pull the door closed. There was a clutching in my chest as I felt the impact of what I had just allowed my children to witness. My tirade had forced my oldest son into the caretaker role. I was awash with shame that I had forced him into a position that had once been my source of identity and purpose in that very house. That old energy must live in its walls because for a fleeting moment I could sense the rush as it enveloped me and left me doubting if time had passed at all.

Quickly, my focus returned to my mother as she accusingly stated to me, "Now look what you did; you just kicked them out of my house!"

My sorrow was instantaneously replaced with monumental disbelief at her assessment of the situation; once again she held no responsibility for the scenario. She accused me of words that never passed my lips, and it was I who was to blame for everything yet again. It was the same blatant denials and behaviors that made me feel like I was the crazy one when I was a child. This time, however, I was able to see her warped perceptions for what they were. For a brief second, I became fascinated with trying to understand that level of instant denial and projection. That I had lived that level of insanity with them for more than twenty years was mind-blowing to me now and, I realized, mind-numbing to me then.

Afterwards, on the way home, my oldest son refused to sit beside me in the previously-coveted passenger seat and instead sat in the back with his younger brother. Again, I felt utterly ashamed of myself as a mother. "You scared us," they shared. They weren't fearful I would harm them, but in the moments prior, who I had been was frightening and unknown to them. Naturally, I apologized and explained I was simply overwhelmed from anger that had been building within me for years.

I had scared my children, something I deeply regretted, but after further reflection I made the conscious choice to cease mentally berating myself. I knew and understood the intensity of that encounter and the years leading up to it. In no way was I saying that it was okay, but instead I was saying that I could follow the fuse that led to that unfortunate explosion.

Oddly enough, the fear my children felt gave me an appreciation for myself and the life I had created for them. Uncontrollable rage was a common theme in my childhood home, and vicious fighting was something I had witnessed many times over. I thought for years that that was how anger was expressed and had become blind to its power to frighten and paralyze others. I was so grateful it wasn't normal to them.

Through my children's eyes, I was able to more fully grasp the intense fear that had become a norm for myself as a child. What they had witnessed was mild compared to what I had endured for years. If they could be fearful of my one-time tirade, I could then catch a compassionate glimpse of the fact that I had been scared beyond description as a little girl.

A greater sense of gratitude filled my awareness as I analyzed the situation even further. While I made a grave error in judgment that day, I needed to put it into perspective. It was a day in their life, maybe fifteen minutes maximum, and I took responsibility for my behavior. I was grateful that this was an anomaly in their world–I had worked so very hard to see to that–and although my behavior had alarmed them, they still felt safe enough to share that with me. In the strangest of ways, it was symbolic of how very far I had come.

## A Hallmark Moment

I received a card from my mother a few weeks after our altercation. It simply said, "Thinking of you."

*Thinking* **what**? I sarcastically wondered. I found her message lacking considering the intensity of our last visit together.

I had a few more things to say myself, quite a few, and put pen to paper to express what had been on my mind. Below is the letter I mailed her and my last attempt at communication with her:

Mom—

Got your card, don't know what "thinking of you" is supposed to convey, but I'm writing as a follow up to our last conversation. I don't know why. Everything I say or want to say falls on deaf ears; guess I'm just doing it to stand up for myself and make my intentions clear. It fell on deaf ears when I was a child, and it's clear nothing has changed.

My whole point of the talk I tried to have with you was to get an apology and to try to get you to understand the gravity of your actions on my entire life. I could write pages and pages of how I've been affected by your parenting choices. It's taken me my entire adult life to work at and attempt to overcome the pain, trauma, and deep sadness that come with my childhood memories. You see my life now, which is blessed, and see no side effects of my younger years. Let me assure you that the life I have now is through much blood, sweat, and tears on my part and the love and support of Craig. The belief system I had to construct about myself and the world at large were all seen through the eyes of a terrified and enraged little girl. I have to parent myself all over again, reconstructing healthy beliefs so I can enjoy the love and joy that now fills my life. That defiant little girl is the one who carries me through the healing process— she was problematic for you but even then I knew what you guys pretended to know— "having been to the mountain...," was out and out bull. I will never back down. You did what you did, it's as simple as that.

But how can I expect you to understand the depths of my agony when you don't even understand your own? As I said, I'm not trying to prove that you and dad are hellacious people. I understand your choices and actions were brought about by your own pain and trauma but again—that doesn't mean you're not responsible for your actions as the parent or the adult at that time. You want me to give you compassionate understanding but showed me none as a little girl, and continue to give me no compassion for my pain today.

You aren't interested in my welfare, only in defending your actions. "That's what people did then (parented)..." you say. I don't care if the president of the United States went on TV and told everyone to do it; it's still wrong and when we harm or hurt another the mature, responsible, and loving thing to do is say, "You're right. I'm sorry I hurt you." You know now and you knew then that it was wrong–if not you wouldn't have any issue with the neighbor hearing what I was saying that day. (And by the way you started the yelling and were yelling too.). Hell, you wouldn't care if I shared everything with family and your friends if you were so "okay" with it all. But you're not okay with it because IT IS WRONG. It was wrong when you did it and it's still wrong when people do it today.

You then want to believe that you somehow gave us something better than your childhood–maybe you did. I didn't live your childhood but even your "better" was horrific. I think it's sad that you were hit with a shovel, but you're "still standing there," as you say, as a woman who has abused and been part of abusing her child. Whether it was your parents or you and Dad, abuse is abuse–simple.

And while we're on that part of the conversation, let me make it clear to you that I have NEVER slapped, hit, punched, strangled, pinched, spanked, pulled hair, cleaned their mouths out with soap, hit them with a hairbrush or flyswatter, or in any way physically abused my children–and don't you EVER imply again through snide comments like, "So you say ..." or "Yeah right..." or a rolling of your eyes, that I am a hypocrite and have done those things. It is possible to parent without hitting or abusing your child, and I choose to have my children respect me, not fear me, Craig, or for their lives. I made different choices than my parents; it was an option you had available to you too. And any mistakes I've made as a parent, I've been sure to follow up with an apology because children deserve respect, kindness, and compassion. Children aren't to be controlled and manipulated by parents or adults.

I've only touched on the physical abuse, but let me assure you that all the sexually inappropriate things that went on created their own scars as well. You apparently didn't know it, but it's not appropriate to make your teenage daughter model her new bra for your husband, not to mention the fact that a father shouldn't be kissing his daughter on the neck, he shouldn't rest his hand on her breast when he hugs her, he shouldn't stand in the bathroom "to talk" while his teenage daughter is bathing, he shouldn't stare at his daughter while she's bent over the tub washing her hair, and making comments on your daughter's body and growing breasts also falls under the category of sick and abusive. We weren't being "sensitive"; we were being traumatized. I'll leave out the other details of the other sexually inappropriate things that went on in that house.

And the emotional abuse just goes hand in hand with all the other crap you guys dished out. It was constant.

Of course I said it before, but you chose not to hear it; there were moments of laughter and joy. But those times were so overshadowed by the trauma and fear and don't "make it all even" on the playing field. You want me to focus only on the good, taking ownership for that, but won't own up to the flip side.

Terry was sharing details of her first marriage with me and the poor choices she made as a mother, allowing her children to be abused by their dad, etc. She feels horrible and knows her choices have had dire consequences on her daughters' lives and choices, but you know what she did? She apologized. She told them she knows she failed them, she's sorry and they deserved better than that. She didn't make excuses, she realized she fell short on her role as a mother and owned up to it. I have respect for that. I don't respect people who push the blame onto others and won't accept responsibility for their actions.

That's all that was needed was an apology, taking ownership. To know you cared that you hurt me beyond measure and that I deserved better than that–that my feelings were more important than your selfish need to defend yourself. You were a victim of your childhood, but you aren't a victim of the choices you made as an adult...

... my goal, (is) to forgive. Part of my journey to forgiveness is to try to be honest with my abusers so that they might know the consequences of their actions. Simply pretending it didn't happen, one of our family mottos, doesn't create healing, it only adds to the pain. So, I tried to be honest with you, not letting you know every detail of how I've been traumatized but letting you know damage was done. But you didn't like that. An apology would have taken me so far into the process of forgiving, and maybe lifted some of the burden for you too.

Hell, you even accuse me of hurting you and (claim you) lost out on so much because of me. You are hurting not because of me. I'm simply telling you facts, what you know in your heart of hearts you've done. You're "losing out" because of the choices YOU made all those years ago. I'm an adult now, and now I don't have to endure your behaviors, games, and nonsense. I'm not going to "pretend" anymore. I'm breaking the family rules, that's why you feel betrayed. But those rules were all based on deception and control. You always wanted to control us, can't control me anymore.

So I made one last attempt in September, longing for the words, "I'm sorry." Not in a snide and condescending way ("I'm sorry you had such a bad childhood..."), but in a loving and nurturing way. As I said that day, this isn't about the now and how you behave now, it's about the then. The nice now can't make up for the mean then, especially when you can't own up to it. And your behaviors in September show me you still have plenty of the mean right (below) the surface.

*So, as I come to the end of the letter I guess I had nothing to lose by saying this all with honesty. If I didn't say these words, I would be betraying myself, and I've endured too much betrayal for this lifetime. You believe what you want and need to believe, and I'll expect nothing more from you. You are who and what you are; I won't ask you to step out of that mold. And right now I don't have room for people in my life that continue to disrespect and hurt me. Just know it makes me so sad to say because I wanted so badly for it to be different.*
*Kellie*

I never received any type of response to my letter. I've no idea if she read it or tossed it in the trash, but it made no difference to me. Staying in that old role felt far worse than the notion of standing on my own.

Almost instantaneously I was repulsed by the idea of calling her "Mom." She wasn't my mom, nor was he my dad. They are my parents, they brought me into this world, but they haven't earned the honor of those endearing titles. "Mom" and "Dad" denote a sense of great love and benevolence in my mind, and they don't fit the bill for me. A mom and dad don't behave in the fashion that they have and then point their finger at their victim as the source of the family's demise.

As they see things, it was my fault we weren't a family unit. I was the only one who rebelled against those unspoken rules and delusions, the only one who had disengaged from the family. It's four to one, which left me the odd man out and, in their minds, the troubled individual. They all still remain in close and constant contact with one another. My sister is the only one who remained in my life.

At times, it has been lonely not having a family. No one likes to be left standing on the outside. There are instances that I question if I made the right decisions to cut them out of my life; those are the times I remember their moments of kindness and humor. *Should I be more understanding?* I wonder. Briefly, I get hooked back in. They aren't all bad, no one is, but the price to pay for those glimpses of family was just too steep and left me emotionally maimed. They didn't want me on my terms and I didn't want them on theirs; it was time to part ways. It was the only way.

It was difficult to explain to my children the choice I made to not engage with my family. How could I ever convey to them the years of the suffering I endured and how desperately I wanted to fix us as a unit? I didn't want to walk away, but there are limits to how much one sacrifices themselves for another, especially when the other isn't willing to work with you. They saw nothing to fix, and I simply couldn't fix it alone.

My children have wondered about the family they don't see, those who are connected to them in some fashion but people they have never come to know. They had a relationship with my mother for some time, and the grandmother they knew was not the mother of my youth. I'm sure it's difficult for them to reconcile the disparity between their experiences of her and my experiences of her. I've told them what I deemed appropriate and true, and made a conscious effort to not malign the character of my family members while still remaining true to myself. It was a very fine line. They didn't grasp the entirety of it all, and how could they? That level of brutality was like science fiction to them. They had no concept of the trauma of child abuse and its aftereffects; my husband and I made sure of that.

I've often feared that they saw me as a cold-hearted person, because of my decision to not see my family members. Did they imagine I could walk away from them, my children, just as easily? If so, I would say to them, "No, never." But I couldn't spend my energy justifying my every action to them. My hope is that when they're adults they may catch a glimpse of all I dealt with and see I acted courageously for myself and them so that they would never know the same story. Only time will tell how they view me, but ultimately I knew I'd made the best and most healthy choice I could and didn't turn to go until all hope was gone.

## Misplaced Loyalties

My relationship with both my parents had officially come to a close, and next I would find myself under the scrutiny of others as pleasant conversations turned uncomfortable.

Curious minds would ask, "So what are you doing for the holidays?"

"Just hanging out at home with the four of us," would be my response.

I could see the other person struggling to compute what I'd just said, the cog wheels straining in an effort to assimilate what was out of their comprehension. "Oh, have your parents passed?" they would question, this the only reason that would seem fitting in their world.

"No. We're not in contact anymore," I shared with what I hoped was an air of casual acceptance. It was then that they understood that something was out of the ordinary and a simple nod of the head seemed to be the only appropriate reply.

If I could, what I would have wanted to say in conversations such as those is, "I don't know how to have a relationship with someone who can't take responsibility for the hurts they've inflicted." Yet there's this unspoken, and at times spoken, theme in our society that implies that because someone is family, we must endure any and all levels of misdeeds and behavior. You know the saying, "Family is all we got."

"But, they're your mom and dad," some people have said to me when they realize I'm not in contact with them.

Yes, they're my parents and they clearly didn't take that title as seriously as they should, not the other way around. I understand the sanctity of that title, but the respect and love that follows it must be earned; it's not some God-given right just because one brought someone into the world. Nor is it a title that gives anyone free reign to behave as unconsciously as they wish, and still covet the bond with their child. My parents failed to create that bond. Why, I marvel, am I now beholden to that broken link? I didn't create this mess; I'm simply cleaning up my corner of the world that was littered with its remains.

I do have compassion for them, even though they've shown none for me. Perhaps I inflate my importance to them, but I would imagine that having their child completely cut them out of their life is painful and embarrassing. If this is true, I take no pleasure in that. But this was no temper tantrum I had here, folks. This was a well-thought-out decision on my part and made only after I felt I had exhausted all my options for reconciliation.

They refused to take any part in making amends for their actions. That had to be the first step for me, or else it was all still a lie.

My loyalties lie with myself and the family I have since created with my husband. Why is it that we are taught we must sacrifice ourselves all in the name of "family"? Family isn't perfect, but neither is it demeaning, selfish, controlling, manipulative, and abusive. Family, as well as love, doesn't demand.

The truth is, even if my parents were Mary and Joseph, I have a right to not maintain a relationship with them. The titles "Mom" and "Dad" do not mean your children owe you. Our children owe us nothing, and anything we get from them is a gift bestowed upon us, and oft times in direct relation to the foundation we created with them. Bringing another soul into this world is an honor, and if you don't behave in accordance with that then you should be prepared to face the consequences of your choices. That, according to the Gospel of Kellie.

## Role Reversal

My goal and focus had always been to create for my children a world that was in direct opposition to what mine had been. To me, parenting was a sacred act. Along the way, it became clear to me that this wasn't a one-way street; they had something to offer in return.

My role as a parent implied that I was responsible for teaching my children the fundamentals of life, supporting and loving them in their blossoming and learning of themselves and our world. While I certainly hope I have been fulfilling those job requirements, I found this welcomed role provided an added bonus--I have birthed two of *my* greatest teachers. They demonstrated to me that there are other ways of reacting or responding to a situation. There were times they remained clear and focused, when my initial response was one of anxiety and a deep emotional upheaval.

I knew and understood that their responses were based on their life experiences, which are far from mine. I didn't judge myself for my response versus theirs, but instead observed and pondered the energy they possessed in those situations. Their reactions, which were in contrast to mine, allowed me to glimpse what a healthier response might look like, instead of those that had become part of my framework.

Through observing them I was able to gain some frame of reference for an experience I'd never had, nor been able to conceptualize. Silently, I followed their lead. I immersed myself and my mind in the energy they conveyed, allowing them to be my guide in what was a foreign land to me. Through their eyes, I could temporarily create a new vision of the world and myself, and as my blinders slowly fell away, I saw a magnificence that could only compare to the gift of life *they* had given *me*.

## Grieving a Mom But Not My Mother

Releasing the emotional ties that bound me to my mother left me both lighter with relief and heavier with mourning. But the universe was keeping a watchful eye on me, and with my clearing vision I was able to embrace that which it was offering me, not in the form of my children, but this time from someone I shall never meet.

Life was forever giving me opportunities for new lessons and discoveries. There was always a theme to the triggers, some insight I'd be taking to a new level or processing. I have often been bombarded with scenarios and situations that created a stirring within me. The brewing culminates in my emotional well flowing over, as I hear my inner self revealing the truths that lie beneath the storm. Always, the storm comes to a final culmination in some very poignant fashion. The theme of one of my micro-journeys was grieving the loss of a mom.

"I miss having a mom," was what I stated in a simple, childlike truth. And I cried. I longed for the idealized version of that one person in the world who would forever see me as her beloved. Her precious babe. That motherly energy that would hold me when I was wounded, encourage my power and inner beauty, and love me despite my failings. To know with certainty that she had my back, no matter what the rest of the world might say or throw my way. I don't know if that type of mom truly exists or if she's been created as some type of societal myth, but in my imagination I saw her as Maya Angelou.

It was no small coincidence that on one particular Mother's Day, a day I no longer recognized with my mother, I lay flat on my back. My body was struggling to recover from two concurrent ailments, and bed rest was prescribed. I was to allow others to tend to my needs, nurture me in my recovery–the way a mom might. The TV remote became a newly-formed appendage on my body as I perused the channels for a source of entertainment that didn't require too much of my very minimal energy. Initially, I settled on watching the TV shows of my youth–*The Mary Tyler Moore Show* and *M*A*S*H**. I felt myself pulled back in time, reliving the simplicity of those shows and feeling like a young child again. As I was steeping in the memories and emotions of my childhood, I flipped the channel during a commercial and there she sat deep in conversation with Oprah–Maya Angelou, my fantasy mom.

In years gone by, she struck me as the closest version of the mythical mother that I'd humanly observed. I hung on her every word, drinking in her energy and allowing it to comfort me. *I want a mom like that,* I thought to myself. Brilliant, kind, compassionate, sincere, strong, embracing, and honest without shaming. A women willing to own up to her weaknesses, as well as her power, and love you and yours as a whole package. That's the mom I longed to have in my life. The only thing I could do was shed more tears. I cried because I felt held and nurtured as I listened and observed the interview; and I cried because all I had was this TV projection for a mom.

Perhaps my mom recipe was too unrealistic and my mother could never have lived up to those types of expectations, but I wish she had tried harder. I believe that she wanted to love me, and in her own way she gave me nuggets of the nurturing I pined for, and for that I was grateful. I just wished the nuggets didn't come with such a high price tag. *Are the nuggets love,* I wondered, *or just nuggets?* It's my understanding that love doesn't come at a cost. In saying good bye to my mother, I also said good bye to the nuggets, the only version of a mother's love that I'd known.

There was no mining for the nuggets as the miners dig for gold, leaving the silt and unwanted detritus behind. If I wanted more nuggets, I was going to have to accept the hurt, betrayal, and abuse as the price I paid, there was no separating them. That was an expense I couldn't afford. The bittersweet truth was that I didn't have a mom.

One more time, I was left with the knowing deep within that I'd made the right choice for me; I wished it didn't hurt so much. Perhaps it was not my choice that stung, but the fact that I had to make one at all.

## Ouch

My drive to honor myself grew in direct proportion to my blossoming self-compassion, but not everyone, including those closest to me, would appreciate what I would come to know about my life and the positions I took. Those were the times I needed to flex the newly-developing muscle of that self-compassion because sometimes it was the only compassion available.

Another holiday was upon me that no longer entailed the tradition of extended family gatherings. I can't say that I specifically missed those get-togethers, just the palpable festiveness and potential that seemed to saturate the air as the planning took place. The anticipation felt magical, as if imaginary glitter swirled about our days in some wondrous celebratory dance, and that is what I longed for, not the people.

Somehow my mother was casually mentioned in a conversation I had with my son. In noting her absence in our lives, he stated, "Yeah, well you messed that up."

That was a shot to the heart. I felt a desperate need to defend myself in great detail, explain to him the error in his interpretation, but instead I simply stated, "She messed that up, not me."

"Well you're the one that ended it," he retorted with what he believed to be an expert opinion.

"Because it was the healthiest choice I could make," I calmly said as I turned and walked away.

I had to end that conversation then and there. He was quickly pulling me into the deep waters of defense, and my internal cavalry was armed and ready for battle. Part of me felt as though I needed to justify my decision by bearing my deepest pain to him. I longed for his compassion, and I wanted to know that he was on *my* side. Another layer of me wanted to blast him for his childish understanding of the choices I made and the past that haunted me because of her. Both paths were littered with landmines, and I needed to swallow my pain, and my pride, as I remained firm in my parenting role.

Instead, I internally coached myself. In truth I owed no one, not even my son, an explanation for my choice. It was not his job as my child to show me the comfort and understanding I longed to feel, it was my role as a mom to offer that to him. There was no way he could conceptualize what I had endured. That was always my intention as his mom, that he not know a similar life to mine, and clearly I had succeeded.

The Mamie of his childhood looked as threatening as the Pillsbury Dough Boy and bore gifts each time she saw him. This was all he knew of her, and any glimpse I might have offered of her that was in contradiction to that was deemed a hallucination. Over the years I shared bits and pieces from my childhood as questions were posed, but he had no understanding of the complexities that wove and intertwined themselves into the relationship I had with her, or the time and effort I spent attempting to release their vice grip from around my heart.

Even after I ceased connecting with her, I explained to my children that they could maintain contact with her if they chose. I never told them that they could not see her. I knew she was of no threat to them, and I understood that their relationship with her was not the same as mine. I assured them I wouldn't feel upset, and I meant that. The funny part is, for as much as my one son lay blame on me for her absence, he never voluntarily reached out to her. Each year, several times a year, I've asked if they wanted to see her or talk to with her. "Nah," is always the only response I've received. I could be wrong, but I saw that as a reflection of the connection she made, or didn't make, with them; that it was not due to my termination of our relationship.

I could hear my mother's whispers, see her snide look of satisfaction at my moment of discomfort as she said yet again, "You reap what you sow." I suppose this was true on some level; the decision I made to remove her from my life had placed me in a moment of judgment from my son. One of my greatest fears was staring me down. Yes, each and every decision we make has consequences, and in this situation I felt confident that the good outweighed the bad. My hope was that one day, my son might see it in the same light.

## Retreat! Retreat!

As I continued on my path, at some point when I wasn't looking, someone flung open the door to one of my closets, unleashing yet another ghost to shock and terrify me. Just when I thought I'd gotten it all down, this whole healing thing, something else came along to take me to a deeper level of understanding and release.

I attended a retreat that involved working with horses as a means of growth and personal insight. Unbeknownst to me, safety was to be the theme of the day for me. So much so, that I got slammed in the face with feeling completely and utterly unsafe.

The first task of the day was to write our names on the name tags we had been handed and slap them onto the front of our jackets. I proceeded to glance about, reading the labels we had all been handed at birth, but I never made my way to everyone because one woman's name in particular caused my eyes to fly open in alarm. I noticed with grave horror that she had the same name as my mother, with the same spelling as well. Tears immediately sprung from my eyes as I made futile attempts to brush away all evidence of them.

Panic ensued, and I longed to run and hide, somewhere far away from the grouping of those six letters that had come to menace me. It was as if my mother had been in wait to enter my most sacred space, jumped out from behind a bush, and stripped me naked emotionally. I felt exposed, and all efforts I had made to create a safe existence for myself that was free and clear of her had disappeared without a trace. Her perceived presence seemed to say, "You fool, you'll never get rid of me." In fact, I did feel very foolish for allowing my guard to come down. My rational mind was futilely trying to bring an abrupt halt to the wave of terror that was tossing me to and fro. No matter how I tried, I didn't see how I was going to be able to function with this woman and her name in my presence. I sat swamped in a tearful display of dread and worry.

I was obviously in a bad way. Thankfully, I was guided by the host to share my trigger. I felt foolish sharing with the group the cause of my emotional tailspin, but with compassion and understanding, one of the event coordinators had us all remove our name tags. I felt an instant sense of relief and calm flood over me as I watched my mother's name vanish into the trash, the tears disappearing along with it. The fact that my sense of safety could be so easily threatened by just my mother's name rocked my world.

## Retreat Act 2

Clearly, there was still part of me that believed my parents had the power to hurt me. I was unable to remain in my center or with an open heart in their energy or anything that might suggest them. I couldn't bear the thought of being vulnerable in front of this woman that bore my mother's name. I didn't want to expose myself in any way while in her presence. I was overwhelmed with the sense that she, my theoretical mother for the day, would harm me in some way and determined that never would I allow her to see my true self. It was like lying with my belly exposed after having been gutted by my abuser: open, defenseless and raw. My mind wouldn't allow me to go there.

I couldn't trust "her" (my real mother) with me; she had proven that. Then what the hell was she doing uninvited in my world now, the one that I'd created that excluded her presence? It was shocking to me, and I was ill prepared for "her" to be there, much the same way I was ill prepared for "her" treatment of me as a child and the entanglement that was our relationship. As a child, I had been trapped; there was nowhere to run, which was also how I felt at this retreat. There "she" stood, even after all these years of trying to liberate myself from the sticky mess.

At one point in the retreat, after some exercises with the horses, I felt overpoweringly indignant. I was incensed with the fact that my parents hadn't honored my divinity; there's no other way to put it. They treated me with less than I deserved. "Who the *fuck* did they think they were messing with?!" I wanted to shout to the universe with every ounce of righteous indignation I felt. Did they not see, didn't they *understand* my power and sanctity? They were not worthy of the likes of me.

I know, I know how that sounds, like I'm pretty full of myself. But if I'm to be true about the experience, then I must be honest with this larger than life feeling that I was, *am*, worthy of reverence–and damn them–they fell way short on reverie. I felt it pulsing within my body that I was deserving simply because *I am*.

Of course, part of me pondered the situation further and questioned the sense that they weren't worthy of me. Would the embodiment of Spirit truly feel that? *Probably not*, was my first thought. Perhaps it wasn't "they" who weren't worthy, but their actions and behaviors weren't, and aren't, worthy of me? Or maybe it's just the opposite, *because of their actions they are in more need of my divinity so that I might help them to remember theirs?* I struggled to put the pieces of the puzzle together; instead they remained strewn across the pallet of my life as I searched for how it all fit together in clarity and understanding.

I trusted in time that I would get there; there'd been no stopping me thus far.

# Retreat Act 3

A thought came to me later. Perhaps the point was for *me* to claim my divinity. During the moments of indignation I definitively knew my godliness. I can explain it no other way than to say that Spirit was not separate from me; I *was* Spirit and its infinite power.

If I was to claim my divinity, how could they possibly impact me in the way in which just my mother's name seemed capable of doing? Nothing could stand in the way of that essence. The quandary seemed to be how to stand in my power and be vulnerable at the same time. In my mind they seemed at odds.

I knew and understood that vulnerability, remaining true to my thoughts and feelings, took great courage and strength, and I felt I'd explored that avenue, but always with safe people and after the waters have been tested many times over. Wasn't that using discernment and caring for oneself?

I pondered how my power and vulnerability could exist at the same time. Was that even possible? Power felt expansive and invincible, while vulnerability conjured visions of a conscious and delicate emotional flaying. My mind was strongly encouraging me not to go there, but something told me I'd added one more piece to my jigsaw.

Because my mind could not grasp the existence of both, most especially in the face of my abusers, I once more placed my faith in the universe, that it would guide me in the next level of understanding and insightfulness. And so, I asked for the vision to see clearly my next step in whatever form that might take.

## Safety Test Driving

What I didn't see was the blind turn I was to take next. I maintained a death grip on the steering wheel as another basic event of life sent me into internal pandemonium, my emotional tires spinning as I scrambled to bring my spinout to a halt.

My oldest son was learning to drive and taking him out onto the road had ripped open a vast chasm of fear for me. I was petrified, convinced really, that I was doing to die. I didn't feel a shred of safety. Each time we prepared to go out, I felt the tension mounting in my body as my blood pressure soared and my heart beat a fast and furious pace. Once inside the vehicle, I desired nothing but escape, finding it difficult to focus on the instruction and not the many ways in which I was sure to perish.

This wasn't an extreme reaction to my son's driving ability, but a haunting of the shadows that continued to lurk from past. My mind saw nothing but danger as once more I lay in wait for death to find me. While sitting in silence and alone, I allowed a salty river of tears to stream down my face, releasing the long held panic of that little girl that was waiting for her life to end. I couldn't escape it; it permeated even the seemingly serene moments of my day. Body taut, anxiety skyrocketing into space.

I was scared, so very scared as a little girl. How else do I say it? The tears that flowed had been held and compartmentalized within all those years, from a time when it wasn't safe to express my emotion or even bring consciousness to those feelings that consumed me. Finally, the dam broke and the intense sobbing began as our dog, Jabbers, rushed over to comfort me. The release was draining and allowed yet another layer of compassion to birth inside me for the child I once was. It also allowed for a space of calm to return within me.

I believed this particular release of not feeling safe began with the work I had done with the horses a few weeks back. One of the major themes was not feeling safe, and at one point in the session I received guidance to let the tears flow. I thought I had cried my tears that day, but here they were again, flowing so that I might be freed from yet another level of my pain.

One of the last messages I got before I left the retreat was, "It has begun." And so it had.

## Equine Guide

It took me many months to come to clarity as to how my vulnerability and power could coexist, my mind finally able to release its stronghold long enough to allow the insight to sink into my awareness. These words, this book that you now read, are the culmination of those two qualities. I've already done what I had feared to even perceive.

The magnificent soul that had played a starring role in manifesting that moment of grace for me came disguised as a horse, and time was to prove the significance and glory of one more gift he was to share.

While spending the day with the horses, I felt guided to follow one that was wandering away from the group, not unlike myself on many instances throughout my life. His name was Foster. A former racehorse, his chestnut colored coat rippled with the musculature of his purebred status. The coat on his hind legs sported white "socks," and the marking between his eyes seemed as though someone had inadvertently dropped a splash of white paint. His manner was one of confidence, arrogance, and an initial mistrust in the retreat participants who surrounded him. I felt a certain bond with him, knowing that he endured years of physical abuse and neglect prior to his current home. He understood and knew PTSD.

His caretaker had explained how traumatized and untrusting he was upon his entrance to their program. Years later, and with much patience and understanding on the part of the staff, he had made notable progress, though some triggers continued to haunt him to some degree.

I followed him to a field where there were no other horses. I simply watched him from a short distance as he stood close to an overhang where hay was kept for feedings. As I tuned into him, giving him my focus, I became well aware of his wounds as I too began to feel them. I found myself becoming resentful at those who had hurt him, and I felt sorry for him. I wanted to fix him, and it was very clear in my mind that I wanted to be fixed as well, with no more triggers to yank me back to those moments of pain.

It was then that Foster bent his neck to begin rubbing his nose on the overhang, as though scratching an itch. He instantly jerked his head back and gave his entire body a shake. Something unseen had startled him. I intuitively heard him say, "I'll always have triggers, so will you. They will never completely go away. You just have to shake them off." His energy felt very accepting of this fact, not self-pitying in any sense, unlike my prior thoughts and feelings.

This scene played out in my mind many times over the months; each time I was able to tap into his acceptance and very *slowly* make it my own. He had become my guide and role model. Those triggers that were still present in my life were likely to remain for the rest of my life. Instead of lingering in resentment and frustration about their existence, I could simply stop and shake it off, as my dear friend demonstrated.

At the time of my interaction with Foster, which was long before Taylor Swift sang of such notions, I was unaware that animals do indeed shake as a means of stress release, a fact I learned some months later. Of course I've seen them do it many times over, but never understood that it was directly related to stress relief and a resetting of the nervous system. I'd spent numerous years attempting to completely rid myself of the triggers that remain, and have often been left feeling defeated. Most of my healing had been intense and complicated, similar to my personality. Perhaps the gift that was being offered to me was to approach my healing, or lack of, with an air of acceptance and deal with it in a much simpler fashion than I had become accustomed. The pressure I placed upon myself was unnecessary, as well as unrealistic. What Foster suggested was an acknowledgement of the trigger and then just as quickly its release by shaking it off, no longer allowing myself to linger in all the thoughts and feelings associated with it.

He taught me that not all healing had to be, or should be, a gut-wrenching event that left me spent both emotionally and physically.

# Not Amused

The triggers I speak of were hiding around every turn, ready at a moment's notice to spring into action and catapult me not forward, but back in time. In all honesty, sometimes it was exasperating, and I wondered if anything could ever be simple again.

Have you ever noticed how many strangulation scenes there are scripted and aired on film? I have. The answer would be, well, *a lot.* I know this because each and every time one pops up on the screen, I have to turn away. Even the initial fictional glimpse of one character strangling another creates instant nausea and panic within me, not the captivating suspense the writers were hoping to create. I used to make myself endure the whole scene, telling myself it was all make-believe, but eventually I came to realize the trigger and the memories it held were exponentially more powerful than my logic. The most loving thing I can do for myself is to look away and hope the scenes that follow can distract me enough from my own internal full-length feature that has begun playing across the screen of my mind.

As silly as it might seem, I have also used what is playing out in a show or movie as a personal confirmation of sorts for that small part of me that struggled to fully accept the fact that my parents tried to kill me; that part that is looking for some exception in this equation. Certainly I've never witnessed strangling in a show or movie as a means of greeting another or expressing love. When one character strangles another, it is only with the intent to murder them or, at the very least, use it as a threat.

I remember the day I sat in therapy with Hailey and said to her in a voice of astonishment, "My parents tried to kill me." She gave me a simple, consoling, and affirming nod, as compassion filled her eyes. I sat in a sort of stunned silence as I took time to try to comprehend the implications of what I had just said.

Did I think my parents woke with a plan to kill me? No, certainly not. But their strangling me could seem to have only one intention. Why was it important for me to fully accept that yes, in those instances my parents tried to kill me? Simply put, it validated me and what I endured. There was no other interpretation of that action, then or now. It was not buying into the denial and delusion that my parents still hold today, and one I held for most of my life as my mind battled to conceptualize the unfathomable, bouncing between the opposing beliefs of, "Yes, they did" and "No, they couldn't have."

Being able to hold my parents, of all people, in the same space and definition as people who tried to kill me takes a vast degree of mental gymnastics as the psyche grapples with what seems to be at odds with the natural order of things. What this acceptance was allowed an opportunity for continued and more profound healing as empathy gradually unfolded, like the petals of a blossoming rose, for those parts of me. Ironically, by embracing the horrible truth I begin to free myself from its stronghold.

# Cowardly Lion

There were many lies and beliefs I had come to identify with throughout my developmental years. As I continued with my weekly therapy purges, I became more adept at knowing and seeing the deceptions and distortions for their truth.

While I knew, and through time clearly understood, that my father's actions were far from the normal or acceptable range, I continued to wrangle with who he was as a man. It took me most of my life to figure out that my father was a pussy. That's right; you heard me. I said it.

As a child, I always knew his physical attacks weren't "nice," to put it simply, but I never understood just how unfair they were. Again, my husband planted a seed in my brain, this time about the powerhouse a human male can be, and its germination took many years.

I would listen to him as he watched sports and assert, "Ooh, that one hurt!" or "Did you see the hit that guy took?!" I would question his exclamations, wondering how anything could hurt with all the protection athletes donned. And did it really hurt to have someone body check you? He would assure me that padding only provided so much protection, and yeah, it was painful when another guy rammed their body full force into your own or brought to the ground. How did he know what I could not seem to grasp?

Well, he was a guy. He played sports in the past and had played recreationally with his friends as well over the years. In listening to Craig and his friends, it seemed that they knew and appreciated the physical power they possessed as men.

And then I became a mother. There were times I playfully tickled my sons and had to dodge and manage their flailing limbs as they laughed hysterically. They were no competition for me and my strength, an adult versus a child. Huh, that made me wonder a bit more.

My husband stands slightly shorter than I and is at a comparable weight, but still I know he has the physical strength to overpower me if he chose, as I experienced during times we light-heartedly prodded one another.

"Are men really that much stronger than women?" I pondered in a therapy session. Indeed they are, Hailey confirmed, even quoting some statistic to drive home the point.

It was with the melding of all these scenarios that slowly I began to understand my father wasn't the mighty warrior my child had transformed him into. He was a coward. He far outweighed and outsized me and my family members as I was growing up; there was no competition and very little hope of doing any form of damage close to what his advantage allowed. His was a barbarous attack. Add his rage into the mix, and it was like a kitten trying to defend itself against a rabid lion. You get the picture, and I was starting to get it too.

But I had to bring my little girl, the youngest version of my inner self, into the knowing and show her all that I had learned. It took a lot of convincing and sharing as my child couldn't even imagine him as anything other than brave, for she had confused violence with bravery. It was so embedded in my psyche, presumably because it was created at such an early age, that it still takes extraordinary concerted focus and effort on my part to release the image of him as a fearless warrior. I can hear her whisper in my mind, "But Daddy is so strong and powerful." For my part, I must explain once again that there was nothing brave in any of his actions. She understands it best in the terms that he was a bully and that he wasn't "fair." He stole others' power, but in no way was he powerful in those moments. That's a mentally twisted concept for me. By nurturing this more factual image of him in her (my) mind, I took another step towards releasing a perceived power he still had over me. We were on to his game now, and at any point I, the adult, could call his bluff.

In fact, I did just that. I envisioned myself stepping in as an adult during violent scenes that flash from the past into my mind. I saw myself step into the image as the adult that I am now, and with all the force I could muster I yelled at him, "Knock it the fuck off, you big fucking pussy!" and then I shoved him off the person he was attacking.

In those scenes it's about me asserting my power and putting him in his proper place as a weak and troubled man. I have to say I've found pleasure in this exercise because I'm not cowered in fear, traumatized, or assaulting him for the sake of violence. Instead, I reclaimed my undeniable truth and knowing, and damn it felt good. This time, *I* was the force to be reckoned with.

## Fruitless Fantasies

Certainly all of the meandering conversations of my mind haven't ended in a place of personal empowerment. Sometimes I sought a fierce vengeance.

I had been reflecting how the traumas of my childhood have affected the simplest functions of my daily life. It was then I remembered how I used to fantasize that for every time my father's behaviors affected my day I would be able to harm him in some fashion also.

I daydreamed of a way to hurt him for each and every instance I struggled or had to manage my thoughts, behaviors, or actions because of him.

I wanted him to suffer both physically and mentally. More than anything, I wanted him to be fearful of when the next attack would occur—anyplace and anywhere. It brought me pleasure imagining his anguish. But I never thought of the perfect system of punishment; nothing ever seemed to fit the bill.

I guess it was because there was no way of hurting him that would truly take away any of my sorrow or pain. I would still be left with the truth that I needed to deal with this on my own, and he was free to live his life oblivious of my day-to-day hardships.

Nevertheless, when I recalled how I used to imagine forms of torment for him, I fell into that role again. I spent, or I should say wasted, five minutes attempting to formulate his punishment that had eluded me in the earlier years. Once more, I felt my sleeping giants, rage and resentment, stir until they embodied every inch of me. I felt my entire body clench as the animosity stampeded through my veins, growing in ferocity with each heartbeat. Still inside my brain was the file that contained all that history and my mind was willing to lead me down that all too familiar trail.

I marveled at the ease with which I could sink back into that hole, and then took a conscious leap out of that pit. It no longer felt comfortable for me to dwell in that place of contempt. I wasn't going to do this to myself, nor did my prescription for forgiveness allow for the mental masturbation.

The gift? It permitted me the opportunity to see yet again the great distance I'd traveled between then and now. My mental juggling act reconnected with the truth of who I knew myself to be and reminded me that this was to be a lifelong process, this healing. If I let my guard down for an instant, I could quickly be swept up by the tides of my past.

I've been there, done that. No need to return to the scene of that tragic accident.

## Treasure Hunting

It's all about the lessons, and they were never-ending as I processed and progressed with therapy. This particular go round of therapy was noticeably different in that having removed the top layer of rubble and raw emotions, I sensed and saw with greater wisdom and clarity the rich and fertile soil that held the untold wealth that would sustain my continual growth.

I believed, and in fact have always known, with all of my being that the childhood I had wasn't some nasty twist of fate, but that it had a purpose for my higher good. The trick was to wade through the muck and rubbish to discover the answer to the eternal question, "Why?" The only choice presented to me was to explore the hand dealt to me or sit paralyzed amongst its wreckage. Paralysis was my biggest fear; there was no way would I remain idle.

I'd even toyed with the idea that my parents perhaps sacrificed for me on some soul level this lifetime. Perhaps they agreed to be "the bad guys" so that I might learn forgiveness? I knew there was a bigger picture of which I'm unaware. There were valuable lessons to be learned amongst the hideous mayhem, and as I've combed through the remnants, I discover the gems.

The most precious gem I discovered is to trust myself. Always, always, always listen to my intuition and knowing. Others have had their own agendas when they've bullied me into denying my experience. My family's entire system was designed around denial, denial of self and events so that those in charge could continue their reign as dictators. While part of me had to swim in that vast sea of self-deception in order to survive, there was a stronger part within that held onto my truth and knew it was just a game. My truth knew and saw their actions for what they were, not what they silkscreened them to be. I had to bide my time until I could unearth the gem that remained a constant flicker deep inside.

The lessons didn't stop just at the discovery of the jewels. Life, and people, would give me opportunities to put it to use so that they might not be buried once more. A gem wasn't some museum artifact meant to be put on display; no, this was a working and breathing entity. It was meant to be pondered, polished, and chiseled to new depths of revelations. Just when I thought I'd grasped the lessons conveyed in its beauty and luster, another situation came along that allowed me to put it all into practice, but always with a before-undiscovered twist.

This could be frustrating and awe inspiring at the same time. "Not again," I muttered with discontent. "Can't I be done with this lesson?" I grumbled to no one but me.

Over time I learned that if approached with consciousness, the duration and magnitude of the teaching lessened each time, but clarity deepened. "Practice, practice, practice," the parental universe seemed to be saying. After all, practice is the only way we've accomplished anything in our lives.

But some days, I simply wanted the emotional stretching and fleshing out to be over. I craved simplicity. I fantasized about walking away from the past to start anew, but it circled back for another round, like a case of genital herpes. And yes, sometimes I relied on humor to carry me through and onward. I found laughing at the absurdity of it all to be a necessary part of all of this and saw it as a step toward increased mental health that I was able to take a step back and put it in its proper place. That was truly a tricky part of self-exploration–knowing how much time to devote to the past in order that it might have some level of healing and perceiving as opposed to rummaging and ruminating in the past, to my own detriment.

The past was comparable to an avalanche some days, and it could take me into the realms of the days gone by like some wild amusement park ride as the mind willing replayed the hurts and traumas. My mind wanted to make sense of it all. Surely if I watched the old film reels one more time, it would all become crystal clear to me. I'd be able to under-stand all the hows and whys. That was the addiction, trying to compre-hend the incomprehensible.

I found no perfect recipe that quantified the right amount of time to be spent in dealing with my wounds.

Gem: there is no right way, only a conscious way. Some days I would pull the emergency brake on the ride of my past and say, *Not today. Today, I will not try to understand anything else about the then. I surrender to not knowing. It's done and over.* Sometimes I couldn't bear to think about any of it for one more second.

Instead, I spent time perusing a news story or magazine article to remind myself that things are glorious. Rather than recite my own story, I would take the time to read about another's plight and know things could be worse, and that no one escapes some pain in life.

Gem: witnessing another's pain brought into sharp focus all the gifts that have been bestowed upon me in today's world. Gratitude was the name of this jewel, and it's one I took out and admired every day, but it too must be developed into a habit in order that it maintain its shimmer.

Some days were about taking that ride to the past, but nowadays it was a conscious choice versus previously being blindly strapped in for a helter-skelter voyage. Foremost in my mind was to keep an open eye for the lessons I was to learn on the trip I was about to embark. What was I now ready to see or uncover that had previously remained obscured to me?

Gem: taking the ride wasn't the goal; it was how that ride could lead me to healing or hell, my choice. Learn or simply run myself through the meat grinder one more time. I chose the gem of wisdom.

# Gifts

As my heart continued to mend, a burgeoning capacity for love toward my "girls" came with ease instead of determined focus. I soon realized I owed them the opportunity to be heard, and not just from a paid professional. One of the greatest gifts I gave to myself was the telling of the secret to another who was still in contact with my parents–a gift that sat unopened for almost forty years before I held it in my hands, blew off the dust, and unwrapped it with trembling fingers.

Andrea and Craig were the first to hear about my childhood, and as time went on I began to share my past with others in my life, mostly close friends. Apprehension filled me each time I dared to share with someone. Ever alert, I would home in on them with an eagle eye to assess any untoward body language or unspoken words, searching for their judgment. What would others think of me once they saw how tainted and disgusting I was?

Thankfully, everyone received my sharing with grace, but each time I was surprised that they didn't begin to treat me differently based on what I had divulged. I then did what I do best; I analyzed that observation. Ever so slowly, I understood and stopped identifying my worthiness in association with my parents' behaviors; it was their behaviors that required examination, not my worth. While that might sound obvious to you as you read that last sentence, to me it was a revelation.

The funny thing is that these initial people were my safest choices to share my story with, but I didn't see that at the time. Not one of them knew my parents. I kept everything tight-lipped around relatives or mutual acquaintances. Until one day, I could no longer.

I always had an inner knowing of the mutual acquaintance who would be the first to hear my story. Lynn, a friend of the family, has known me my whole life. I couldn't say why she was to be the one, just that it felt right that it would be she. Time after time I played out in my mind the details of my sharing. What would I say? How would she react? Would she believe me? Would she think this was an act of revenge? Would she think I was crazy? My trepidation was all-consuming.

I clutched "the secret" tight to my chest each time I happened to see her, year after year, waiting until I felt the time had come. The signal that I was ready to share hit me with an undeniable impact. I started to repeatedly hear in my own mind, *"I can't keep this [secret] for them anymore."* It was as if it appeared out of nowhere. I soon realized it felt physically and emotionally impossible for me to contain "the secret" anymore. I sat on the edge of my bed and wept with the exhaustion of carrying this burden for so long, feeling as though I had been hauling around the weight of the Earth each and every second of my existence.

For my entire life, I had protected them from themselves, never allowing others to see the side of them they dealt to me in spades. While growing up, my parent's shame felt like my own, and so I tried to protect them, and me, from exposure and further scrutiny. But I was done protecting them. This wasn't an act of defiance or revenge; I simply lacked the strength to hold on to it anymore; it was slipping rapidly from my grasp.

My conversation with Lynn became one of my most pivotal healing moments. There were no generalities in what I told her. Simply labeling my experience as having been sexually and physically abused didn't do justice to what I had withstood; it gave distance to something that was extremely personal in its assault. Instead, I gave details of all those moments that had been replaying in my brain all my life. I showed her the widescreen edition of me and what had transpired when I was a child.

My telling to someone who knew my family and me both then *and* now was a miracle cure for me. It was as if I had a chance to revisit the past, teleported to that time in space with them, and in the telling I no longer stood alone in that period. Someone was there as my witness. Despite my greatest concerns, that she would think I was insane or spiteful, she held a space of support and kindness.

Though she couldn't fix what had come and gone, she did allow me to be seen and heard in the most supportive fashion. Who could ask for more? She didn't call me crazed, but instead said, "You're a beautiful soul." Oh, what I wouldn't have given to hear those words as a child, and there I sat with just that opportunity. To say I allowed those words to fully sink in at the time would not be true, but instead I gradually allowed them to wind their way into my depths, nourishing me much like the water that weaves its way through the soil to bring life to the plant. Someone from "then" had seen and listened to me "now" and by doing so brought me life, a life free of the ever-present anger.

It was in that gift that I was able to release the tethers that kept me rooted in my animosity towards my parents. "The secret" was the last thing we shared as a family in present day. I would often sit in self-judgment wondering why, with all the work I had done with my issues, the anger always lingered. Overnight the anchor that kept me wallowing in the fury was released. My chest felt lighter, and breathing simply felt easier. There was finally a space between me, them, and the past.

What I learned was that in keeping "the secret," my inner being still felt connected and controlled by my parents and, thus, still enraged. I had spent my entire life trying to be free of their tyranny, and there I was forty-plus years later, still playing the game. Still playing by those rules of protecting them and sharing nothing, lest others see in me what my parents did, that I was the difficult one. Perhaps others would see me as vile for all that had been done to me and the blemishes it created. I was opening myself up to expose the core of my vulnerability, and it had become instinctual to me to not let that guard down. But that's what this healing journey had been about–authenticity–and if I was to be authentic, then I had scars that remained.

Fear kept me secretly bound to them all of my life. Some layer of me still feared their retribution if they found out I had told another about our lives together. My child's mind still gave them the power they ripped from me all those years ago. I saw a battle looming ahead because every time I stepped out of line they tried to pull me back into the web of deceptions. I had to remind myself that I was an adult now, and they no longer had a say as to what I do and share about my life. This was no longer going to be about them; it was time to take care of me. The secret and the shame didn't belong to me; I had to give it back to its rightful owners.

No longer was this going to be about them and their reaction; it was my time. My goal had never been to cause them embarrassment and pain. I came to a realization that I was not their protector, and truth be told, never should have been. It was a sick turn of events that left me in charge of their emotional wellbeing and happiness.

Numerous times my mother shared with me how deeply *I* had hurt *them* with my accusations and distancing from the family, her fantasies of being grandparents most especially squashed. They told me I was a challenge to parent. "We always had to treat you different," they would say. Their actions showed me I wasn't worthy of protecting. They force fed me a steady diet of shame. They tortured me on all levels of my being in many different ways and many different times. They confused and disoriented me, smiling one minute, sharing a kindness, and then snatching it from me in yet another act of cruelty. I owed them nothing, and if I ever had, I had paid it back to them one thousand times over.

I was more loyal to them than they ever were to me.

## Memorials, Farewells, and Arrival

Only after releasing that final thing that continued to keep me bound to them was I free from the unspoken pact which had been formed between us all those years ago. When looking back at all those events in my childhood, I began to see them as a memory, a distant and unpleasant occurrence. No longer did I have to cling to my anger in defiance or self-preservation.

I realized that my anger had become my own personal memorial for all the pain. Part of me clung to the fury as a means of honoring what had come to pass. It seemed to me that if I dared to relinquish my resentments, I was somehow saying what had happened didn't matter. No one was my witness or savior back then, and so I stood guard with a justified wrath at my own memorial for my slain little girl. It wasn't okay with me, and I wouldn't forget.

My role of standing guard at her tomb in outrage had vanished along with my sharing. She, I, finally had a witness, and I no longer had to soldier on in full warrior mode. Someone who knew her bore witness to her story and pain, and it mattered to them. They cared. She could rest in peace, and I was free to more fully embrace my life as I no longer was the watchman of my past.

There are parts of me I'll never regain; pieces of me died in those younger days, and I grieve for what can never be again. There were no words to describe my mourning; grief had battered me until I resembled a car that had seen its final days in the crusher at the scrap yard. The remnants of the grief I felt as a child came flooding out of every part of me, held in all these years by the dam constructed of rage. Tears were the only language I had to convey the loss as I peered ever deeper into the chasm.

Dramatic? Yes, it's been a dramatic life.

There was nothing left to say but goodbye. In my mind's eye I pressed my lips to her grave and kissed her farewell. Finally, I could sit in this vulnerability without self-judgment or analysis from my mind and simply say it was a sad, sad situation. Naturally, it left me wondering "What if..." but I wasted very little time on that fantasy as it distracted me from my present life and self. There is only "what was."

This wounded warrior was part of my identity, but by no means all. Now I will honor that little girl, and my losses, with gratitude and delight for the present day–so that her suffering wasn't in vain. That was the very least she deserved.

After all, this was the moment I'd worked so hard to get to, freedom. "I made it. I finally made it," kept replaying over and over in my mind as I sobbed with emotional exhaustion and relief.

I arrived.

# A New Dawning

My arrival at one of my destinations was only to lead me to the next. Up to this stage of my recovery, forgiveness had proven to be an elusive nemesis. I imagined it somewhere off in the distance, always bobbing and weaving in a wicked game of hide and seek. But it seemed that the spilling of our family secrets had cleared a path for me, and now I had it in my sights.

As the armor of contempt fell from me, the soft, gentle energy of compassion that I used to nurture myself began an expansion. Its graceful unfurling lead to me to open my heart even further until it wasn't just me that I could hold in this energy, but my parents as well.

No longer swaddled in the chains of my rage, I was then able to gaze upon them with an air of understanding. Simply stated, I felt an empathy for their pain because I too was well acquainted with its company. That they were the masterminds behind much of my misery wasn't lost on me, but I was willing to set them free as well, no longer bound by my expectations or the belief that they had left their debt to me unpaid. I let go of the hope that they, and our past, could or should have been different.

What I had given birth to was still so new and fragile that I dared not gaze upon it or cling to it too tightly for fear that it might dissolve. But it did light a new spark of hope and possibility: that I might be much closer to what had seemed an impossibility–holding the hand of forgiveness.

## Humanity

With the hopeful promise offered by the infant stages of forgiveness, I also found a shift taking place in my acceptance of my human state. My first step was to embrace the road I took to get where I stood, to honor the unpaved route strewn with the emotional ruts that threatened to halt my expedition out of the there and into the here. What that meant was that I was able to forgive myself as well, forgive every human thought, feeling, and action that joined me on my travels.

Of course, my parents were constantly by my side as I didn't walk away from twenty-plus years of varying abuses and begin writing in my gratitude journal, posting on my vision board, sitting peacefully in meditation, and instantly knowing and understanding the meaning of it all.

I didn't, and I'd spent many years berating myself for just that. Why couldn't I just fall into love and forgiveness? I used the knowledge that the past has no hold on today as a weapon to assault myself for not moving swiftly enough through that past and into understanding for myself and my parents. I shamed myself for allowing my childhood to affect me in the present, and I felt even deeper humiliation for the malicious feelings that resided within me.

I found that I first had to be honest with the hatred, distrust, murderous rage, agony, grief, sadness, and longing that blocked that understanding. It was a showdown with my demons as they dared me to face them head on. And I did.

As you've read, I spent many moments, even in my adulthood, envisioning violent actions towards my parents in rage-filled revenge. Am I proud of those thoughts? Indeed not, but denying them doesn't make them go away. I had to first own and give them expression if I was to make way for a more nurturing and loving existence. I had to clear those emotions and thoughts in an effort to make way for the new.

*Perhaps there's another way?* I pondered that, too. Perhaps I'd simply been following the wrong path, and if another was in my shoes, they would approach the situation with much more grace, empathy, and wisdom. Perhaps, but I've yet to meet that individual, and I can only know what has brought *me* from darkness and into light.

It's a fine line I walked, this healing. I had to honor the sludge I lugged around with me, but by no means was my intention to stay there. That's not to say there weren't any moments of lingering, but my intent was always toward healing and *not* remaining a victim. With that intention I could only, and eventually, move forward, however slow the pace might be. And it felt gruelingly slow.

There's a movement about that seems to suggest if we only envision our healing and bring conscious awareness to our thoughts, all will be well. I haven't found it to be that simplistic. That's not to say there isn't truth in these types of practices. I utilize various and many forms of these techniques daily, but there's also another side that needs to be explored and indeed requires recognition if these tools are to be of greatest benefit. I would suggest that we use these forms of intention and healing in *conjunction* with an emotional cleansing and recognition, all the while keeping our dial set to healing.

Take the time to meet your past, chat awhile, and explore the lessons and riches awaiting there. Then very politely say, "Thank you, but now I must be going," and leave with those riches clasped tightly in your hand so that the past may be of service to you, not a detriment.

## Spirituality

By now we know our earthly time is comprised of opposites, and it was time for me to no longer utilize spirituality as a means of escape from my human side. I was ready and willing to find the middle ground.

Exploring spirituality, not a religion, had been a significant tool that carried me through this sometimes treacherous terrain. Through the wise words of many spiritual gurus of the past and present I found myself and my core: my truth, not the drama.

It was in the teachings offered by others on this Earth that I felt at home, and a deep thirst was quenched. The revelations in their sharing rang true to my heart and allowed me to begin to see myself as I was born–divine. In truth, that divinity had gone nowhere, but I believed the actions of my parents defined my worthiness. It was through spiritual explorations that I remembered that all was not lost, nor was I. I was, am, powerless no more.

Without any doubt I knew, on some level, that I chose these life events with my parents. I've not a clear vision of the purpose of it for all who are involved, but I knew there was meaning to be had for everyone–whether their eyes were open to it or not. I trusted in the process and the Creator of All, of which I am part.

If it stood true that I sought to embrace and witness my own divinity, then I too must welcome my parents'. There was not an ounce of doubt in my mind that they too stemmed from the same source as me and are no less, despite their actions. Their actions didn't change their core value, just define their wounds–as was true for me.

It was in moments such as these that I felt no ill will towards them; instead, there was the continued bubbling of compassion. I sent them blessings and prayed that they find their truth and peace, however that might look for them. I gave up trying to define how I believed they should be, and accepted them for who they are and what they choose. Their expression of the divine was not the same as mine, nor could it ever possibly be.

For me there was no question that somewhere in time, perhaps in a distant place and time, we shall meet again. What roles we will play is unknown, but this part of our dance was complete. I sensed there are others to be resolved and played out somewhere in the far distance. The bonds we share are intense and deep; they simply could not be discarded, but it remained my hope that our next encounter will be filled with greater love and understanding for all. I know I'll be stronger and pray to be wiser. Perhaps they will too.

To them I say, "Namaste."

# Motherly Love

The middle ground between my human and spiritual essence could best be found in the world that surrounds us. It was in nature and connection to our Mother Earth that I stayed nurtured and nourished. Taking walks soothed and healed me. It was outside that I could drink in all the creations that presented themselves in this ever-changing and rich world that we call home.

My favorite thought to ponder was the fact that I am this minute creature walking on the top of a huge ball that floats in space, the size of which I can't even conceptualize. How spectacular and awe inspiring was that? It made me giggle just to marvel at all the forces in place that were involved in making that happen.

The birds and trees always left me with something to admire or see anew. I took in the vibrant color of the foliage, the shape of a tree trunk, the rustling of leaves, the pattern of a bird's feathers or the soft sound of their wings beating in the air as they took flight. That's part of what I love about nature; there is so much to see that each outing was an adventure in spying something that didn't capture my attention during my last jaunt.

The sky held wonder in the shape of its clouds and colors. When I gazed into the sky, I was immersed in the expansiveness of the universe and myself. There were no constraints or boundaries to contain me. I was limitless.

Nature doesn't struggle but flows and accepts itself and its circumstances; it was my reminder to do the same.

As the sun warmed my skin, I connected to my belief that I too am made of the same light and energy. Once again, I sensed my own power as it radiated outward in a blissful greeting to the world.

The Earth as a whole has been the mother that never abandoned me, but has instead cared for me every day, each moment, of my existence. This was to be my healing balm, nature and all its grandeur, of which I remain an integral part.

As I took in the miracles that surrounded me and that which is me and my life, I released my longing to return home and leave this world behind. I came to understand that this indeed was home, perhaps simply another room to explore in its vast expanse. No longer must I ride on the coattails of Craig to know and feel the wonders this human life had to offer. Instead, I donned my own with an enthusiastic anticipation.

## Strength in Numbers

After several years of sharing my ups and downs with Hailey, I knew once more that a good-bye was in order. Naturally, with it came some sadness as I left the safety of her kindness, understanding, and support. I could no longer tolerate listening to myself or my story. While that might sound a bit harsh, what it actually was, was healthy.

Throughout my time spent working with her, I felt a strong compulsion to push myself deeper into the memories, trying to uncover those pieces of events that remained cloaked in the darkness. I was compelled with the desire to know more and more of the details that were part of my life's trauma. The unknowing left me unsettled and internally restless.

I was always trying to part the curtains that hid what my brain once deemed too devastating to remain in the bright light of my consciousness, but only found myself franticly fumbling for the veiled opening. Initially, I was resentful that I was not permitted a pass to those realms of my personal being, but as my therapy with Hailey came to an end, I reached a level of resignation.

My brain had decided long ago what was too harsh a reality for me to face; it was the guardian that had allowed me to maintain my sanity. Each and every time I attempted to forcefully pull more from my obscured memories, I was traumatizing "my girls." I finally understood that what was required of me was a trust in those levels of me that had cordoned off the pieces that created a picture that was too frightening to face. I chose to stop torturing myself and accept that there were some things about those points in time that I may never know, and that it was for my greatest good. Instead, it was time once more for me to go out into the world, my tool bag in tow and stocked with various means of caring for myself.

It was through my time with Hailey that I began to more consciously nurture my relationship with all my inner kids, bringing their needs back into my line of sight. In tending to those distrusting, scarred, and petrified parts of myself I eventually saw, and later captured, periods of self-love. I knew I would come to rely heavily on that self-love because I understood full well that my journey was far from complete. There would always be more to process and release, but hopefully with less intensity and duration.

While I would no longer visit Hailey weekly, I did begin a practice of daily visits with "my girls," the five distinct parts of me that represent various ages and needs. Our relationship with one another had improved greatly since I was no longer in contact with my mother. The termination of that relationship allowed my connection with them to solidify further as I was no longer subjecting them to one of their abusers. Who could blame them? My past actions proved to them that I was not completely trustworthy while she remained in my life.

I made a point of envisioning them all so that they could feel seen and important. Our morning routine consisted of moments of affection in the form of a hug, kiss, or cuddling for the youngest that reside within me. My thirteen and eighteen-year old simply enjoyed being physically close to me and taking in the sense of family we all shared. I then visualized each one us being filled with the energy of health, and lastly our bodies were filled with the white light of safety. Although my sessions with Hailey ended years ago, this routine is something that I still commit to on a daily basis.

Creating a sense of safety for myself and them was a great challenge because I had no internal frame of reference for what that might feel like. For years and years I tried to envision feeling safe, but I always came up short. I eventually realized that I had created an externally safe world and home for myself today, and that letting that safety *into* my being was how I was going to be able to develop and foster feelings of safety.

So instead of turning inward to manifest safety, I scanned my environment for direction. What I first noticed was a chickadee perched on a tree outside of our living room window. Using my empathic abilities, I focused on feeling the bird's sense of safety. I realized it was not naïve to the harm that might come to it, but instead trusted its own self-preservation observations and skills to come into play if and when necessary. Until the time it was necessary, it relaxed into the beauty and safety of the outdoors. I focused on embodying the chickadees energy–for weeks.

In time, my attention was drawn to our dog, who graced my lap every morning as I sat relaxing and tending to my inner world. He was the epitome of safety and letting his guard down. He too trusted that when need be, he would be taken care of, and so I imagined his calm creating that reference for my inner world too–for months.

Finally, an energetic healer guided me to create a visual for that alarm in me. What I saw was something similar to a home security system that sat low in my abdomen. I then imagined that box disintegrating, and in its place I filled that space with a white, expansive light that has come to represent safety to me. It was this final vision of white light that I utilized each day with my internal family.

It was a long and convoluted road to get to that point, but I'd had years of internal landscape that continued to challenge me and force me in the direction of new techniques and skills.

## Serious as a Heart Attack

How far I had traveled on this lifelong trek was soon to be called into question as once more the telephone became the catalyst for my travel down another trail.

I received a phone call telling me my father had had a heart attack. A quite serious one at that; it had stopped his beating heart. The lack of oxygen caused him to seize and remain unresponsive for a period. He remained hospitalized in the ICU, on the mend from a stent placement. The first thought that struck me, *He came back for a reason.*

I remained collected as I asked my sister multiple questions about the situation and the impact it had on the rest of my family. I felt grateful that she took the time to share with me this information, as most times I am left out of the loop of family communications. She had been spot on when she said, "I thought you would want to know." I promised to send him healing thoughts, and I did.

After that phone call, I shared with Craig the events that transpired, and I remained eerily calm. I felt nothing about this cataclysmic occurrence for my father. I didn't want to rush to his side, and in fact, thought doing so just might give him another heart attack. There was no sense of rapturous vengeance or justice—that he got what he deserved. There was also no anguish. It was simply a fact that was shared with me. He had been out of my life for so long that the news was similar to hearing that an acquaintance of an acquaintance went knocking on death's door. I felt a general caring for his suffering, but not concern.

Over the years I'd imagined receiving this type of phone call, fantasizing about how I would react. Now I know, and it was much more anticlimactic than I'd anticipated. *Was that due to all the work I'd done to heal over the years or was it some form of shock?* I wondered.

I talked to my grandmother about my feelings, or lack of, and she suggested maybe I would want to send him a card. I quickly shot down the notion, bolting upright in our office chair, telling her I really had nothing to say.

I had nothing to say to my father, a statement that was weighted with deep sorrow. I talked more with Craig, and he mused, "What would you say? 'Good bye'?" That sentence, along with my grandmother's suggestion, and the knowing that he came back for a reason, replayed over and over in my awareness.

## Open Hearted

As I woke the following day, I noticed that initially I still felt at peace. As my mind slowly came to, I continued to hear the voices of my husband and my grandmother and the phrase, "He came back for a reason."

A vision then came to me: *I stood at a memorial service for my then-deceased father, and I became keenly aware that I had a regret. I dove deeper into the picture before me, attempting to gain greater clarity as I pondered the source of the regret. I realized my regret was that I had never said good-bye to him.*

At this realization, I began to bawl. As the tears streamed down my cheeks, I allowed myself to finally say good-bye to the fantasy of my father, the man he could never be, and felt a deep desire that he find peace. That I never brought direct closure to our relationship was the regret I pictured in the scene at his memorial. I had simply walked away. Our relationship was left lingering; there was no ending paragraph to our story.

I would never suggest that the reason he came back was for me. But perhaps, I contemplated, now that he was back, there was something I was meant to do. I knew immediately what step I was to take, exactly what my grandmother and husband innocently implanted in my psyche. I would send him a card, and in the message I was to say good-bye. There felt an urgency, and it seemed as though it fit into the perfect order of things down deep in my marrow. There was no question. The action felt as though it was to be the gentle closing of a door that had been left blowing in the wind.

I immediately sat at the computer and what follows are the words my heart spoke:

*Randall–*

*I got a call last night that you left and came back. It made me wonder why. I'm always looking for an understanding in life's events. This pondering made me realize I never said good-bye; our relationship was simply severed. I don't regret that severing, but I feel in my heart I do need to give you a proper good-bye.*

*My good-bye consists of saying thank you for the gift of life. I know I wasn't a welcome surprise all those many years ago, but the truth is some part of your being agreed to bring me to this experience, and so I thank you for that. It's a spectacular place, this thing we call Earth, and I believe it's the one thing we do share, our wonder at the workings of nature. I know you inspired that marvel in me. Thank you.*

*You also inspired in me my deep passion for music and dance. I still recall watching you sing and dance when I was little, and it was in those moments that you were the dad I loved. It was then that your heart was open, and you seemed to be your most true self, the man I knew remained under guard inside you.*

*Determination and strong will, yes, I share that with you too, and those are the tools that have carried me through. I've relied heavily on those traits to come to this point of the letter, forgiveness. I'm writing to say I forgive you.*

*That's what I've been working on these twenty plus years we've been apart, forgiving. I had to work hard. And I do; I forgive you. That's not to say that your actions were ok, that I didn't deserve better, because I did. What that means for me is that I now hold compassion in my heart for you, for you too were once an innocent, open-hearted child, and somewhere along the line someone changed that for you. I stay focused on the forgiveness and not the resentment. I know you acted from your wounds, not the truth of who you are.*

*Perhaps you don't need this, my words or forgiveness, but I share it with you anyway because to me it seems a necessary part of what once was our relationship.*

*What you do with this, I have no clue or hopes. It simply seemed like this closure needed to occur and these words written. Please know I wish you health, happiness and above all else, I pray you find peace.*

*With great sincerity,*

*Kellie*

When I first began to type, I was faced with a quandary. I went to type "Dad" and was brought up short. I couldn't type that word to him, and in fact the little girl within demanded I not address him as such. It was too scary and not the truth. Father felt too formal, and thus, I was left with calling him by name. I think that's a fair representation of our relationship today, adult to adult.

After writing the letter and sealing the envelope, the fear bubbled to the surface, as though someone had poured peroxide on my emotional wounds. I suddenly felt extremely vulnerable mailing my abuser words spoken from my heart. I asked my angels and the universe to give me some type of confirmation that this was for the highest good of myself and my father. I didn't want to act on impulse or cut short the process that might still be unfolding.

I shared my letter with my husband, my grandmother, and a close friend. They all felt what I had hoped my words would convey, the spirit of love. I took a deep breath and proceeded to take a walk to the mailbox. As the garage door rose, I heard, "Hello," and I immediately screamed, grabbing at my chest. It was the mail carrier, making a delivery to our door because it was raining and she didn't want a package to get wet. She held out her hand, taking the letter and my control with it. It felt as though the universe was going to hand deliver my message, and I had received the confirmation I sought.

It became clear to me that I needed to tell my father I forgave him simply because he didn't know that I had. I had tunnel vision on my destination of forgiveness for longer than I was actively in his life. Now that I had accomplished what I set out to do, I needed to tell him just that. That was the next step in my journey of forgiveness.

I would guess that in his world and operating system, I still sat festering in hatred towards him. He had no clue that I was attempting to heal and was not hell bent on punishing him. I needed to release him and me of that dynamic energy, and the only way of doing that was to share with him that truth. I didn't do it so that he would feel better, but instead so that he could see the battle between the two of us had come to an end.

It was a cosmic twist that my mother had the final say as to whether he received my letter as she would get the letter in their mail and be the one responsible for handing it to him—or not. One of the people he brutalized in his life was in full control over whether he received a message of forgiveness. She, as one that brutalized me, also had an opportunity to honor me in a way that she had never been able to do before by sharing my words with my father. This time, would she follow her heart or her fear?

It almost made me want to laugh out loud as this realization occurred to me.

If he received my message, I'll most likely never know, as in the past the letters I've sent to them have gone completely unacknowledged. I only had control over my intent, and I'm clear that my words were sent with nothing but healing intentions. How they interpreted my words and my actions was up to them.

In the interest of full disclosure, I must admit that for about a minute I wondered what my family thought about my role, or lack of, in the events that transpired. Were they hoping that with this life-altering event I would come to my senses and present myself bedside to my father? Because I didn't, were they thinking I was the ultimate bitch? Did I disappoint them yet again?

It was then that I questioned this line of questioning; did it really matter what they thought or wanted? Who was I to think my actions even mattered to them at all? And the final moment of clarity came when I said to myself, *Let's face it—he did try to kill me, and logic dictates that in that instance he's an individual I owed nothing.* And with that the internal inquiry ceased.

## Irony

Just to be certain I meant what I said to my father, "I forgive you," I was thrown another unexpected zinger by the universal jokesters—something new to ponder on the forgiveness front.

While perusing the Internet, I quite unintentionally stumbled across two articles that suggested some people don't deserve forgiveness, especially those who have never owned up to their trespasses. This, only days after I professed mine in black and white to my father, who had never taken responsibility for his actions.

My first thought was, *Shit! You mean I went through all this work for nothing?!* My mind quickly leapt from that caravan because I knew in my heart that all of this was not in vain. Instead, I dug some more to further unearth more fully my motivations for forgiving my parents.

I knew I didn't send the letter to my father to bring him comfort. I wouldn't be upset if that was an outcome, but I didn't do any of it for him. Everything I'd done I'd done for me—so that I might feel complete.

My initial journey began because I simply didn't want to be like him, and I was fast approaching that manifestation on some levels. I wanted to run from any part of me that resembled my father; survival mode was fully engaged. I should have just walked in to Andrea's office saying, "Help, I'm becoming my father." As I traipsed through the debris on the path from which I came, that which seemed more than capable of swallowing me whole, my focus shifted to forgiveness.

Forgiveness initially entered my awareness because I felt societal pressure that I "should" forgive. It seems the virtues of forgiveness are preached to us at every turn. If I didn't forgive, then what did that say about my character? Stewing in malevolence seemed to keep me sitting in the same low ranks of my abusers. I wanted to be better than that.

As I continued with my look back, I noticed that my goal of forgiveness transitioned into a means of proving my superiority. I wanted to cram my noble heart right in their faces. As I sat up on my perch, I wanted to declare with the spirit of a town crier, "I am so loving and generous of heart, that I have forgiven a piece of shit like you!"

Good thing I kept going in this process.

Next, it became clear that I wanted to forgive to prove to *myself* that I was in truth a benevolent individual. I had judged myself and my plethora of venomous emotions. I felt a great deal of shame surrounding the rancor that knotted me up inside. If I could forgive them, then it would prove that I was not only loving, but maybe even more importantly *loveable*. I unconsciously, and wrongly, equated being loving with being worthy of love.

The years passed, my frustration with failing to reach my goal of forgiveness escalated, and with it defiance soon reared its all-too familiar head; I would forgive to prove that those *fuckers* didn't control me anymore. They had ruled my life for far too long and forgiveness would be my way of proving they had no effect on me. The truth was that they had a monumental impact on me, and the more I fought that, the greater it twisted me within. I was trying to will myself into forgiveness. I surmised that I had stayed in this operating mode for many years, my wheels spinning me almost imperceptibly towards the benchmark I had created for myself.

The breaking point I've mentioned before was telling Lynn about the dark contents of my family album. I had finally honored the fact that indeed they had had an impact on me. By breaking the sacred rule of not airing our dirty laundry, I unwittingly released myself from the shackles they had placed upon me. I was then free to forgive, for I was no longer begrudgingly bound to them through maintaining our secrets.

With that, I realized because I finally had had the courage to show myself some compassion and share the truth of my experience, what naturally followed was a greater capacity to compassionately *feel*, not just intellectually *know*, their pain and its manifestations. Wholeheartedly, more accurately stated as openheartedly, I had to own my own truths before I could see another's. With great clarity, I saw that everything that had happened to me was no longer personal, but was understood as being truly about them and their personal torments.

Of course, I understood all too well the experience and complexities of being wounded. Soon the relationship was emotionally no longer between a daughter and her parents, but instead one adult recognizing emotional sickness in other adults, theirs still appearing to be their driving force.

Now, however, I no longer had to feel the direct impact of its unrelenting momentum because the door to my cell was unlocked. I was free from being their emotional prisoner.

With the resentment fading I had greater space and capacity, literally, for a more expansive love and contentedness to continue to enter my world—and that, simply made me smile.

Did they deserve my forgiveness? The articles suggested not, but it was not about what they deserved; for me it was about what *I* deserved, and I deserved peace.

## Simple Math

As I continued to familiarize myself with forgiveness, who and what I was *to my father* shifted and changed inwardly for me, but outwardly I caught a possible glimpse of my importance as well.

In a conversation with my sister, she shared that the cardiologist determined my father lost a third of his heart function as a result of his heart attack. That was a significant loss.

A thought soon popped into my mind: I am one of three children, a third, if you will. Symbolically, I wondered if I represented that third of his heart and what he had lost. I would like to think I once held some space in the domain where love resides.

Energetically, with the death of that third of his heart, is that what moved me to bring conscious closure to our relationship by writing a letter? Or had that part of his heart where I had once dwelled become dead to him? Were those events necessary to bring that awareness to me—that I no longer had a place in his heart?

I'll never know. But what was clear to me, is that without that third of his heart, his life will never be the same.

## Dream Destination

No longer consumed with the necessities of rehashing and replaying my traumas, I was afforded the opportunity to continually strengthen and know my newly-discovered relationship with forgiveness. It seemed it required just as much time and attention as my past had previously demanded.

I used to think forgiveness was a onetime thing, a destination to be reached. Soon enough, I saw that it too was a process. It took dedication and effort to maintain this place of forgiveness, frequent practice to remind myself that I've visited this place before, and this where I chose to stay. The roadside reminders remained posted along the way telling me to let go, as I sought to further release both them and me.

It's like visiting the beach of my dream vacation. Once I reach that beach, if I stand idle in one spot for too long, the tide will eventually wash away the sand beneath my feet, the foundation which supports me. It is then that I risk the danger of being thrown off kilter or carried out to sea, no longer living my dream. So, too, I found, it is with forgiveness.

Once reached, it requires continued steps and actions to maintain my place of balance in forgiveness, continual awareness, and actions lest I get swept away once more by the tides of those years gone by. Those tides will pull me back to the place where my mind lives in the land of, "But don't you remember?" and "Don't ever forget." A place where I felt righteous in my wrath towards my parents, a place that I knew intimately and one that was full of the false promise of feeling powerful.

Yes, I learned that forgiveness too requires effort to maintain its brilliance and place in our hearts and lives. It should come as no surprise, I suppose, as the past and pain too were tended with years of dedication and painstaking labor. But that stark land and its desolate gardens were no longer a place of dwelling for me. I've walked through that terrain and no longer find its hills and valleys to be a place of comfort.

I discovered that forgiveness is an island in the land of self-love and self-compassion, a place to be visited often and with fervor. I made, and must continue to make, the choice to board my boat, so that I might travel to the isle of forgiveness through daily focus, conscious efforts, and visualizations. My new hope was that it might become my home away from home, and a permanent destination in the land of me.

## Simplicity

I obviously wasn't the model for Rodin's sculpture entitled *The Thinker*, but I had felt our kindred nature when I first set eyes on it as a teenager. My pervasive analysis of anything and everything proved to be a great asset, as well as a downfall. While I had perfected my ability to meticulously scrutinize, it was quite cumbersome and eventually proved to no longer be a staple in my life. I was being called from a complex practice to one that spoke of a more simple nature.

Quite miraculously, for me, some days I had only one focus. When I found my mind wandering into murky waters, I asked myself only, "Does this thought serve me? Does it take me to a place of happiness?" If the answer was "No," then I disallowed its chattering within me. After spending years being complicated, the simplicity was refreshing.

Enough said.

## Today's Truce

The death of one thing often leads to the birth of another, and I was soon being asked to reinvent who I had always known myself to be, an embattled warrior.

The time had come to lay down my sword. I no longer had to go fisticuffs with the carnage laid behind me. I stood victorious, not because

I won anything, but because I was courageous enough to endure each hellacious step. I've had many self-doubts and criticisms flow through my brain, but the one attribute of my being that I'd never wavered on was bravery. I was unflinching as I traversed the terrains of my youth, seeking the higher ground and truth that I knew awaited me. Many times I fell on my journey, but always I would pull myself to standing and shuffle on. I refused to allow my past to become all that I was, and I fought to reclaim who I knew myself to be.

Today I choose to live not from my wounds, but from my soul. When I find my mind wandering to what was, where it's always willing to travel down those dark alleys, I redirect myself by asking, *What is? How would my soul see or handle this situation?* This is my new mantra, one I've not perfected, but choose to practice repeatedly.

I've no doubt events of the past shall seep through the cracks of my life again, but now I know I'm better equipped to not allow them to bring me to complete destruction. Now I shall build myself up with those new-found *(Or are they reclaimed?)* pieces of myself that were previously lost in my life's explosion and proceeding implosion. Perhaps that was the point of the whole journey, discovering me.

Is it possible that without the fodder of abuse I wouldn't have been as motivated to live from my truth? Without the fuel of rebellion would I have fallen into a lull that was a mediocre version of myself? I had to suffer the extremes of who and what I wasn't in order that I might more fully know who I am? Or shall I say, who I choose to be?

For now it is a choice, to repeat the past and its drama or step beyond its boundaries. Allowing my brain that's been hardwired to replay and repeat, to run and ruin my life, or pressing the stop button long enough to hear the whisperings of my heart and soul–that is where I am being led again and again. Because of the masterfully crafted steps I took toward healing, I now have the choices that had once been torn from me, the choices I had forever craved. No more does my life run on an unconscious autopilot. For me there's no going back, only forward.

# Gifts from Heaven

Removing myself from the battlefield left me primed to take in the wonders of my new landscape and its offerings of love.

It was during a meditation that I received a most amazing gift. My only plan had been to flow with whatever made itself known to me. As soon as I closed my eyes, doors appeared and proceeded to open wide in front of me. Light shone brilliantly from the space behind the doors, and I crossed the threshold into what seemed like the brightest blue sky. As I gazed down, I noticed I could see the Earth below. I could sense the power that the planet and its people possessed, as well as the pain.

My paternal grandmother quickly joined my side and gently took me by the arm. She was younger in my vision than when she had passed. She encouraged me to look more closely at the Earth. I bent forward, as if peering down at a passing insect, to get a closer view. It was as if my vision instantly warped from macroscopic to microscopic; I was seeing others on the planet as if in a movie, not just the planet as a whole.

The person I saw was my father as a young boy, and what I witnessed was a condensed version of the abuses he felt from his mother. I saw a dejected and hurting little boy who just wanted to please his mother, but it was always in vain. It was then my grandmother spoke to me and said, "I was cruel and unkind."

I was filled with sorrow for that little boy, and my heart ached for what he had endured. Quickly, I was given the vision of my father as a man, the abuser he became. I too saw myself as a little girl being shamed and hurt, both physically and mentally. My heart went out to me as well as memories flashed through my awareness.

It was then my father spoke directly to me and said, "I hurt you because I hurt."

My attention was again drawn to the sky where I next met my maternal grandfather, as my grandmother faded in the distance. He too appeared younger than when I had last seen him.

I was led to the next experience, but this time I was permitted to see the unkind acts perpetrated upon my mother by her father. I saw how afraid and somber she was, desperate for love. My grandfather spoke too and said, "I did many things that I shouldn't have. I wasn't right in my mind." Once more compassion awoke in me for the child I had just been allowed to witness.

Again, I was taken to re-experience my emotional traumas, this time those that resulted from the way my mother had treated me. She spoke to me and referring to my father said, "I want to be part of his team because he's the leader here. This is the first time in my life that I felt powerful."

It was as if I had been given the motivations behind both my parents' behaviors through their spoken words, and none of it had anything to do with me or my worthiness. I had been given the opportunity to *feel* so that it might become more ingrained and crystallized in the mortar that was now holding my truth.

My grandmother returned to stand beside me and my grandfather, and she explained, "What happened to you is a result of what happened to them. What happened to them is a result of what happened to us and on and on, back through time."

The domino effect was clear to me and I was just one of the many dominos affected by this chain reaction. I would like to think of myself as the last one to fall, that the cycle ended with me.

I wasn't left standing there alone to contemplate any of this. Instead, my cousin Fred, whom I adored, came to share his love with me–assuring me his love is still alive today even though his body is not. And a sweet surprise was a hug with my great aunt, Helen.

Next was a visit from my pack of dogs that have passed. I touched and felt every one of their unique physical characteristics that remained embedded in my memory: Regan's thick fur coat, a combination of shepherd and husky, that I would run my fingers through in the direction opposite its natural growth. His crystal blue eyes and unique greetings that sounded as though he was literally speaking the phrases, "Hello" and "I love you." How he would lay his head on my lap or gently give me kisses on the inside of my right wrist.

The marshmallow-like muzzle of our sharpei, Barckley, that I loved to plant kisses upon and how he would come up underneath my right hand with his head and demand to be pet. The wrinkles that wove channels on the top of his head. His coarse, short coat that I would softly balance my hand upon and wiggle back and forth in some vain attempt to get his fur to balance perfectly straight, similar to the game I played as a little girl with anything made of plush.

Barney's large floppy ears that I would gently bend and roll, or sometimes sit calmly stroking their ultra-soft, thin edges. His smell that I would intentionally inhale again and again as I buried my face near his. How he would bay out of the kitchen window for me whenever I got off the school bus.

I was also allowed to relive their very different gifts and personalities that they had shared with me when they were in physical form, each with their own lessons for me. Their love, I knew, had saved me many times over.

Standing behind all of my departed loved ones shone the army of spirits that supported and guided me each day and for all eternity. They appeared as indistinct visions of light and energy, a twinkling display of untold wonder.

It became clear to me that I too was a vision of light just like them. I too was spirit. When I saw myself as that vision of light, I felt the greatest sense of peace and calm I have ever known. No one and nothing could harm me.

Lastly, my spirit parents, beings of light that I'd envisioned times before to fill my parental void, came into my line of vision. They stood beside me to offer their unconditional love in the form of smiles, reaching out to hold a hand and pulling me into a hug with an outstretched arm. These are the parents I came to love and trust. I felt as though I am forever safely wrapped in their limitless affection and nurturing. It was with this sense of caring, safety and support that they returned me to Earth.

The meditation ended as I walked through the same doors through which I'd entered. I was back in my body, as tears of gratitude flowed for the love and understanding that I was fortunate enough to receive.

## Super Powers

I continued to keep my mind, eyes, and ears open to new possibilities, and I was never left wanting. Despite the vast degree of time and effort I had dedicated to my internal mending, and the bliss I had begun to encounter, there remained components within that were still haywire. The guinea pigs in my gut still came to call. *What was I to do with them?* I asked in exasperation.

I began to try a spinoff of my sensory exercise, but in a preemptive fashion instead. Sometimes I found the simple act of thinking, *I am safe*, and then observing my secure surroundings in order to anchor that observation, helped to prevent my alarms from being triggered to full alert. The key seemed to be to acknowledge that safety *before* my brain clicked into that old anxiety mode of waiting for catastrophe.

Often when trying this technique, I would notice the guard come down; it was then I could once more actively engage with the pleasures of my day and my well-being. Those fractions of a second where I felt safe were a real marvel for me, and I loved that I could utilize this practice anywhere at any time. Because this was quite foreign and new to my system, I had to complete this simple act many times over throughout my days. It almost felt like it was my super power that I'd just discovered; that's how potent this simple exercise was for me. As if now *I* had the upper hand that once belonged to the omnipresent apprehension.

Pa-pow!!

## Practical Application

I guess there's no point in learning anew if I never get the chance to use it. Once more, the powers that be planned a pop quiz for me to see how seriously I had been taking my studies.

While visiting my grandmother, I had to briefly see my mother, an accidental encounter. It astounded me how instantaneously I could be kidnapped from the present via an emotional time warp. When I glanced at her, I saw awkwardness and dispiritedness. I attributed that to our lack of communication and relationship with one another, and in a flash my heart seemed to crawl within itself, contracted by guilt and an all-too memorable pain.

The heartache came back just from one quick glance. Witnessing her humanity took me to the morose mother of my youth, when her misery was mine as well. As she sat in her SUV, she no longer physically looked like the mother of my childhood. Age had left her looking weaker and more fragile. I wanted to do nothing more than jump out of my vehicle and just make it better for her somehow. Just as quickly, I knew that wasn't what I needed to do to take care of myself because that was no longer my starring role. Instead, I took a deep breath and chose to tend to my hurt instead.

First of all, I made the observation that maybe she wasn't feeling anything I'd imagined she might be experiencing. Truthfully, I didn't believe this with great gusto as I had spent many years enmeshed in knowing her emotional energies, but I allowed myself to be open to the possibility that my radar might have been taking a reading from the past versus the present scenario. I also had the awareness that although she wasn't abusive in that moment, the potential was right there in the mix. Our last conversation confirmed that. She was still the same woman who showed me no mercy many times over, her possible mournfulness didn't take that away.

And just in case my mother *was* feeling everything that I had surmised, I comforted my little girl that had tears falling from her eyes because yet again she saw her mother hurting. I assured her that their relationship was a sorrowful issue but it was not hers to fix, nor did she create it. I let her grieve as I envisioned holding her close, kissing the top of her head.

When I got home, I shared the experience with Craig, getting a hug, and with that I let it go. The fact was that our relationship was a wretched situation that will not change anytime soon, and so the best I could do was allow the despair to flow through me and get the comfort I needed in the moment.

There was nothing left for me to say or do, and with that I moved on.

# Surviving Victim

The more I embodied forgiveness and healing, the more driven I became to speak out, trying to add a modicum of sanity to an insane topic.

I took part in a discussion about domestic abuse at a local women's shelter. One of the women referred to herself as a victim of domestic abuse. She was quickly corrected by another who was donning her best cheerleader smile and reminded that the term to use was, "Domestic Abuse *Survivor*."

Give me a shake of those pom-poms!

That statement left me a bit perturbed. Okay, more than a bit. Yeah, yeah, yeah. I knew, the statement was meant to empower. The goal was for the individual to stand in her sense of power instead of wallowing in the victimization. But…

To me, it felt like a denial of sorts. Speaking personally, I *am* a victim of abuse, and *I* am a survivor. Semantics, some might say, but each statement rings with a different truth. I was a victim; that's why it hurt, and to deny that also denies the aftermath that followed suit. The remnants that remain are from a place of victimhood, which I clearly endured.

Now, I stand here today because in the very core of my being, I am a fighter and because of that, a survivor. For me, survivor embodies that energy that gets up again and again, no matter how many times they've taken a KO punch. It's a quality of me personally, one I fully own, but it doesn't negate my victimization at that time.

What was empowering to me was to *honor* my *victim*, knowing that as I trudged through my personal battlefield I was utilizing and honing my *survivor skills*.

# Forgiving Again and Again

For me the road to forgiveness, and its refining, was key to my very survival–both emotionally and physically. Without it, I would have drifted further from myself and all those in my life as both my body and mind suffered.

Because forgiveness was all so new, I found myself hesitant to trust its strength and stability. Many times I questioned its frail nature: what if it was just temporary? What if I'd been fooling myself?

As I pondered these questions, I felt my mental energy literally being pulled away, into some dark and distant tunnel, as my mind tried desperately to cling to the experience of forgiveness. I didn't want the calm to end. I soon became riddled with apprehension. I begin to speculate that this fragile beginnings of forgiveness would come crashing down if I had to be in my parents' presence for some reason; that they'd always have some hold over me. I imagined their absence was the only thing supporting the vessel of peace I held gingerly in my palms, and if I but glimpsed their physical essence, it would slip from my hands. Just as quickly as my mind was whisked away into fear, I put a stop gap in its place and consciously chose to not focus on that possibility, but instead the feelings of forgiveness that were present, no matter how delicate they may have been.

Focusing on the forgiveness was the best way I knew to make it grow in my life and in my heart. I have found that over time the forgiveness felt more solid and real. Patience, Kellie. Patience to allow this newfound energy to gradually and calmly become part of my truth. Patience for myself as I remembered there is no one who can take my power or destroy what I've worked so diligently to create.

This will be the next step for me, bringing this healing into the very presence of their faces and not flinching or withdrawing in pain and memories. Instead, I hope to stand strong in my truth and with an open heart but with a clear knowledge as to how much of that open heart I will hand to them. Words don't need to be spoken, and if they are I can say what is needed from my place of center, not with energy of my dear old friend Rebellion. This will be my test, as old habits awaken most often when confronted with those individuals who anchor that energy and experience for us. It only feels natural to put on my emotional armor when around them and fling energetic daggers in order to keep them at a safe distance, both emotionally and physically. Will I stand in my truth or allow myself to be swayed into a war that has long since ended?

Only time will tell, and so once again I pulled my wanderings from drifting too far into the future and always on the present. This was an exercise I performed time and again and will do so, I suspect, until the day I die.

## Head Games

Never was I left without the need to put to practice all that I worked so hard to learn.

Before I ended my time with Hailey, she had helped me to see the light, the phrasing I might use to more fully embrace the "me" at the end of it all. Despite all my efforts at healing, I still felt as though whatever continued to linger from my abuse was a string that kept me connected to my parents, and that kept me from fully accepting those parts of me. It felt frightening to me, as though I was being asked to once again allow my parents into my world. This felt incredibly unsafe and alarming to me.

I saw the lasting fragments of my childhood abuses as life-long damage, wounds inflicted by them that I had to carry around and witness for the rest of my days. "How could I ever embrace and accept that?" I asked.

Perhaps, she suggested, I not view them as wounds, but instead survival skills I imparted in order that I might endure.

It was one more mind game I was playing with myself, I knew, but it allowed me to feel empowered. Survival skills were something I had control over, albeit unconsciously for the most part, something some part of me chose to evoke versus something that was thrust upon me and embedded into my being by them. That I could live with.

I believed it might also help during moments of flashbacks and triggers as I can remind myself that they are survival skills that I don't need anymore, not another infliction and replay of all that they'd done. It was through this perception that I could potentially gain even more emotional freedom from my parents and our life together, but it too required laser-like focus as I strained to bend the construct of the old mental infrastructures.

I personally devised another technique that I kept at the ready for those places in time when old habits come to call. Yes, they still have my number—a direct line in fact.

There were still times that I found myself pulling away emotionally, collapsing into myself in an effort to feel safe from everything and everyone. Sometimes, for no outwardly logical reason, I felt myself pulling back from love. I think it will always seem most natural to observe the love in my life, keeping it at a safe enough distance so I theoretically won't be left unaware of potential abandonment, never allow the love fully in for fear that it will one day be taken from me. I literally took this lesson to (my) heart. With all that I am, I believed that I could never fully trust others' intentions; this had been the impact of those early years.

But it was a new day, and with it a new mantra. I no longer wanted to live keeping love at bay. It wasn't fair to me nor was it fair to those in my life today who hadn't abandoned me and our love.

I devised another trick to manage this foe, one that I still use today—when I find myself pulling back out of a previously unconscious habit I tell myself, "You're punishing *(fill in the blank)* for something someone else has done. That's not fair."

Fairness is of utmost importance to me. I feel it's important that I treat others fairly and simply can't tolerate others' unfair actions. It was with this treasured value that I manipulated my mind as well.

Sounds simple but it has allowed me to shift the energy of my fearful brain from one of withdrawal, to my open heart that allows the particular love of the present day to touch and soothe me. "Oh yeah," my mind registers, "they're not the ones who hurt me." It's instantaneous as my focus on being fair feels much safer than pressuring myself to be receptive to love, a much scarier proposition.

# Rx: Daily Brain Scan

Diligence was, and forever will be, key to my continued commitment to healing. Without that commitment I knew that like an infection left untreated, the old will flourish once more until it oozed its way into every crevice of my life.

I came to accept that I cannot let my guard down completely, and so every day I focus on my intentions of emotional and spiritual wellbeing. Every day I practice some simple form of meditation. I don't invest hours in meditating, but allot some time in my day to calm my mind and support my intentions of living from my center. This practice reminds me that I am more than my thoughts or my past, but rather a divine and radiant being on this planet. I feel empowered and capable when I take the time to practice these moments of focus and clarity.

Every day I make a point to feel gratitude for the people and events of my life. Sometimes they are the simplest things: a particularly picturesque cloud or the tweeting of the birds outside my window. And always they are the most grand, the laughter my children bring to my day or the smile my husband beams at me as he enters the door while returning from work. I spend my day looking for things to add to my mental gratitude log for that day. I find it fun, another treasure hunt twist.

Every day I read some inspiring words or quotes. Again, it is not something I spend hours indulging in, but instead I set my intention for those words, no matter how minimal, to inspire the light and healing within me. A written truth, if you will, that resonates with how I choose to live my life. Whatever I read always seems fitting for where I am at the time and brings my mind into a focused direction instead of being left to its own wanderings. Those teachings and words always felt fitting to me, like little beacons of light guiding me along the runway of my life as I continue to explore and learn.

Every day I perform exercises to increase the flow of energy throughout my body, qi gong or some other practice that I'd been instructed in performing. These practices allow my body to relax and let go, much like the words that I read bring a calm to my mind.

You'll notice a theme, every day. It's easy to get distracted by my list of things to do, but I make the commitment to myself and make myself the priority, not the things.

I allow for leniency in my routine on holidays, vacation, or if my physical energy is running particularly low. Obviously, I have a tendency towards rigidity and defiance, the two qualities that I called upon frequently to bring me to this place. By allowing myself to take a break, I remind myself that the world is fluid and that I always have a choice; there was no mandate. I'm so defiant that sometimes I even defy myself, and so this was my way around those self-imposed limits.

Despite my best intentions, sometimes I still fall short of my aspirations. Usually, that is because the reptilian part of my brain rears its prehistoric head, my monkey brain chatters and screeches in its most primal fashion, and/or those neurotically anxious guinea pigs begin scampering about in my gut.

I adapted this visualization from a neuropsychologist by the name of Rick Hanson. He referred to parts of his brain in a similar fashion; the guinea pigs are my adaptation, and it helped me to simplify those parts of me that were acting out and wreaking havoc in my life. He had his own images for those particular parts of his brain, and by the way we all truly have a reptilian portion of our brain, and so I envisioned my own internal zoo.

My reptilian brain doesn't think; it only reacts to a perceived threat, as if my life depended on it. Through its traumatic molding, my brain readily concludes that it's under threat, despite what I may cognitively know and see. The image I have is one of an aggressive alligator. When my alligator is acting out and snapping, I picture it transported to cool, clear waters as it basks peacefully in the rays of the sun.

My monkey brain looks like a maniacal chimp, head thrown back, teeth bared, and arms flailing while shrieking its discontent. To calm that beast, I simply envision feeding my chimp bananas as it relaxes in a tree where it is caressed by a gentle breeze and the warmth of the sunlight.

Last but not least in my animal menagerie are the guinea pigs I've described earlier. When they require redirection, I envision gently scooping them out of their prison and wrapping them in a soft blanket as I sit gently rocking them. I whisper softly to them, "It's okay. I know. We're safe."

This whole process takes but a few minutes and takes me from warped speeds to a place of serenity.

What's the point I'm trying to make? The process of healing and enlightenment requires continual practice and concerted effort. There is no finish line that I have stumbled upon. The only person who could make me and my journey a priority is me. I reach into my bag of tricks on a daily and frequent basis in order that I might live a life that is closer to my truth and the freedom to be the only thing I longed to be–loving and loved.

## Reprogramming

Although therapy was no longer a weekly part of my schedule, I did not rest on my laurels in any way; I simply continued to re-route my energies into the pathways for deeper understanding and clearing. What I was doing was building an even more stable and fertile bed for forgiveness to take root and mature.

I was at the point of healing where some of scars had lost their ability to define me. That's not to say they didn't impact me, but instead I began to take a scientific approach as to how they sometimes affect me. I began to read about neuroplasticity and it provided me with enough insight and education to understand that what continued to remain from my childhood events wasn't a matter of my poor character, but was a product of how and what my brain had or had not been fed.

Science gave me the space and understanding to be kind and still more forgiving of myself. It was as if my parents literally sculpted my brain to its deepest levels, the neurons' networking and messaging being left to their seemingly incapable hands. My thoughts, feelings, obsessions, triggers, fears, etc. remained a direct result of the tinkering they did in their all important role as parents. They developed, or didn't develop in some cases, all the connections for the make-up that became me.

Initially, this did indeed enrage me. I was left with what appeared to be quite the defective operating system, yet it was up to me to fix. "What the fuck?!" I wanted to scream, and internally I did just that. It simply wasn't fair. I wanted someone else to repair the mangled mess that had become me, but there was not a box to check for that option, and time had proven that my parents weren't the people for the job. Fair? No. But if I didn't tend to it, who would? I made the conscious choice to not be part of the list of people who had abandoned me.

No longer was my brain and its table of contents my nemesis. Instead, it became one more aspect of me that was held with empathy. No more was I fueled by frustration with myself for not always reacting to situations the way I would have wished to or had recently learned. I saw that, of course, my brain would behave this way because that was how it had been forged and organized. Just like a computer, my brain did as it had been programmed. My responsibility today arises when I note the incongruous nature between who I know myself to be, the educated and healing Kellie, versus how my brain is reacting.

This was where my work took a turn, and I began to make efforts to redirect my brain to more healthy thoughts, choices, and presence in the current moment. That's not to say it was easy and didn't require very intentional, multiple efforts, but it beat attacking myself for "being this way." The real question, I began to grasp, was how could I *not* be this way? My brain was naturally doing what brains do when faced with traumas and abuses.

After spouting about this more profound sense of self/brain acceptance, I have to say there are some programs within that I didn't know how to rewire. Abandonment was one of them. I still fully expected to be abandoned—it seemed to be entwined in my genetic code, and a genetic engineer I am not. In my present day, I have people who show me their continual commitment and devotion, yet some part of me believed that one day they'd leave me, that it was all just some crazy waiting game. One day, some day, they will decide that I am not worth it because, as always, I'm too much and never enough.

It infuriated me as I knew this deeply-held belief masking as truth had nothing to do with those people presently in my life. I knew it, but yet...I just had no frame of reference for what it felt like to not be abandoned;

it's as if my computer lacks that chip. "Huh?" is the only response my brain could muster as I attempted to poke and prod it into releasing this program. My system of operation seemed to be "enjoy 'em while you got 'em", because ultimately I will be standing alone, wherever the end may be. In my own scientific terms, it sucked.

I wanted to know what that deep sense of security felt like. Don't mistake this for dependence. I'm talking about trusting deeply in another that they won't knowingly and intentionally leave me high and dry. Giving them the level of trust that they had my back, and wouldn't get tired of it or me. It's still a landmark in my own growth that I hope to reach.

I'm no fool; I know no one can make promises for an eternity, but while they're in my life I'd like to experience that trust with abandon, no pun intended. What I must do instead is focus on the facts and directly challenge the old pattern. I consciously identify ways in which my husband, for example, demonstrates a commitment to me daily–in fact several times a day and year after year. When my abandonment sensor has been activated, I run through that mental list of ways that I've been loved. I've got my own little banking system and so far, the love is in the black.

## Scammed and Slammed

Welcome to my life and this never-ending process of dealing with my abuse. At this stage of the game, you would think it might be all under control, that I had banked enough in my reserves to maintain a steady state. But reality threw me a curve ball, and I crumbled to the ground once again, struggling to find my footing in the here and now.

I received a phone call in which the person on the other end informed me that I was being sued by the IRS for fraudulent claims for the past five years. I was suspicious because the caller had a thick foreign accent and it sounded as though he was calling from a large telemarketing center, I could hear the mutterings of other people talking in the background. "No," he assured me after I called his identity into question, "the room that I'm in is full of police and lawyers at work."

*What? Police and lawyers going about their jobs en masse?* I wondered silently.

It seemed as though he could hear my thought because he went on to rattle off his name and badge number. Initially, I felt no urgency, thinking to myself that my very experienced CPA husband could take care of this misunderstanding. He claimed the department had made several unsuccessful attempts at trying to contact me in writing.

Next, he told me that I was not allowed to interrupt him or verbally challenge him in any way as he laid out my felonies. "You can write it all down if you want," he suggested. He then proceeded to list all the charges against me, giving dates and financial numbers to validate his claims. My body soon began to register panic, my innards twisted and my bowels strained to contain the contents that had turned to mush and threatened an exit.

"Whoever did your taxes was being deceptive," he accused. Of course, that "whoever" was Craig. He claimed my husband was not being charged with anything, only me. With great conviction he told me that within thirty to forty minutes of our phone call, the authorities would be at my home to arrest me. "The best thing you can do is cooperate," he stated.

The only response I had was to say, "But I didn't do anything wrong. How can someone arrest me? I don't think this is legitimate." Now feeling bewildered and quite fearful, I told him I needed to call my husband.

"No one can save you," was his response. I promptly hung up the phone, hell-bent on trying to get in touch with Craig.

By the time I got Craig on the other end of the line, I was in hysterics. I was shaking uncontrollably, and he didn't recognize my panic-stricken voice. He assured me that it was all a scam and that I was safe, but with the words of the complete stranger the past had come to call too, whispering in my ear all the messages and fears of my childhood until I could hear nothing but the alarms of my emergency broadcast system sounding. The memories spoke to me, the words louder and more piercing than anything Craig said. This was their frantic and rambling message:

*I've done something wrong. I don't know what it is, but I'm going to get in trouble. I'm so confused. How can this happen? What is happening? This is how my body felt every time I was in danger. I am in danger. They're telling me there is nothing sordid going on; it's all my imagination. Is it my imagination? I can't trust myself or my observations. I am the crazy one. I can never trust anyone, even those I love. It's naive to completely trust anyone. Someone else has done something terrible, and I'm the one who will pay the price for it. I can't trust authority. I am not allowed to question authority. I can only take what is being dished out. I'm powerless. This is all my fault. I'm the only one to blame. Someone's coming to get me. Someone always comes to get me. I'm not safe. I'm all alone. I'm being ripped from my home and what I believed was a safe place. There is no safe place. There's no one to help me. There's no one.*

I wanted to believe Craig as he pointed out the flaws in the scammer's claims; he sounded logical, but I knew logic rarely had anything to do with actions of others. Instead my thoughts raced. *He's wrong. He doesn't know what people are capable of the way I do. I am **not** safe*, seemed to boom louder than his voice. I knew I had pulled him out of a meeting and felt guilty for bothering him and taking him away from something that was surely more important than me. Filled with shame, I decided to tell him I could calm myself down.

I was wrong. Instead, I sat on the living room floor sobbing and wailing as the terror mounted. In some distant corner of my brain I had the clarity to understand that I was in the midst of an emotional flashback–a PTSD extravaganza–but it was much more powerful than my logical self. I desperately wanted to call him back, but more old messages began to rattle in my brain: *Don't be a problem. I'm always a problem. He's going to think I'm psycho. I feel psycho. Am I psycho?*

Thankfully he texted me moments later, "Are you okay?" he asked.

I hesitated as to how I would reply. I dug deep, found some courage and decided on an honest response, "No, I'm not. Can you call me?"

Again, I felt inconsolable. Craig remained level-headed despite my cries of, "Someone's coming to get me! Someone always gets me!"

He suggested I leave the house if I was petrified of someone showing up.

"No!" I cried, "I'm afraid they're out there waiting for me." There seemed to be no escape and I was trapped once again in my own hell as the past continued to repeat itself. Waiting, always waiting as something or someone dreadful hunted me down.

I tried my best to show him how this seemingly-unrelated event had slammed me into the throws of old trauma. Enduring the flashbacks and replay of old messages as I attempted to educate and explain things to Craig was akin to mental Olympics.

Eventually the high level of hysteria began to very minimally abate, and I felt strong enough to end my phone call with Craig. As I pushed the button on the phone that cut our connection it gave its telltale beep, that noise signaled my brain that I was once again alone and in very grave danger. The high level panic was back.

I found myself begging to anyone and everything. I pleaded with my guides, angels, and the universe for help, mercy of some sort. In a flash of lucidity I wondered what tools I could use to help myself. I determined that tapping was best suited for the occasion. Tapping is a technique that I knew would help in deactivating my amygdala, that part of my midbrain that was signaling the alarm. I proceeded to cry, tap, and pace throughout the rooms of our house like a caged beast.

I had been told that someone would be there to arrest me within thirty to forty minutes of our conversation. Some part of me hung onto those words, and I began to reason with myself—*I can relax a little after a half hour has passed, and I will know for sure if I am safe after forty-five minutes.* I continued with my routine of pacing, crying, and tapping with an ever watchful eye on the clock. At the thirty-minute mark I felt a slight relief of pressure; maybe Craig was right and no one was coming to get me. I told myself I only had to endure the heavy sense of anxiety and fore-boding for fifteen more minutes, there was an end in sight.

With three minutes left on my mentally ticking clock, our dog began to bark incessantly. I stole a cautious glance out a front window to see what had alerted him and discovered that someone had pulled up to the front of our house. *Oh my god, they're here! What am I going to do?!* was my first reaction. It was then I noticed some writing on the side of the truck that advertised its purpose as a utility locator. *Maybe that's the only vehicle they had to come get me. Maybe they're trying to trick me,* I feared.

I struggled to focus on the logic of that statement, hoping it had none despite what the hysteria was telling me. I hid as best I could and remained planted by a window so I could watch the person sitting inside the truck. He sat inside his vehicle for five painful minutes, and when he exited I could see he was marking underground wiring for our utilities. I began to relax a bit as the forty-five minutes came and went. It did seem as though he was no threat to me, until I saw him take pictures of our mailbox and the front of our house, the camera seemingly pointed in the direction of where I hid. I felt sure he could spy me peeking out the window. I wondered why he needed pictures of where I lived. My paranoid brain concluded the snapshots would somehow be used in the file that was being created for the case against me.

Craig called yet again just as I was watching the stranger who seemed to have randomly thrust himself in my day. As Craig and I continued to talk, I watched the man get back in his truck and pull away. Craig assured me that this man's appearance was legitimate and coincidental, and not a sign that I truly was under threat. For his own sense of sanity he was going to come home to check on my level of wellbeing face-to-face.

Again, my old patterns spoke of my shame, "No, You don't need to come home. I'm okay."

It felt as though I had bothered him enough, but he insisted on laying eyes on me to assess my current state. Upon seeing him, I was quite glad he did come home because I soon realized to physically see him was settling for me and further helped to pull me into the present moment. I was gradually coming back to clearer awareness.

Later I received two more phone messages from the same people. Of course, I disregarded those calls, but they did cause my heart to race again. It seemed the past was replaying one more message: *Just when I think it's over, they always return to haunt me. I can never be completely free of them.* I was easily brought to tears the rest of the day if I dared to replay the day's events in my mind, but I was steadfast at redirecting my brain. I was left feeling emotionally and physically spent, and I knew there was more to come as my foe had always proved to be as relentless as me.

You see, the reactivation of my trauma was the perfect fuel for a more intense bout with my dysautonomia. In the weeks that followed I was left with increased fatigue and muscle weakness. Even everyday walking left my muscles sore and shaking. My postural hypotension, experiencing dizziness upon standing, made a return. I lived in a constant state of nausea and irritable bowel symptoms. Every sound seemed like the strike of a hammer to my overactive nervous system.

It felt, and always feels, like an endless circuit because the gastrointestinal symptoms and fatigue I endured are exactly how my body reacted and felt when I was a frightened and stressed child. My brain interpreted that information as confirmation that I was still in danger, and thus my system was in a continual loop of activation as my brain fired up my autonomic nervous system, which in turn added fuel to the brain's hypervigilance. On and on it would go.

I'd been through the cycle enough to know that only time and patience would get me to where I wanted to go. The haunting messages of my past sat perched on my shoulder at the ready, primed to launch into their cacophonous chatter if I dared to turn my mind's eye in that direction. Distance from the event left me feeling a bit foolish at times because I could see how others might struggle to connect the phone call with my past. All I know is that a portion of my brain holds my trauma, and its main hatchways gave in and were ripped from the hinges, with very little control on my part.

All that was left to do was remain diligent in tenderly caring for my body and my mind. My already low-key exercise was scaled down even more, and I made continued efforts to process the messages and body memories through tapping, writing, talking, and self-compassion. I was steadfast in my efforts to reserve any self-judgment and criticism.

What lingered most strongly for me was the phrase: *Someone's coming to get me.* It seemed as though someone had always been waiting around the corner, ready to spring into action and grab me. Married to that core belief was absolute certainty that I must remain extremely diligent in not letting down my guard. The hypervigilance for my safety has forever felt absolutely paramount to my very survival. There was a strong mental desire to release myself of this burden, but emotionally it felt as though I was being asked to stab myself in the heart and have faith that I would live. My psyche simply refused to release its death grip on its mantra: *I have to protect myself, I must be ready, because an attack can come at any time. Someone's coming to get me.* I felt as though I might hyperventilate at the very notion of releasing it. It was a huge quagmire that left me feeling a bit hopeless.

When sharing my dilemma a dear friend reminded me of a technique I have utilized to deal with my anxiety: instead of trying to get rid of it, accept and embrace it. Literally envision myself holding it. In my emotional upheaval, I had forgotten this approach. It sounded counterintuitive to releasing myself of this burden, to hold it, but if I acknowledged and validated the feeling, it could begin to relax and let go—much like a person who simply longs to be heard. Fighting it and trying to force its exit only made it grow stronger, again much like an individual who is being denied their experience.

So, I personified the mantra, and what I saw was a younger version of myself crouched and cowering in a corner, shoulders hunched tightly and eyes darting about in a primal panic. I assessed what was needed, and I settled with the phrase, "That was scary. People did hurt you and come to get you." When I said those words, she paused long enough in her vigilance to take a deep breath, drop her shoulders slightly, and make hesitant eye contact with me. For the first time she felt the wonder of being heard and validated. I stood in front of her in a protective stance, conveying that I had her covered and would take the watch. She let out a deep sigh of exhaustion and relief and then dared to close her eyes to rest.

It was an involved process for a complicated issue, and one I needed to incorporate frequently in my efforts to heal even further. Again, I utilized tapping sessions to further cement the newfound visualization into my awareness.

I also reflected on what was positive about the whole mess. While I was certainly taken to an extremely dark and terrifying place, the good news was that some other level of my psyche remained strong enough to alert me to the fact that I was receiving a surprise visit from the phantoms of my past. For me there was no doubt that all my years of growth and healing had come into play and prevented me from slipping any deeper into the black hole.

Of course, Craig's unconditional support and love warmed my heart and was a touchstone for reality and healing. I believe that incident might be the most raw and wounded he has ever heard me because it was a culmination and explosion of so many aspects of my trauma, not simply piecemeal expressions of my pain. His nonjudgmental approach and not treating me like the problem allowed me to further deepen my sense of trust towards him and myself. I still found myself grappling with the past and its level of depravity as once more the thought occurred to me that, *Wow—it really was that bad*, as my latent denials and programming slipped just a tad further in their hold over me.

I took a deep breath and did what I'd always done, moved onward.

## Ask and Ye Shall Receive

As I continued to whet those skills that would consistently move me onward, I began to sense that my next step in recovery was this book you now read. There was no doubt that all that I had travailed was meant to serve me and, perhaps, it would do so for others as well. The time had come for me to release myself and my story on a much larger scale. On another level, if I was to continue to distance myself from those events, then I needed to get it out of my head and into the ethers of the universe for a healing that no longer rested squarely in my hands. I continued to knead and stretch all of this in my mind throughout the months that followed, and soon enough the cosmos were answering my call in a most extraordinary way on an ordinary day.

I entered the local Kohl's store to buy myself some new sneakers. For no reason in particular, as I made my way through the store I began to think about my book. *Should I? Shouldn't I? What would the title be? Can someone, something, give some type of sign?*

Having found what I came for, I next stood in line to make my purchase. While waiting, I happened to glance down at the writing on the end of the shoe box and saw the word "Relentless"–the name for the style of pink and brown Nikes I was buying. I felt a jolt zip throughout my body, and I knew *that* was my book title. It then stood to reason that if I had a book title, then I too had a book, the pages of its manuscript floating about within me. All that was needed was my intent to bring them to order and life.

In the coming days the word "relentless" ricocheted off the walls of my skull again and again. I came to know its perfection in describing the essence of me, my purpose, my life in every aspect and my healing. Persistent and unyielding. Determined and never, ever lying down in submission.

That one word allowed me to appreciate what it took to get me to where I was standing. I have an internal drive to make my way, however slowly, through anything. You can tell me no, but I most certainly will find a way around whatever obstacle you've place before me. I'm not to be controlled, nor will I bow to anyone. Don't mistake my calm demeanor for acquiescence; I'm simply watching and waiting for my moment, which will surely arrive.

The heart of a soldier beats in my chest. As I matured and grew, so too did my arsenal, once only comprised of assault weapons, and all served me well in my survival and my intent to speak my truth.

The sneakers were symbolic of my ever present focus to continue to walk my journey with persistence and tenacity driving me. It's a life-long trek, a single step taken a million times over, best to adorn myself with the most comfortable footwear for the job.

I still have the sneakers, and I've no plan to get rid of them or my dogged nature anytime soon.

## Unprofessional Advice

Of course this is a world of opposites and always people and situations come into play that might make us question ourselves and our decisions, that is if we allow it.

While in the process of formulating this book, someone very well-versed in the book publishing business shared her take on my story by saying, "Oh, I hate to read things like that," as she grimaced in displeasure.

My internal response? *Grow up. Things "like that" are happening to children all over the world. It's exactly that train of thought that allows abuse to continue. That attitude keeps abuse in the dark and is just what abusers need to continue their actions–secrecy and shame.*

She next advised, "Maybe you can leave out the details [of the abuse]."

I was aghast at that suggestion, and I fought the urge to bark at her, *Fuck you. I never had the luxury of cutting out the "details."* The whole conversation left me in a foul mood for a bit, but then I realized this was exactly *why* I should be writing my story. People simply needed to know and not be allowed to hide their head in the sand any longer. I needed to be the voice for those that had been buried alive.

That same day I received more sage words from another editor and gatekeeper to the publishing world, "Nobody cares about you and what happened to you, especially if you're not famous."

Well, she was right on that account. I'm not a household name, but people should care, and not because it's me. People should care because I represent many children and adults in the world who are hurting just the same as me, some even more so. Those suffering children oft times grow up to be suffering adults that the world as a whole has to deal with on a daily basis. We don't wear identifying labels, and we're allowed out in the bright of day. We are the people you marry, those who teach our children, and might just be your neighbors or coworkers. We're not an exclusive brand of fame and fortune, but instead are part of day-to-day existence and have a far greater impact on your life than a Hollywood star.

## Questions Answered

My life had taught me that not all who claim authority possess it. I would not crumble under the words of those two women disguised as professionals. I left their company even more determined to put my words on paper.

Certainty and clarity continued to bolster me as I buckled down to write, though old fears threatened to strip me of my confidence. In the process of writing, one question kept calling my attention, like a splinter left embedded in my psyche that remained a tender touchpoint.

It was during a discussion with another woman that my family history arose. I posed the question to her that continued to niggle the back of my mind. I was curious about her potential insight. "Why exactly did my father strangle me during the incident with my flute teacher?" my words dripping with the dread I felt. I had always presumed it was triggered by a sense of guilt or perhaps feelings of powerlessness, because he felt as though I had put him in a position that he didn't know how to fix or face. That made sense, but it just felt unresolved somehow.

She gave a slight hesitation in her response, as though it pained her to tell me, "He was jealous."

*Jealous?!* Her words were a wrecking ball released into my gut, and the nausea and tears were there to drive it all home. I knew I had been given the answer I sought. There was no more wondering. I was grateful for, and left feeling violated by, the information.

It resonated with a somber truth. I was a possession, a thing. Abusers often don't or can't see their victims as people, but instead objectify their intended targets, making their actions and behaviors easier to justify and inflict. That night my two abusers were battling for what they believed to be theirs—me.

I struggled to explain why this was important for me to know. The best explanation I could offer is that it gave me some understanding as to how this occurrence unfolded; it made it seem less random and answered the question, "Why?" It was still sick and crazy, the event and the motivation, but it allowed my mind to rest a bit because it felt as though I had a greater grasp on the whole mess now that I had that missing piece. Somehow a bit of my power from that night was returned to me.

As we sat together, another query sprang to my attention, and I decided to ask another question of her regarding the letter I mailed to my father after his heart attack, "Did he read the letter?" In my mind he had either read the letter and chosen not to respond to me or tossed it in the trash once he saw the return address. Her answer was one that had never occurred to me, perhaps he still had the letter, and it was unopened.

Her response seemed fitting and more in keeping with my father's behaviors. Despite all of his efforts at bravado, his actions often proved to be cowardly. It would take a lot of courage to read that letter and perhaps even more guts to throw it away unread, never having the potential opportunity to digest its contents. He is a great pretender and need only pretend he had never received my letter. To know that perhaps he didn't possess the bravery to read my words left me feeling somber, as I was able to see my father's vulnerability with greater clarity once more. I also felt heavyhearted as I realized he wasn't able to receive a gift that might have brought him some degree of healing; it felt as though it was a symbol for his lack of self-compassion and just brought back to my awareness how truly terrible my father felt about himself. No one who feels worthy would act in the fashion that he had demonstrated for so much of his life.

Over the years, there had been glimpses of his low self-worth, flickers of remorse or self-doubt that were quickly washed aside with the persona meant to intimidate and assert control. Those instances left me heartbroken. I longed to hold his hand and take him away from the places and memories that haunted him. It was through my own pain that I could relate to him, my heart aching tenderly for him as I imagined him unable to see any way out of the darkness. But time had shown me that he wasn't asking for my help and this wasn't mine to fix, only one more thing to accept.

## An Unanswered Question

Silly me, had I not learned by now that there was never just one more thing?

For a year or more the face of one of the girls, now a grown woman, who had bullied me kept popping up on my Facebook feed. Facebook listed her in the category of people I may know, and of course Facebook was spot on. Each time I saw her smiling face a pebble of fear was tossed against the window of my mind.

She appeared to be sharing her heart with the world; one of her main concerns and interests was animal welfare. She listed new age and seemingly enlightened books on her page that discussed the importance of focusing on the present moment and the use of our thoughts to create that which we seek. I was pleased to see what appeared to be steps toward self-awareness.

And then I got an idea.

Why not reach out and ask her to offer an explanation as to why I was chosen as their target all those years ago? Perhaps she might offer answers to one of my long held mysteries. I shared my idea with some and was told to just let it drop, but since when did I do as I was told?

This was my message to her: "*...I've seen your face many times over the years on FB, and today I decided to ask you a question I've wondered for a long time. I remember you quite well for the bullying & intimidation you and [names of the other two girls involved] inflicted on me in middle school. What you didn't know at that time was that I was being physically & sexually abused, and school was my respite—until the three of you* turned your attentions to me and brought me to what I felt was going to be my breaking point because then there was nowhere I was safe. I tell you this so you know where I am/was coming from. What I wondered then, and think about each time I see your face on FB, is why? Why did you guys pick me? That's all I want. I don't recall doing anything to you guys that might have instigated your actions, but if I did, I would like to know that as well. Perhaps the answer is simply that you were a kid going through your own stuff. If you can take a moment to answer my question, I would appreciate it. I wish you well."

I received no response. Perhaps she hadn't finished reading the self-help books she'd listed? Or was her compassion only deemed fitting for the animal kingdom?

I didn't find my message to her unkind or attacking at all, but it was honest. And although I still don't know the impetus for their actions, all was not in vain because I was left with a sense of empowerment. I had reclaimed my power from those events.

That I was able to address one of my bullies and honestly share my hurt birthed in me a sense of support, one that I was in dire need of. I returned to the hall of my middle school, took the hand of the teenager I once was and stood up for her. The bully's reaction, or absence of, was not nearly as important as my own action.

What I did accept was that it seemed no healing was to come from her, but that which I had offered myself was dependent on no one and will remain timeless.

## Ho'oponopono

If acceptance was in order than I had one more very important step to take on my trek of forgiveness—owning my role in the conflicts my parents and I faced over the expanse of my life. This was not something that I had consciously concluded, but yet another instance of the universe's gentle nudge.

Translated, the phrase Ho'oponopono means, "To make right." I most definitely wasn't in search of it, but this Hawaiian healing mantra presented itself in my path and continued to enter my world in various forms for over a year. I chose to ignore it and what it had to offer, asking forgiveness from those with whom we have been embattled.

I'd seen variations in how the phrasing was arranged but the one I learned goes like this: *"I am sorry. Please forgive me. I love you. Thank you."* This was to be repeated while calling to mind the relationship that was strained and the image of those involved. Of course, I saw my parents' eyes locked on me, but I turned my back, unwilling to seek their forgiveness of me and feeling instead that it was they who should be looking to be forgiven. My level of forgiveness was being put to the test, and it stalled a bit at the starting line.

My ego was all for disregarding Ho'oponopono, but in time my heart was victorious, and I was ready to envision my parents while repeating the prayer, with one little twist. I changed the first line to *"I apologize,"* as that sat better with me. "I'm sorry" felt as though I was professing something about my state as a whole, i.e. "I am a sorry state." Whereas "I apologize" is an act which I am committing. If I was going to do this, I meant to do it without reservations and with authenticity.

Some lingering resentment made itself known for the first week or so that I began this practice, and my mind fought their image, but I continued to direct my focus on having a soulful heart. I intentionally saw them as the truth of their souls, and in time I willingly and joyfully asked them to forgive me.

Knowing my childhood story, some friends wondered why I would take this step. It's pretty basic; I was taking ownership for all the hurtful energy I had sent their way over the years. I believe it's understandable that I had malicious thoughts and ideas in regards to them, but ultimately it was not my truth, nor were the actions they took their truth. This was yet another layer of forgiveness, and this time I was freeing myself by owning my part in our unhealthy dynamic.

And I did feel freer, and lighter, as I took responsibility for my antago-nistic feelings and fantasies. As I released myself, the tiny spark of love that I still had for them grew into a flame and allowed one more of the many layers of hurt to dissolve.

I do love them. I always will.

# Thank You

Along with my newfound sympathies came an appreciation for those things they had unknowingly, dare I say unconsciously, gifted to me. Releasing anger's clutter left an open space that was soon filled with heartfelt gratitude.

At first I found I began to envision the moments of happiness that were sprinkled about my life as a child. This was a place I was not capable of going to in years past, my heart still bruised, tender and guarding itself from further injury. But with the retirement of my personal sentry, I imag-ined once more those instances that made themselves known and called them what they were, acts of love that they had bestowed upon me. It was those memories that brought a sad smile to my face as I saw the sweet promise held in those moments, and the knowing that it would never fully come to pass. What's done is done.

As I continued to dig through the gift bag they had left me so long ago I discovered, oddly enough, that one of the greatest gifts my parents gave to me was the lack of an apology, a fact which escaped me before. As I unwrapped that which they had given, I saw its many facets.

My entire life I longed to hear genuine, heartfelt remorse from them, but nothing ever came, nothing for my hands or heart to cling to. My magical thinking lead me to believe that if they truly expressed regret for what they had done, it would somehow feel like they didn't really mean all those hurtful things; maybe it was all a horrible mistake.

Perhaps with the arrival of an apology, the pain would spontaneously disappear, and the floodgates of unbridled love for me would finally open. For me, their lack of apology was a confirmation that they intended every hurt they inflicted. Many of my attempts to describe the aftermath of my life with them had come out in what felt like generalities and so possibly, to them, it didn't sound all that horrendous. I could be far more honest with you as you read my words than I could have ever possibly been with them.

Secondly, in my efforts to get an apology, I shamed them. I wasn't conscious of this at the time, but now I see I approached many of my efforts with a *Look what you did to me* attitude. I was trying to shove in their face all the shame they had dished out to me over my lifetime. It was really no different than the times they rubbed Barney's nose in his own feces after he had an accident in the house. All of their abuses were based in the core of shame they carried within themselves, and I was just adding to the pile. Of course I knew from my own experience that no one reacts well to shaming, and instead they felt cornered and went into protection mode for themselves. They became so concerned with self-preservation that there was no room for my needs. We were all fighting for our own survival; nothing had changed.

Lastly, I truly don't believe they were capable of owning or seeing the degree of dysfunction we lived. Denial is the buttress that allowed them the mastery to fool themselves. In their mind, one kind act on their part far outweighed any wrongs, and instead confirmed for them what stellar parents and people they were. To be able to admit or own the destruction that lay in their wake would psychologically destroy them, and instead validate their worst fears about their own worth.

By not apologizing, they fueled my persistence to heal and forgive, to be free of the legacy that had been handed to me. They fed my fury, which in turn pushed me further and deeper into new levels of self-discovery and healing. I was on a mission to get as far away from them as possible. I was determined that I would somehow learn to forgive. Forgiving wasn't for them, but instead a destiny I longed to obtain in order that I might purge myself of the power they held over me. Forgiveness was my get-out-of-jail card; it just wasn't free. The price I had to pay was one of dedication and fierce determination to not give up on myself no matter how taxing the path.

The burden was overwhelming at times but couldn't compare to what I had already endured. I survived it all once; there was no way this was going to take me down. I set my sights ahead and never looked back.

The realization also dawned on me that if they had shared heartfelt remorse, I never would have divulged "the secret." I would have felt too guilty to share with anyone all that had come to pass. In my mind I would have still owed them that protection, and thus, I would have remained entrenched in their wretched game. I never would have found my way out of the cobwebs of my life.

No longer did I fantasize about them spilling their regrets to me. Instead, I put a bow on top of their lack of apology. I smiled and sent thanks that the mountain I'd been stumbling up had led me to the pinnacle moment of forgiveness and ultimate freedom. I envisioned myself standing on the top of that mountain, arms outstretched, head tilted back in surrender and basking in the glory of the sun's rays that shine as brightly as me, and I feel as if I've conquered the world, or at least mine.

## My Own Hero

Amongst my inner world lived one who beats to her own drum; the importance of the rhythm she kept was as significant as that of my heart. While writing this book, I remembered the image of myself as Motorcycle Mama, a name I'd given myself at the age of four, a time that I believe was months before I was first molested—my kindergarten picture telling that tale.

I had received a tricycle for Christmas. I donned my big brother's new denim jacket and fluorescent orange beanie, my body drowning in their enormity, but not my spirit. I tooled around our kitchen on my speedy new tricycle, pulling on the tassels in my imagined efforts to adjust my pace—the white ones reducing my speed and the red allowing me to accelerate. My mother and siblings happily laughed at my fantasy play and audacious display.

With clarity, I remembered feeling utterly indomitable, my jubilance and power bursting forth to fill the room as I raced lap after lap around the kitchen table. There was not a speck of doubt in my mind that I was a force to be reckoned with. My spirit, *me*, was boundless. That's the little girl I believe helped me get here. Nothing could stand in her way or hold her back. She kept the fires burning within and drove me into the future on her red trike, tassels blowing with the power of her intention, to claim our life. My little Motorcycle Mama, *she* is relentless.

And she's my hero.

Motorcycle Mama

My dog Barney

Me in Kindergarten

Me after cutting my hair short (this is the
image I held of myself for most of my life)

*"We delight in the beauty of the butterfly, but rarely admit the changes it has gone through to achieve that beauty."*

–Maya Angelou

**And the Journey Continues ...**
Stay up to date with Kellie Springer, RN through her blog found at www. kelliespringer.com.

**Connect with the author:**
Website: anamcarakellie.com
Social Media:
Twitter: https://twitter.com/AnamCaraKellie
Facebook: https://www.facebook.com/Anam-Cara-Kellie-2334436735 29375/

**Author's note:**
A few short weeks prior to the release of this book my father passed and left me with more to process. Like I said, my journey continues.

CPSIA information can be obtained
at www.ICGtesting.com
Printed in the USA
BVOW03s2112280317
479709BV00001B/30/P